GUSTAV KLIMT : Drawings

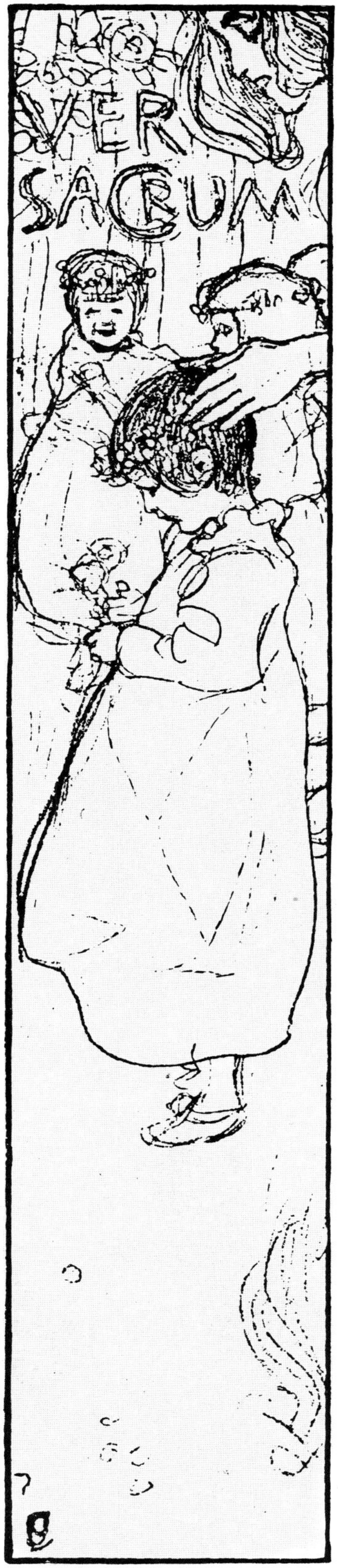

Gustav Klimt, illustration
for *Ver Sacrum*, 1899.

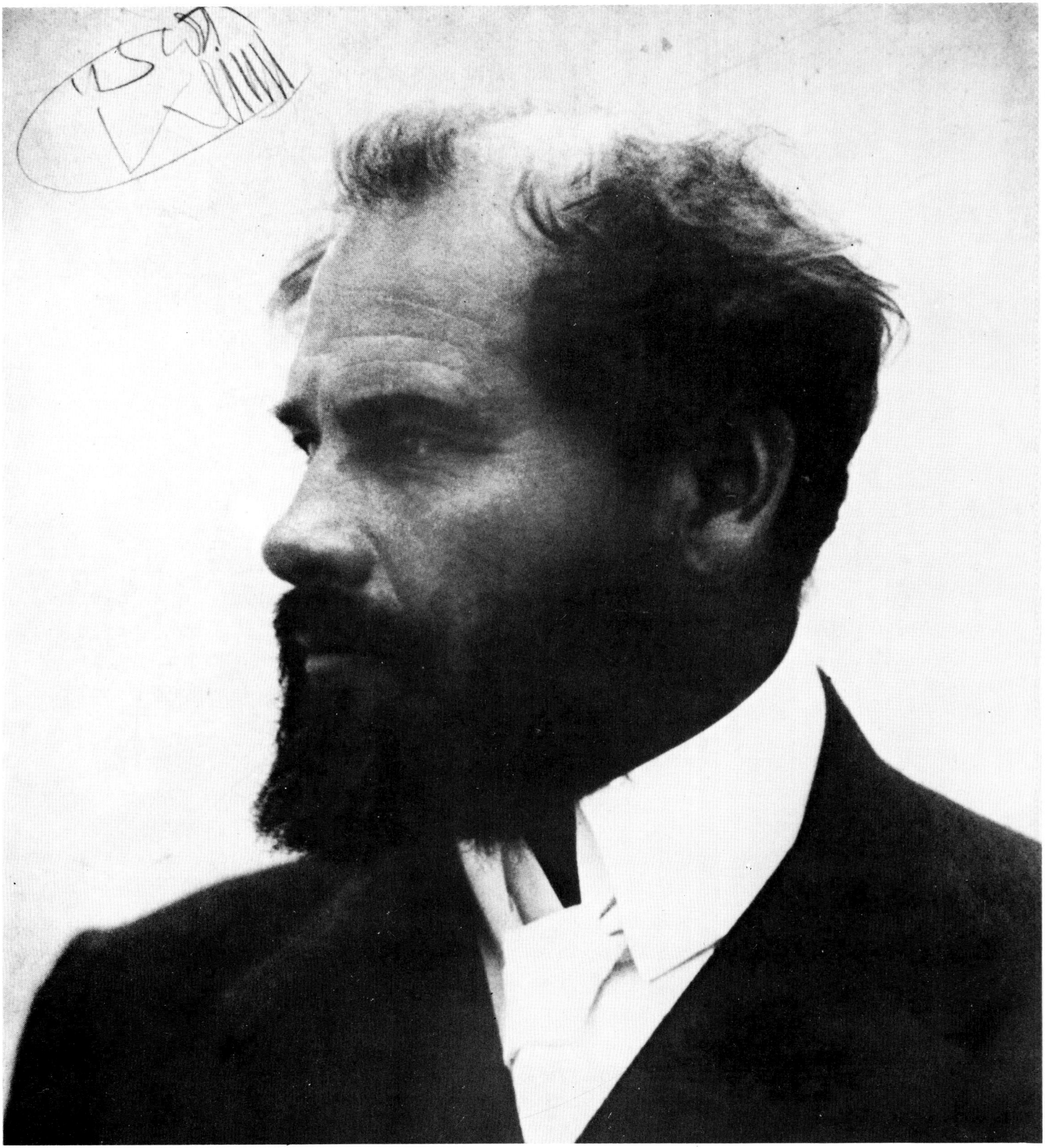

Gustav Klimt, *c.* 1908.

GUSTAV KLIMT: Drawings

Edited by Serge Sabarsky

Gordon Fraser · London

First published in the UK in 1984 by
The Gordon Fraser Gallery Limited, London and Bedford

ISBN 0 86092 078 X hardcover
ISBN 0 86092 079 8 paperback

Printed in Italy

BRITISH LIBRARY CATALOGUING IN PUBLICATION DATA
Klimt Gustav
Klimt: drawings.
1. Klimt, Gustav
I. Sabarsky, Serge
741.9436 NC245.K553

ISBN 0–86092–078–X
ISBN 0–86092–079–8 Pbk

Contents

Curriculum vitae..

Bin geboren am 14. Juli 1862 zu Baumgarten
bei Wien, katholischer Religion und ledig.
Ich kam im Jahre 1867 nach Wien und
absolvierte daselbst eine achtklassige Bürgerschule.
Oktober 1876 wurde ich als ordentlicher Schüler
der Kunstgewerbeschule des Österr. Museums
für Kunst und Industrie aufgenommen und
besuchte daselbst durch 2 Jahre die Vorbereitungs-
schule unter den Professoren Rieser, Minnigerode
und Hrachowina und erhielt die weitere Ausbildung
in der Fachschule für Malerei von Prof.
Ferd. Lauf berger, verblieb daselbst bis
zu dessen Tod 1881 und setzte meine Studien in
derselben Fachschule unter Leitung des Prof.
Berger durch weitere 2 Jahre fort.
Dies sind im Ganzen 7 Jahre, nach welchem
Zeitraum ich im Jahre 1883 mit meinem
Studiencollegen Maler Matsch und meinem Bruder
Ernst Klimt ein eigenes Atelier bezog.
Schon während der letzten Jahre der Studienzeit
hatte ich in Gemeinschaft mit Maler Matsch und meinem
Bruder Aufträge erhalten und ausgeführt.
Im Jahre 1880 Plafondbilder für ein Palais am Schottenring
ferner Plafondbilder für den Cursalon in Carlsbad
1881 Plafondbilder für das Palais Zierer nach Skizzen
von Prof Berger. 1882. Plafondbilder
und in Gemeinschaft mit Matsch und meinem
Bruder den Vorhang des Reichenberger
Stadttheaters.

SERGE SABARSKY

Introduction

If all that you make and all that you do
By the masses seem never well taken,
Do your utmost to delight the few:
The attempt to please all is mistaken.
SCHILLER
(inscription on the painting *Nuda Veritas*)

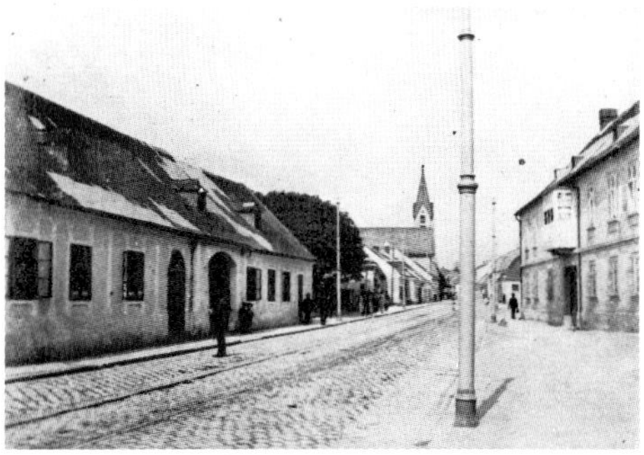

Klimt's birthplace in Vienna, Linzerstrasse 247.

At the turn of the century Austria enjoyed a tremendous flowering in the fields of music, literature and the performing arts, but it was also a time notable for the visual arts. The most renowned names of the period were Gustav Klimt, Oskar Kokoschka and Egon Schiele; Klimt, the eldest of the three, was the first to receive public and critical acclaim. In fact Klimt was destined to become in a brief space of time the idol of the Viennese establishment and the hero of the avant-garde. Such was his success that people today tend to think of the Vienna of the early 1900s as the era of Klimt.

Gustav Klimt was born on 14 July 1862 in Vienna, the second of seven children. His parents were of humble origins and life was often a struggle on the father's meagre wages as an engraver. There is little information about Klimt's childhood; it is known, however, that Gustav as well as his brothers Ernst and Georg displayed a certain artistic talent at a tender age. At fourteen Gustav received a scholarship to the new School of Arts and Crafts at the Museum of Art and Industry, and the following year his brother Ernst also gained a place there.

In those years the two brothers and a fellow student, Franz Matsch, formed themselves into a type of artistic clique, and were commissioned by one of their instructors to collaborate on the painting of frescoes in the main hall along the side of the staircase of the Kunsthistorisches Museum in Vienna. As soon as they graduated the three received further commissions to do a number of works including frescoes for the central theatres of Fiume, Carlsbad and other cities in the Austro-Hungarian empire. In 1886 they were entrusted with the prestigious task of painting frescoes on the ceilings and lunettes of the two main staircases of Vienna's Burgtheater, a quite complex undertaking which earned the three young men the highest recognition by the emperor and the much sought-after gold cross of merit.

Unlike so many artists of his own and other generations, Klimt was blessed with early success. However, although he had established himself as a painter of stature with his earliest works, it would not be hard to discern in these frescoes a certain academic quality. In fact it was precisely by painting in a style which offered no surprises that the three friends earned their earliest commissions.

Autograph curriculum vitae.

It was only towards the end of the century that Klimt gave birth to the style we shall always admire – the symbol and quintessence of the Jugendstil and the Viennese Secession.

Within the Austrian empire theatre, music and opera were traditionally held in high esteem, while painting was treated as the ugly duckling of the arts, as much in official circles as by the public. Artists struggled for recognition in this stagnating atmosphere, and the struggle was hard and generally fruitless. In addition, artists were not at all happy with the way in which their own groups were organised and even less with the internal bickerings which were continually breaking out within them and which seemed to carry on interminably. In 1897 Klimt decided to leave the *Kunstlerhausgenossenschaft*, the group he belonged to at the time, and founded (along with other dissatisfied artists) the Viennese Secession, of which he was instantly elected president.

The Secession did not abandon *a priori* the various academic styles which by now were ingrained in the art of the period, nor did it set out to spark off a revolution. Rather it hoped to revitalise the world of art, to reshape the concept of presentation and to promote the work of its members. Above all it set out to make Viennese artists better known and more highly appreciated within their own country, and to take Austrian art away from its provincialism so that it might be valued on an international level. This approach, which entailed a new type of relationship with the public, turned out to be profitable. The various exhibitions of works by the Secession prompted an immediate and unexpected following, attracting tens of thousands of visitors. The third exhibition was so successful that the proceeds from it allowed the Secessionists to engage the architect Josef Maria Olbrich to design a wonderful new building for them. Under the main entrance to the building were inscribed the words '*Der Zeit ihre Kunst, Der Kunst ihre Freiheit*' (To each age its art; to all art its freedom). This motto, which highlights the guiding force behind the Secession, could nevertheless be adopted by any group of artists. It is interesting to note, however, that it was erased after the *Anschluss* of 1938 when the Nazis occupied Austria. Evidently '*Freiheit*' was not a word they cherished. The inscription was restored after the fall of the Third Reich.

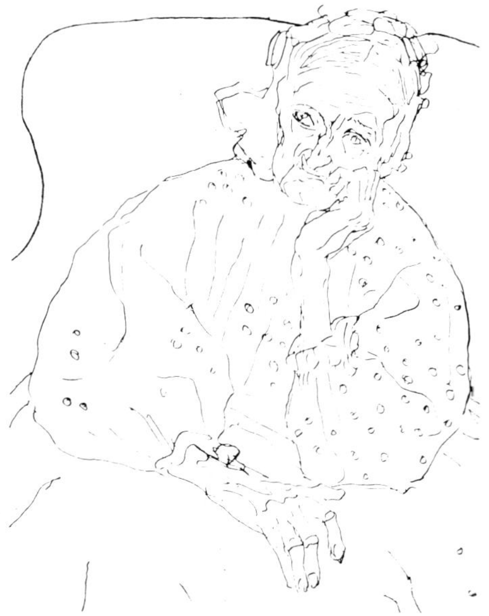

Gustav Klimt,
Portrait of the artist's mother, 1911.

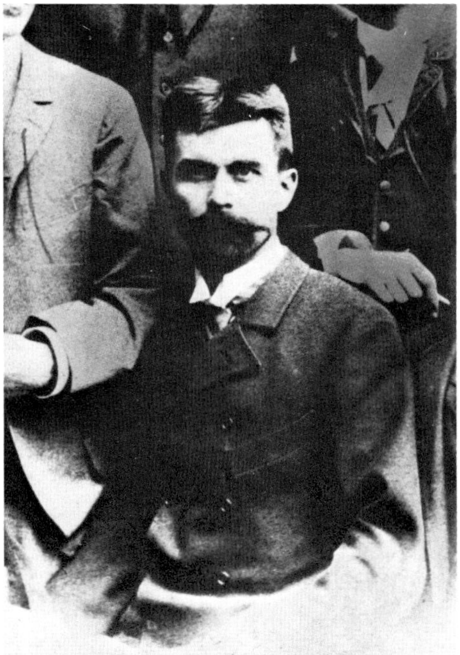

Gustav Klimt, *c.* 1880.

In 1894 the Austrian government commissioned Klimt to do three allegorical panels representing *Philosophy*, *Medicine* and *Jurisprudence* for the ceiling of the assembly hall of Vienna University. Klimt undertook the work in 1897, later showing the panels to the Secession and exhibiting them at several exhibitions abroad. *Philosophy* won a gold medal at the Universal Exhibition in Paris in 1900. However, the Viennese received these unique masterpieces of their finest artist somewhat ambiguously. Though enlightened critics, artists and collectors recognised Klimt's genius and lauded the panels, the general public, influenced by certain members of Parliament, journalists and some university professors who thought themselves authorities on art, criticised the allegorical paintings harshly and did not hesitate to make fun of them. Whereas the German Expressionists or French Fauvists came under attack for their new visual language, in Klimt's case it was not so much his pictorial style as the frankness of theme which created such a stir. The public was accustomed to seeing nudes, but ones with cloth draped strategically around them or ones which 'modestly' covered certain parts of the anatomy. Klimt, instead, painted nudes in natural, realistic poses, daring to depict fat old women, ageing men, even young men holding pregnant women in their arms. Some called his work erotic, others pornographic, others simply ugly; they were unable to sense that his art was ahead of his time.

The harshness and malevolence of the attacks did not diminish as the years went by, while Klimt carried on working on panels and even executed the so-called 'Beethoven frieze' inspired by the *Ninth Symphony*. Klimt displayed this wonderful piece at the Secession's exhibition of 1902, which will go down in history as being the first time that works of different media were exhibited together. Max Klinger's sculpture of Beethoven, for example, was included among the exhibits.

If one thinks of the difficulties and anguish which the University panels brought Klimt, one cannot help but be struck by his perseverence and the spirit which led him to tell the Press one day 'I don't have the time to become involved in these disputes. When I finish a picture I have no intention of wasting month after month in justifying it to certain people. What concerns me is not *how many* like my painting but *who*.' Nevertheless the arguments raged on and with great acrimony, to the extent that the minister of Education and Culture, who recognised Klimt's genius, became so entangled in them that he was finally forced to resign.

In the spring of 1905 Klimt, no longer able to tolerate being the object of so much rancour, gave back the money he had received and reclaimed his paintings, thereby putting a stop to all the tiresome disputes.

These difficulties did not prevent him from collaborating profitably with various groups of artists, but since vexing and difficult problems arose within the Secession, Klimt and some of his friends decided to abandon the group.

In an open letter to the Minister of Education the signatory artists, including of course Klimt, furnished ample explanations for their actions, concluding with this thought: 'No existence is so rich that it is incapable of being enriched by art, and none so poor that it cannot make room for it.'

In 1906 Klimt joined his dissident colleagues to form a new group, the *Österreichische Künstlerbund*. From that moment onwards Vienna's artists endeavoured in every conceivable way to organise exhibitions in Austria and also abroad. Klimt presided over the *Kunstschau* of 1908 and 1909, in which he displayed various works. In addition he participated in several collective shows in Monaco, Berlin, Venice, Prague and other cities.

During the First World War and in the period immediately preceding it Klimt developed the distinctive elements which were to characterise his work of later years, above all the large figures in gold and silver and the patterning in mosaic, the superb decorative portraits and finally the evocative, poetic landscapes painted onto square canvases. In those years Klimt was only away from Vienna in the summer breaks, generally spending them with his faithful companion Emilie Flöge in her parent's house on the Attersee where the artist felt tranquil and serene.

Suddenly, on the morning of 11 January, a tragedy occurred: Klimt suffered a heart attack which left him partially paralysed. After three weeks in hospital it seemed as though he was improving, but he contracted pneumonia, which led to his death on 6 February.

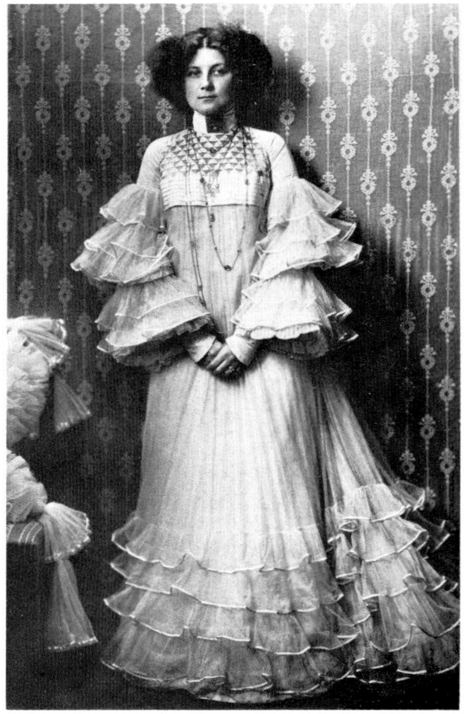

Emilie Flöge, 1909.

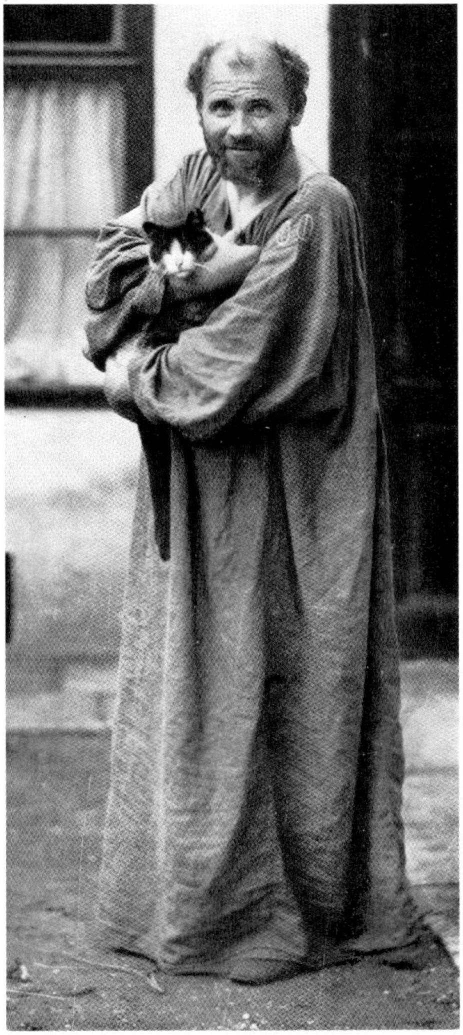

Gustav Klimt outside his studio, *c.* 1912–1914.

Four days later Klimt was buried in the cemetery at Hietzing, surrounded by friends and admirers as well as state officials. The ancient controversies were finally forgotten and the Austrians were now ready to recognise and venerate Klimt as their greatest artist.

Klimt deserves a special place in the art world of his time. While his paintings appear studied, considered and painfully and minutely constructed, the drawings are striking for their immediacy and spontaneity. His pictorial style, although highly original, could be classified as Jugendstil and does not depart significantly from contemporary fashion. It is influenced by Oriental art, and in particular by the art and culture of Japan, which he greatly admired. His drawings, on the other hand, seem free from any outside influence. They are his, timeless and yet somehow contemporary. In his drawings Klimt gives free rein to his psyche, letting internal forces guide his pencil.

Having grown up in the suburbs of Vienna, Klimt was strongly attached to the city and was Viennese in the truest sense of the word. He felt deeply about the way of life and the character of the capital. He enjoyed the company of his colleagues and was always receptive to his family and friends, but grew distant and silent if pressured into defending his work publicly.

He wrote very little about himself or his work and almost nothing of what he said or wrote has survived. Such was his fear of having to answer letters that he would burn them periodically, without even opening them, and his profound reluctance to discuss his ideas on art has become legendary. Consequently it is perhaps opportune to conclude this introduction with a brief extract from Klimt's writings.

'I am good at painting and drawing; I think so myself and others say it also, but I'm not sure if it's true. I know only two things for certain: 1. There are no self-portraits of me. I am not interested in myself as a subject for a painting; I prefer others, particularly if they are of the female gender, but even if they are not. I am certain that there is nothing exceptional about my person. I am simply a painter who paints every livelong day from morning till night. Figures and landscapes, portraits somewhat less. 2. My words and writings are not worth much, even less if I am forced to discuss myself or my work. Just the idea of having to write a simple letter floods me with anguish as if by waves of nausea. I am very much afraid that you will have to do without a portrait of me either painted or in words, but it is not a great loss. Whoever seeks to know me better, that is to say as an artist – the only aspect which is worth knowing – should study my paintings to track down who I am and what I want.'

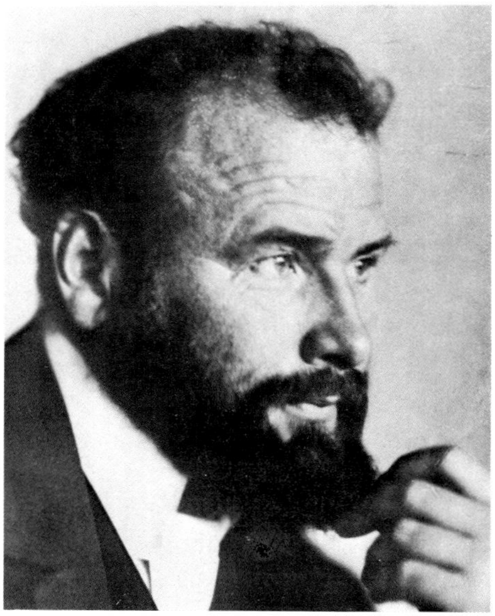

Gustav Klimt, *c.* 1908.

GUSTAV KLIMT

The Union of Artists and the Public

(from the opening address of the Kunstschau 1908)

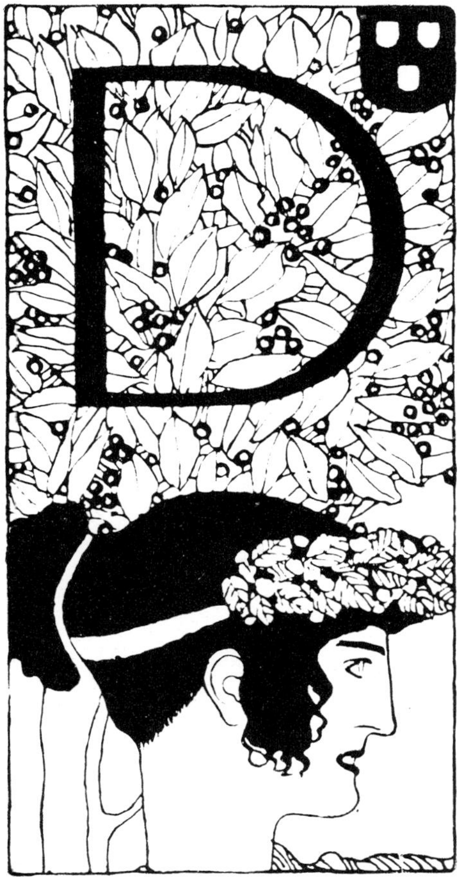

Gustav Klimt, illustration for *Ver Sacrum*, 1899.

We are well known for holding the view that exhibitions are not the ideal way of establishing contact between artists and the public; to achieve such an aim we would much prefer to see support given to public undertakings with regard to art. But until there is overwhelming public reaction to economic and political questions, the exhibition is all that we have. We must be grateful to everything, public and private, which as on this occasion gives us the means of showing that in the last few years, when there have been no exhibitions, we have not been inactive but on the contrary have perhaps gone even further. Having been entirely freed from preparing for exhibitions, we have dedicated ourselves with even greater enthusiasm and intensity to carrying out our ideas.

We are not a co-operative, a consortium nor an association: we are linked in a free grouping, set up precisely with this exhibition in mind, brought together only by the common conviction that no part of life is so small and insignificant that it does not allow room for artistic aspirations, or, to quote the words of Morris, that the most humble object, provided that it is perfectly executed, further increases the beauty of our earth. Only the ever-greater penetration of the whole of life by artistic ideas will guarantee the progress of civilisation.

Our idea of the 'artist' is the same as that of the 'work of art'. We speak of the artist as someone who not only creates but also as someone who enjoys art and who is therefore capable of bringing to life and evaluating artistic creations with his own receptive senses. For us the 'artistic union' is an ideal union of everyone, creators and the public. That such a union actually exists, that it is strong and important (thanks to its youth and its vigour, as well as the purity of its ideas), is proved by the construction of this house and the opening of our show.

Therefore our enemies strive in vain to kill off the modern movement and to defeat it. In fact it is a useless struggle against everything that grows and develops, even against life itself. We, who for so many weeks have collaborated to give life to this exhibition, must (now that it is open) go our separate ways, each taking his own path. But this does not mean that in the near future we shall not meet again, in different ways and with different aims.

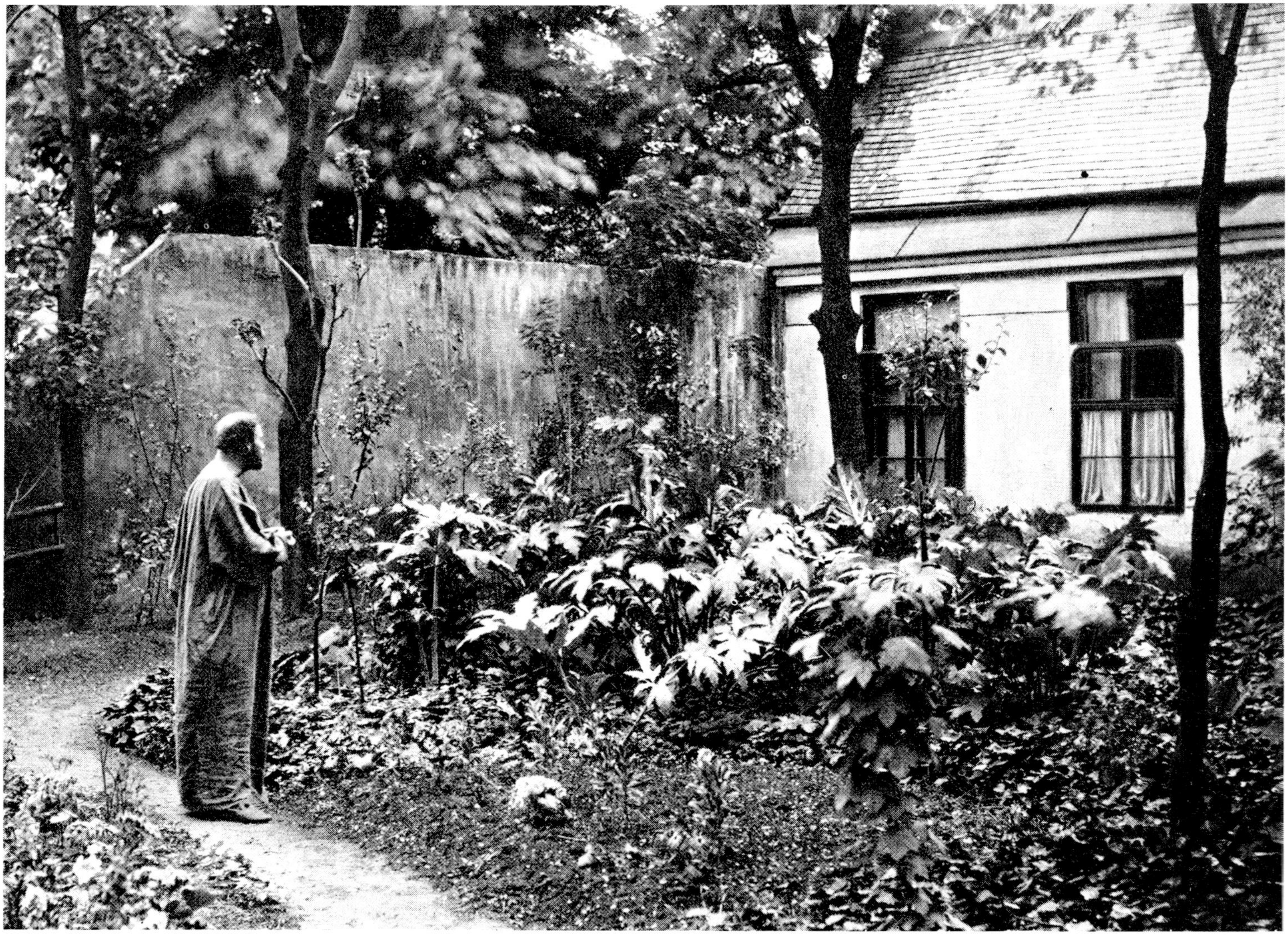

Klimt in the garden of his studio in Josefstädterstrasse, *c.* 1910.

EGON SCHIELE

Klimt's Generosity of Spirit was Genuine

When I went to meet Klimt for the first time in 1907, he was a sturdy man with harsh features in a tanned face. It was at 21 Josefstädterstrasse, in the garden – one of those old hidden gardens which still flourish right in the Josefstadt – spread out in front of a low villa with many windows, in the shade of very high trees. Between the flowers and the creepers a path led to the house and a glass door opened into the hall, where frames and other painters' materials were piled up; from there you entered three communicating studios, whose floors were covered with sketches. Klimt always dressed in an ample blue smock which reached down to his feet, and always appeared in this, even to visitors and models.

In 1911 the area was demolished and Klimt was forced to leave his little house amidst the greenery, where he had seen so many years of joy and sorrow, and to move to a single-storey house in the Feldmühlgasse, at Hietzing. He had two large glass walls put into the north side of the house, choosing and furnishing the area reserved for work astrologically. Each day, having had breakfast at Tivoli, Klimt withdrew to paint and draw without a break from ten o'clock in the morning until eight in the evening. On Sunday morning he would be found taking a walk with Mödling and Baden.

Every year he rearranged the flowerbeds around the house, which was so delightful to arrive at, with its profusion of flowers and ancient trees. Two beautiful heads which Klimt himself had sculpted flanked the entrance door, which gave onto a small hall. From here a door on the left opened into the sitting room, furnished with a square table in the middle and a large number of Japanese prints covering the walls together with two, larger, Chinese paintings. Statues of negro art were placed on the floor and the corner nearest to the window was occupied by a black-and-red Japanese cupboard. This room led to two other rooms with a beautiful view of a rose garden. From the right hand side of the hall one entered a room which was dominated by two skeletons, and from there into another room whose wall was entirely covered by a huge wardrobe, which held his marvellous collection of Chinese and Japanese robes. This in turn led into the real studio, where Klimt showed me the works on which he was engaged.

At Hietzing he painted a series of pictures of women and of full figures, *Love and Death*, *Leda*, *The Virgin*, *The Bride*, *Eve* and many more, even some of the beautiful countryside of Attersee and Lake Garda.

The pictures which he made for the exhibition of Klinger's *Beethoven* represent for me the high point of Klimt's creativity. On six panels, 2.20 metres high and 4·06 metres wide, he expressed everything he believed in.

My Kingdom is not of this World: this work was to have been destroyed when the exhibition closed, but Karl Reininghaus succeeded in saving it just in time and in 1915 it was acquired by the Lederer collection complete with the three hundred preliminary sketches. Even the panels which Klimt painted for the ceiling of the University are to be found in a private collection where they are probably better off than in the great hall of the University.

There are also thousands of sketches in the Feldmühlgasse, of which only a few isolated sheets can be seen and admired in exhibitions.

Klimt's generosity of spirit was genuine; he was not a hermit, and was even very welcoming, though he knew well who his real friends were. He earned a lot, very much in fact, but spent it all. 'Money ought to circulate', he used to say.

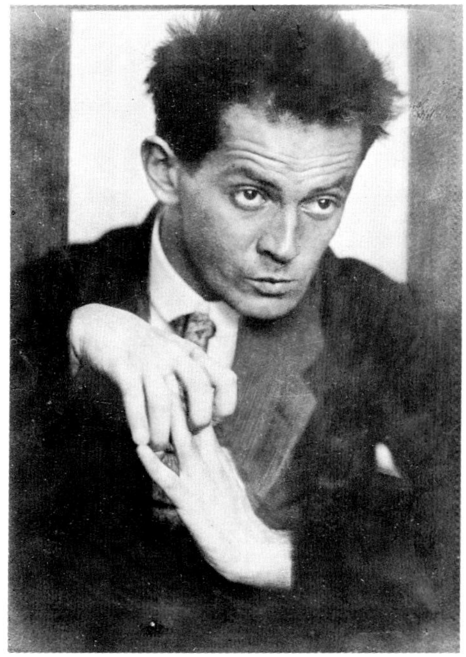

Egon Schiele.

MAX EISLER

Beyond the Picture

The last decade of Klimt's creative life is a period dominated by his graphic works. As well as reflecting (more than contemporary paintings) the artistic development, the perfecting and mastering, the prints (or new style that they represent) influenced Klimt's painting, which now moved from its linearity to a freer and looser style. The beginning of this change cannot be dated precisely, but it was probably in 1908, the beginning of his last ten years, although it had shown itself a long time before, for example in the sketches which preceded the *Danae*. The light, aerial quality, the almost uninterrupted, sinuous line and easy pose of the figures rendered with skilful play on the surfaces are still related structurally to the sketches on wrapping paper from the previous period, yet the more complex movement – the bent leg, the leaning head – gives greater depth to the space; the picture breathes, vibrates, seduces like a living being.

Combining the two naturally heterogeneous elements – impressionism and ornament – Klimt enriched modern art by a particular and significant union. His art becomes the perfect synthesis of graphic art of all periods. Amongst other things it raises the question, through the print, of whether Klimt the graphic artist is greater than Klimt the painter. Only the future can give us the answer.

When his pictorial conception changed, so did everything else. Paper, which was no longer intended for preparatory sketches but for autonomous drawings, was chosen with care; very fine rice paper in two vertical formats, which, however large, were not always big enough wholly to contain the slim female figures, which were at one time cut off by their tresses, at another at their feet. On this silky-opaque, chalky background, the grey of the pencil stands out brilliantly, brought into relief here and there against the white by highlighting with red and blue crayons on the lips and the dresses. At first soft, elongated and spare, the treatment of the pencil has now taken on an extraordinary illusionistic force, creating – even without any other modelling, and with only a few light accents – both the form in space and its pose. Later the treatment becomes more abbreviated and more vigorous, massive and intricate, often repeating itself; the feeling accentuated at the beginning is now transformed into positive expression.

In this period of great maturity Klimt drew opulent figures in movement, reclining on couches, crouching, kneeling or walking, fleshy, with ample gestures, and at the same time discernable under the draperies which wrap around them. The combination of these restless elements is calmed by the compact plasticity of the composition. Often the bodies which Klimt draws are unequivocally erotic. In fact this active moment, in which the passionate frenzy of the senses makes the limbs tremble and the body arch while the faces are still eager, just gratified or already relaxed, is what most interests the author, who directs with persuasive immediacy the animal instinct in the act of release.

It is the final phase of Gustav Klimt's stylistic development. Having moved away from decorative surfaces and matured through the monumental works, his drawing is the ideal form in which to set down his new experience.

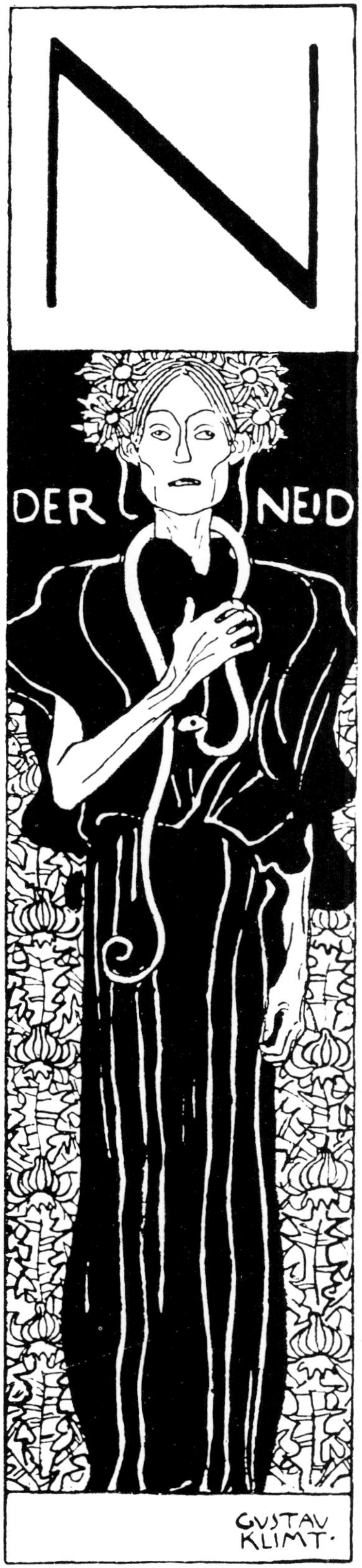

Gustav Klimt, illustration
for *Ver Sacrum*, 1899.

The Drawings

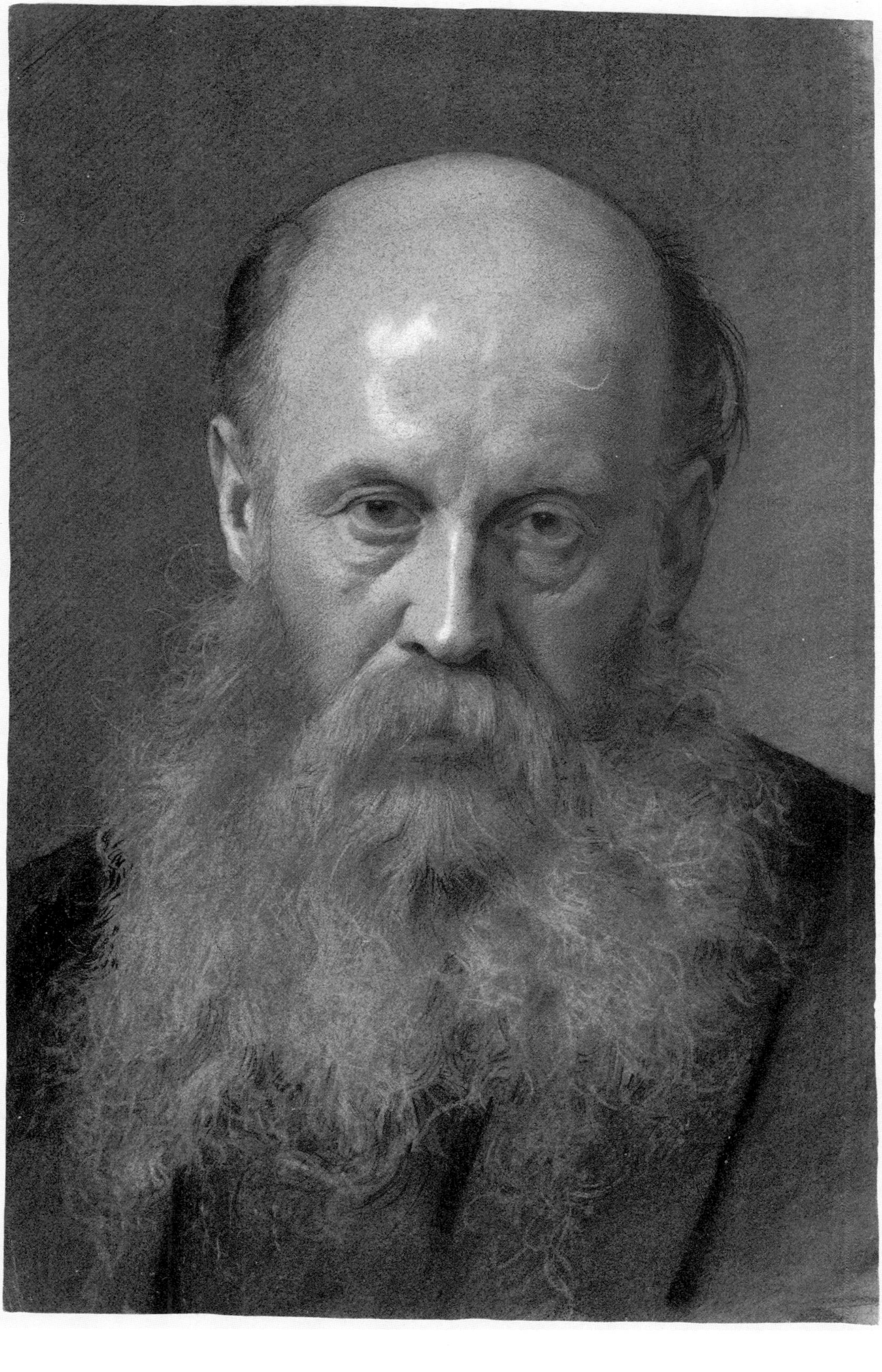

1. *Study of a man with a beard*, 1879.

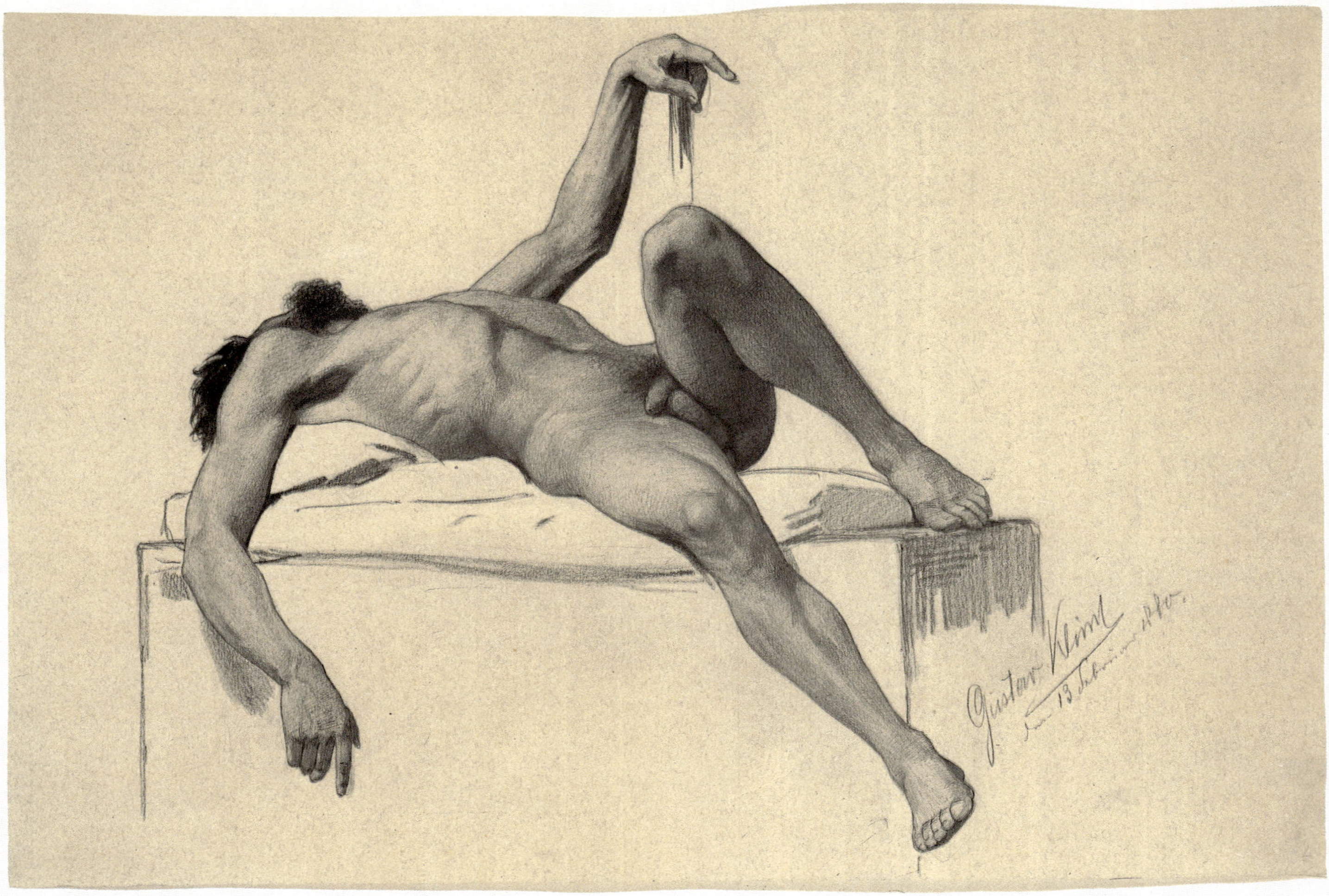

2. *Recumbent male nude*, 1880.

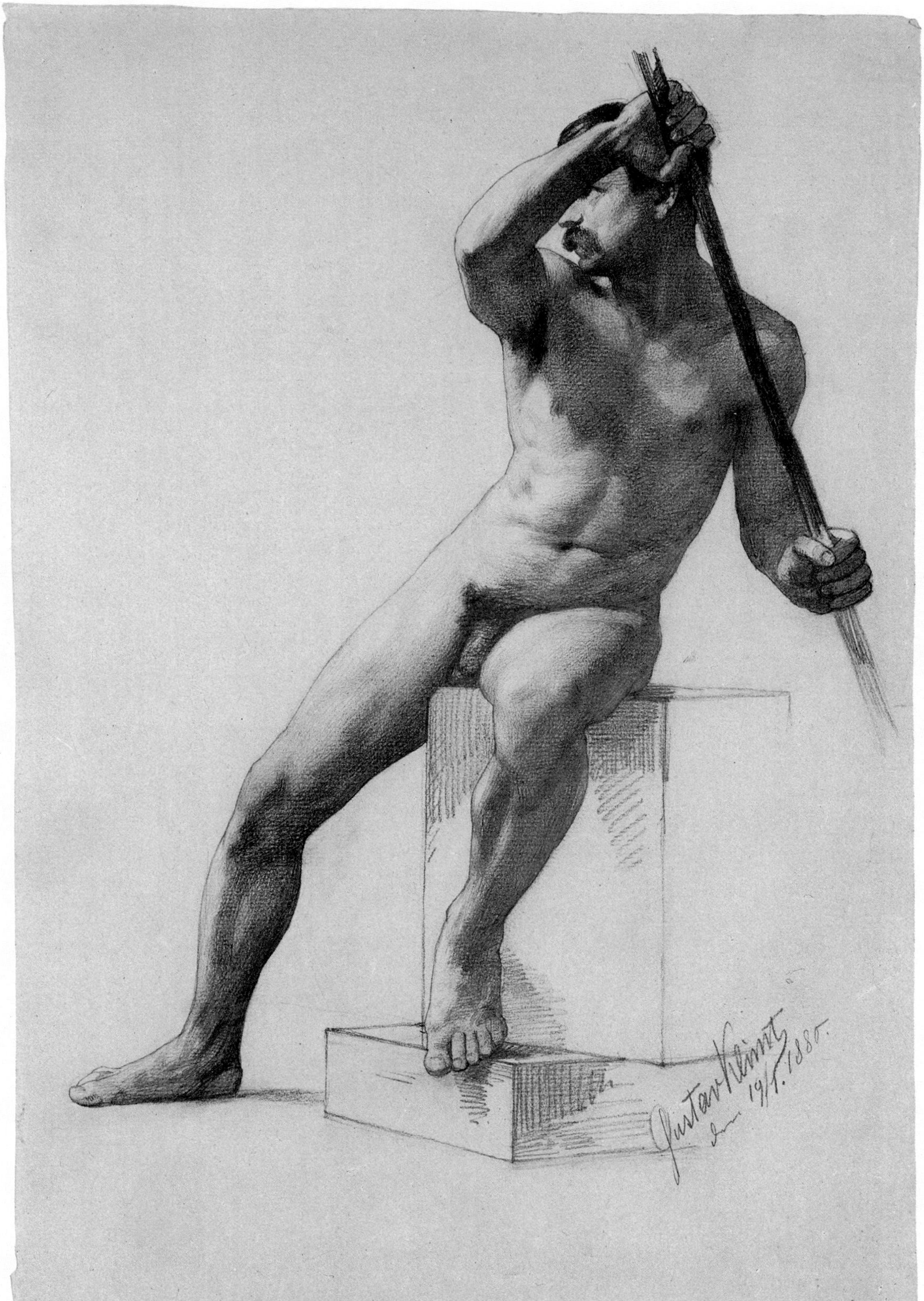

3. *Male nude seated on a pedestal*, 1880.

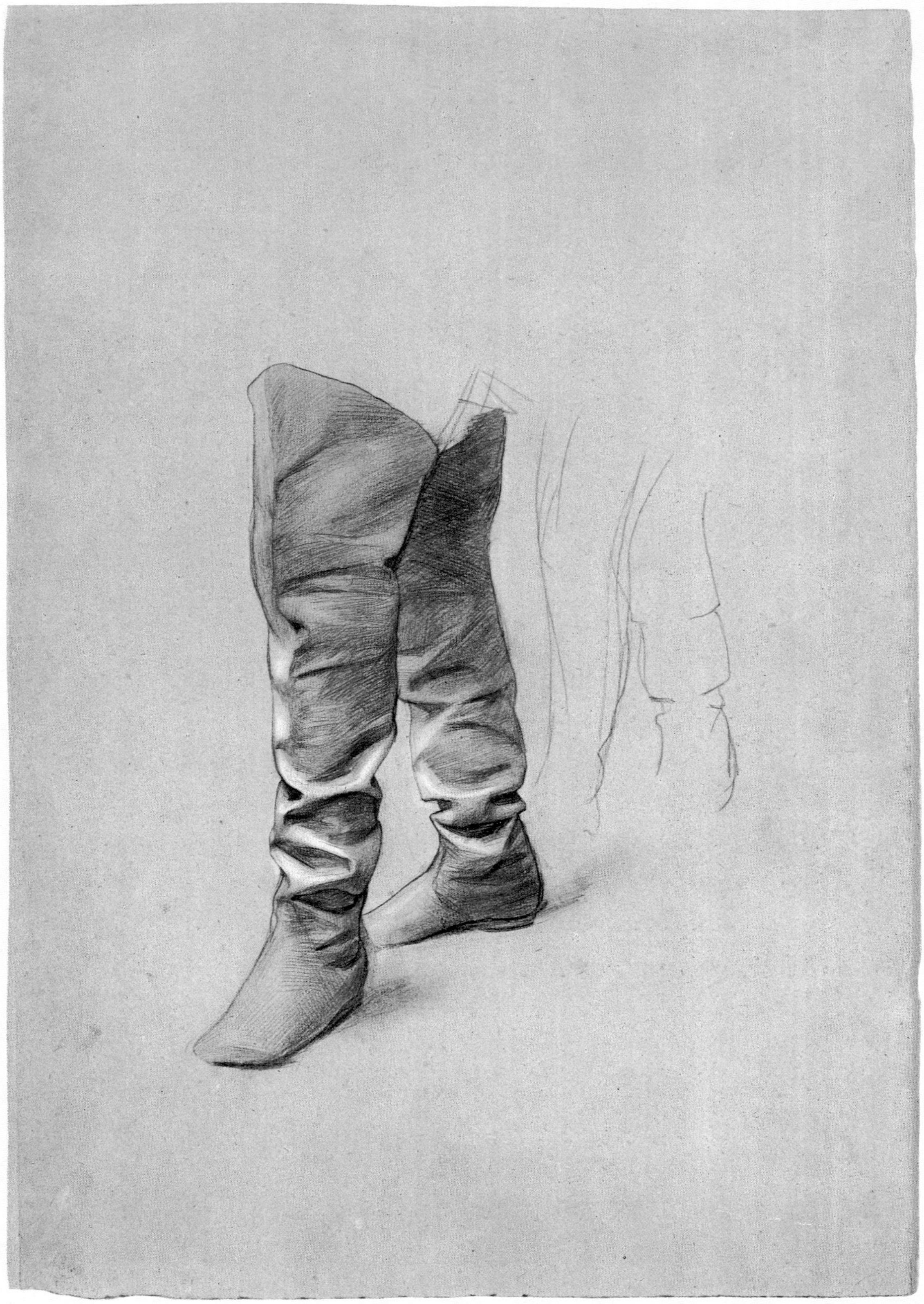

4. *Study of a pair of boots*, 1883–4.

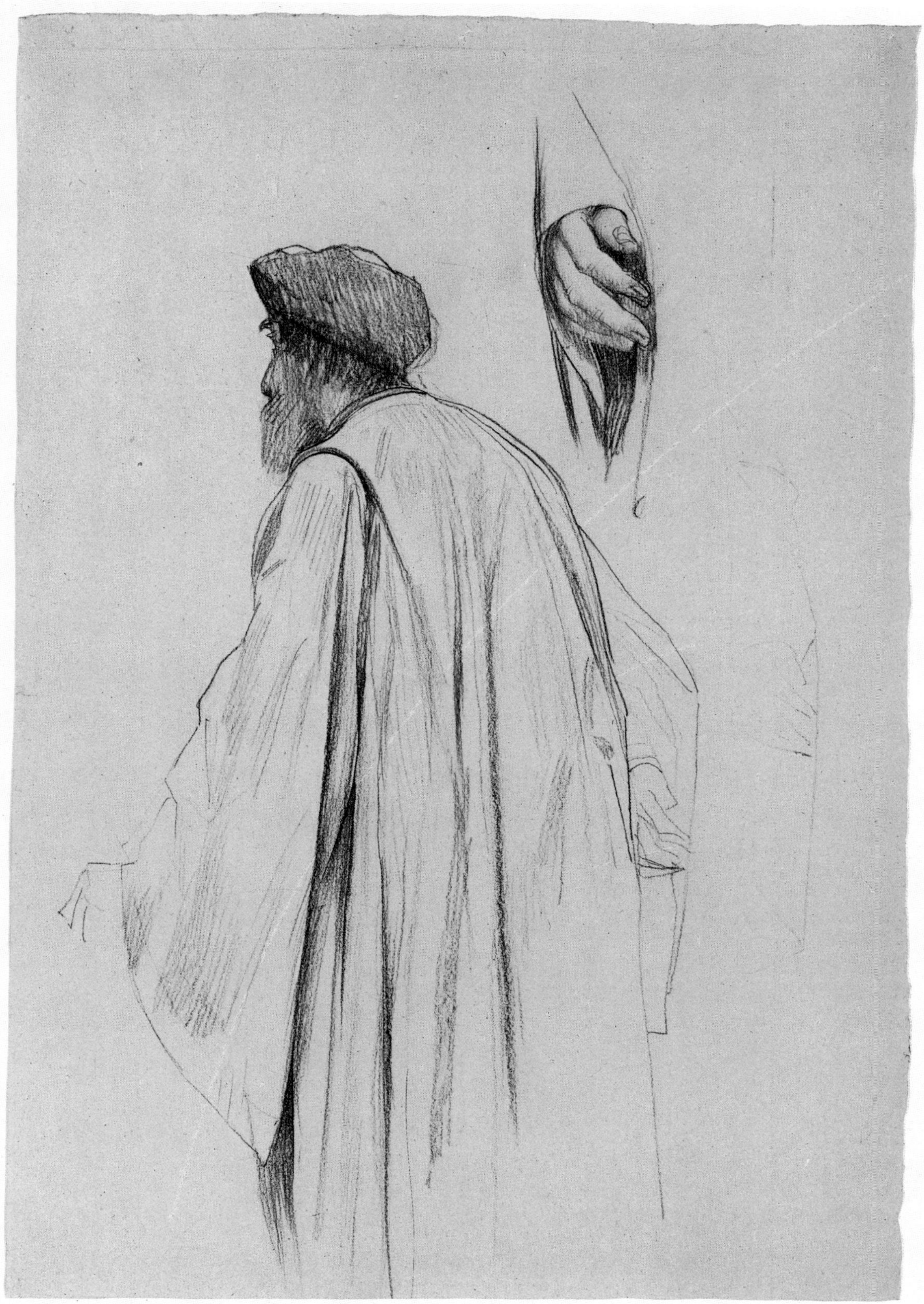

5. *Bearded man standing, back view, with two studies of a right hand*, 1886.

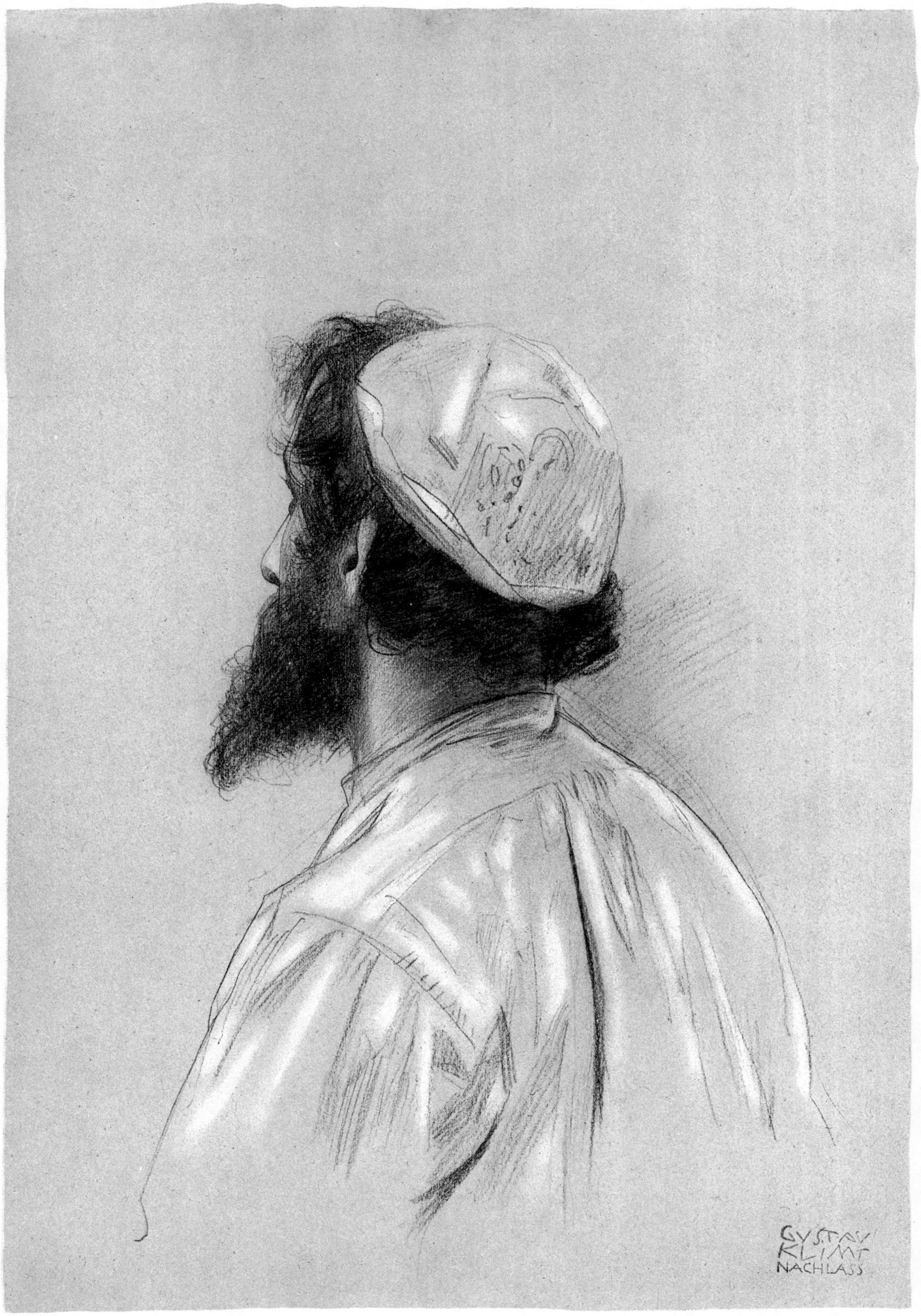

6. *Young man with beard and skull-cap*, 1886–88.

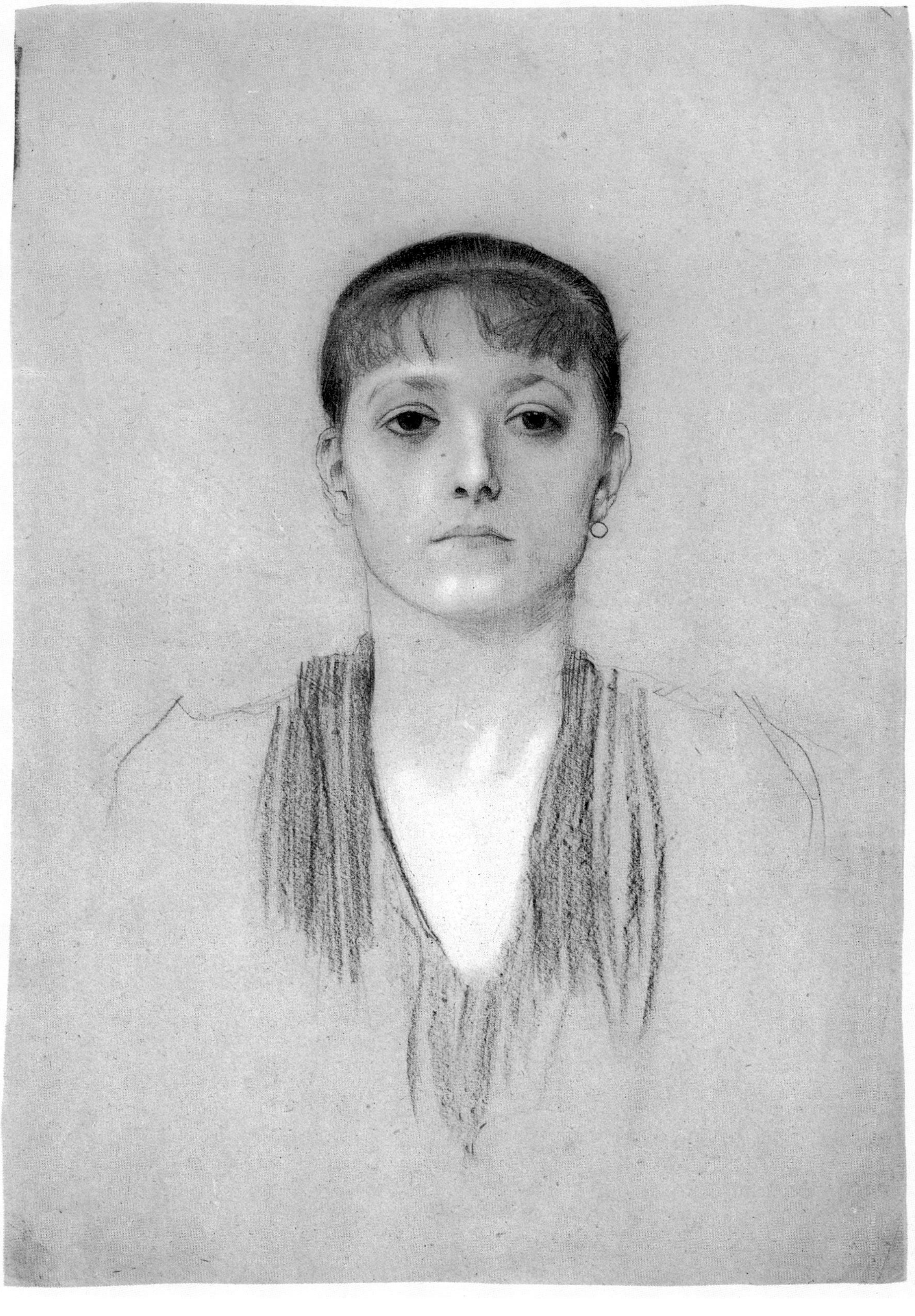

7. *Portrait study of a young woman*, 1890–91.

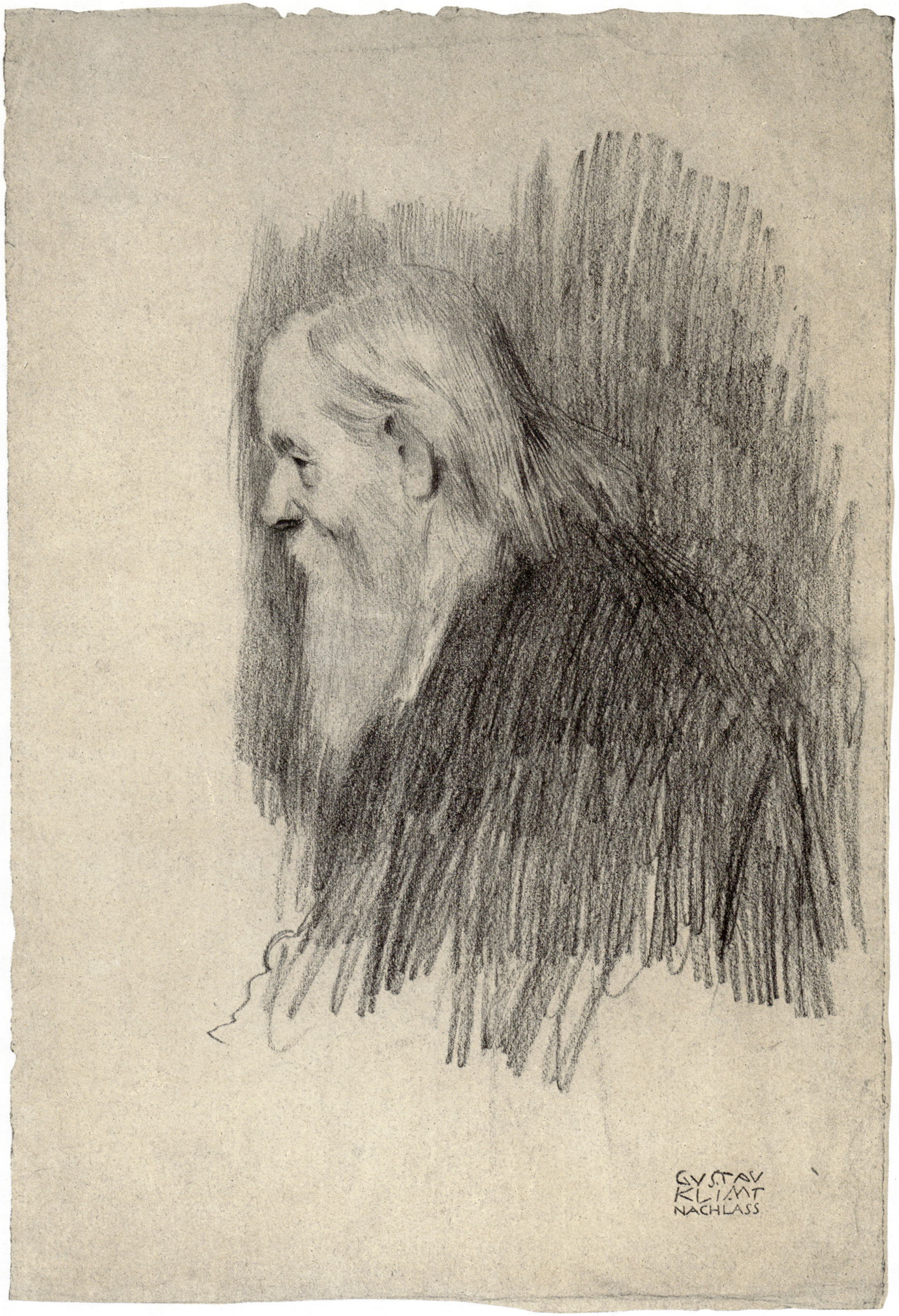

8. *Portrait study of an old man in profile*, *c*. 1890–94.

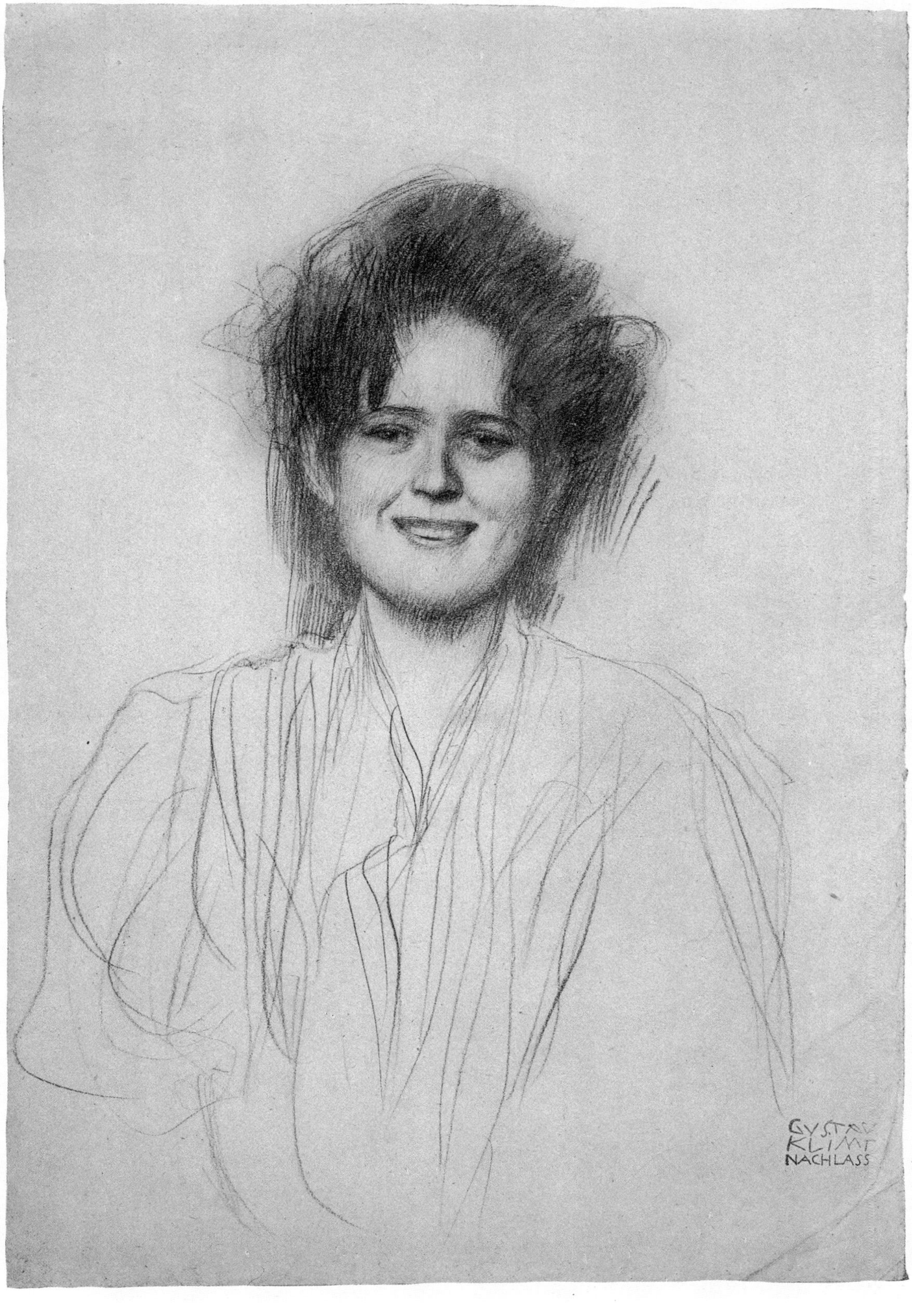

9. *Portrait study of a young woman smiling*, 1895–96.

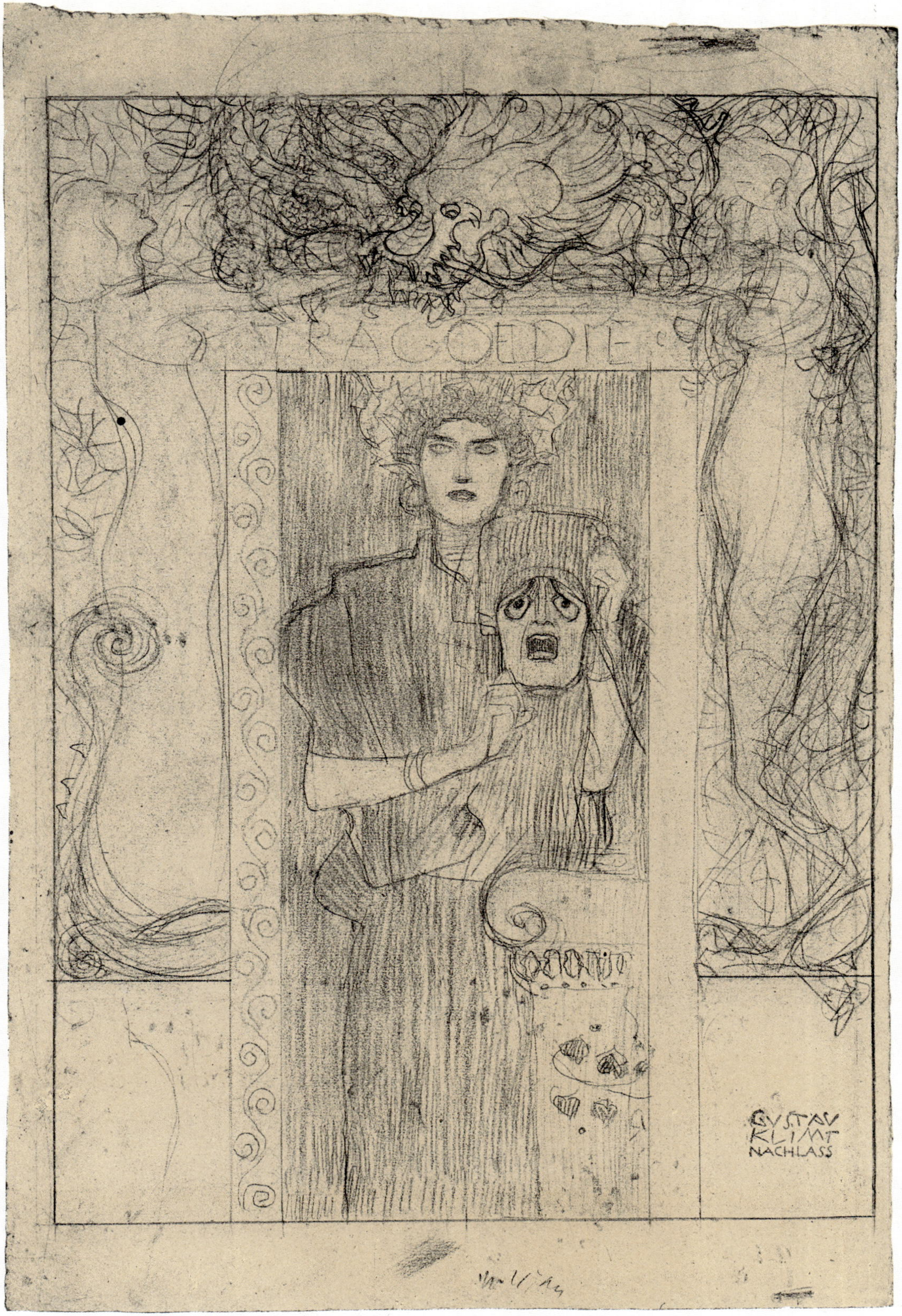

10. *Study for 'Tragedy'*, *c.* 1879.

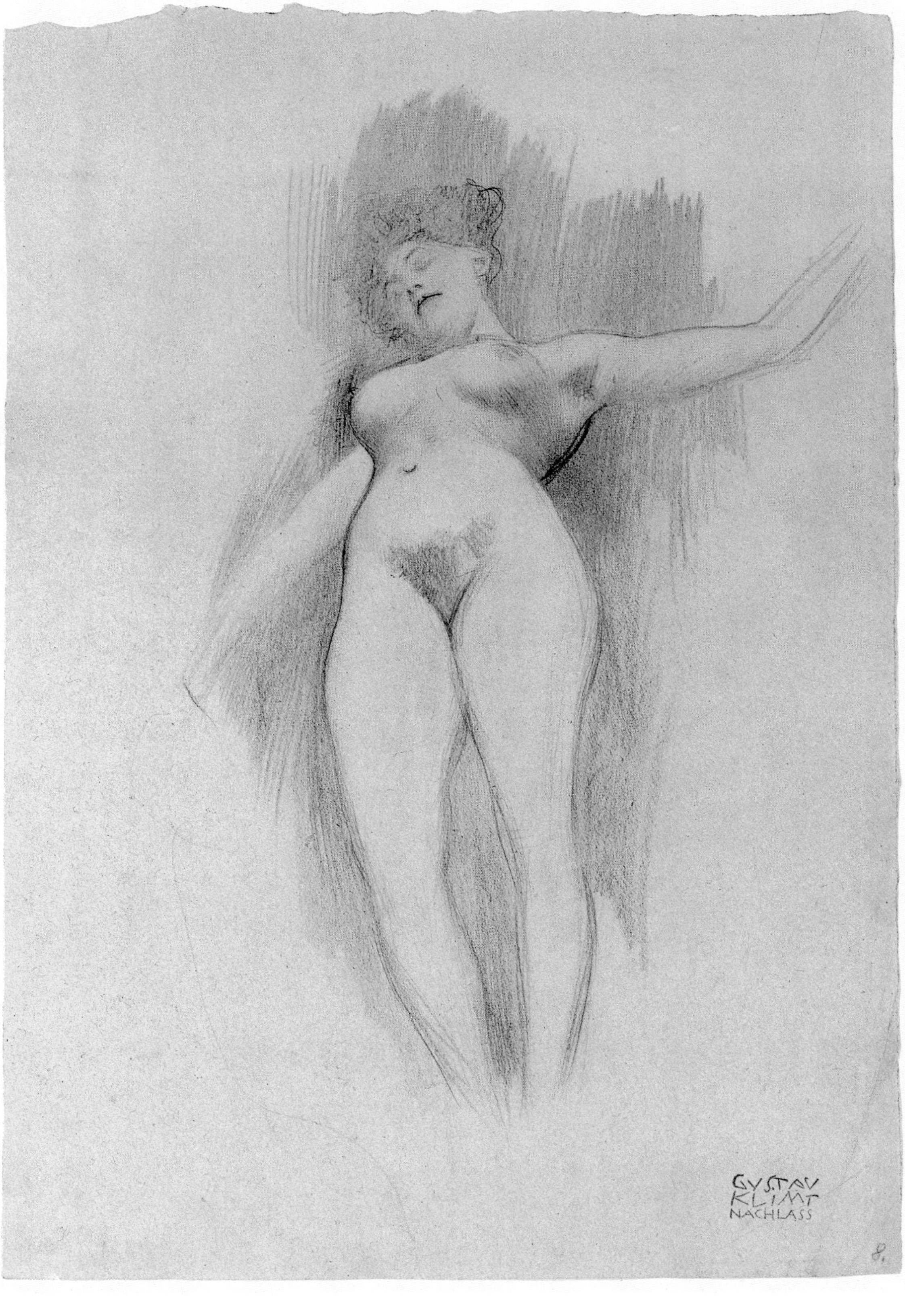

11. *Nude with dark background*, *c.* 1896.

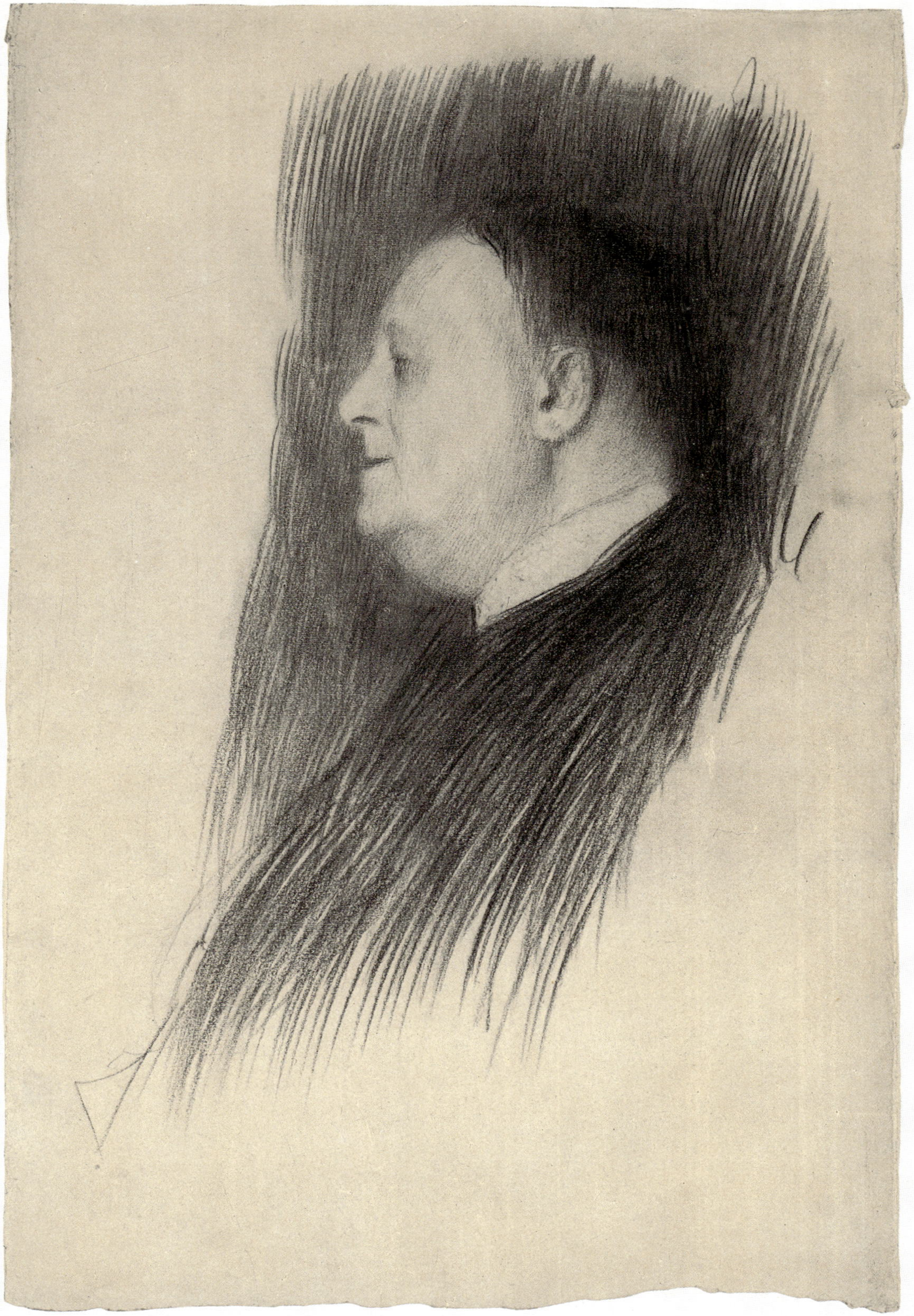

12. *Portrait study of a man in profile*, 1896–97.

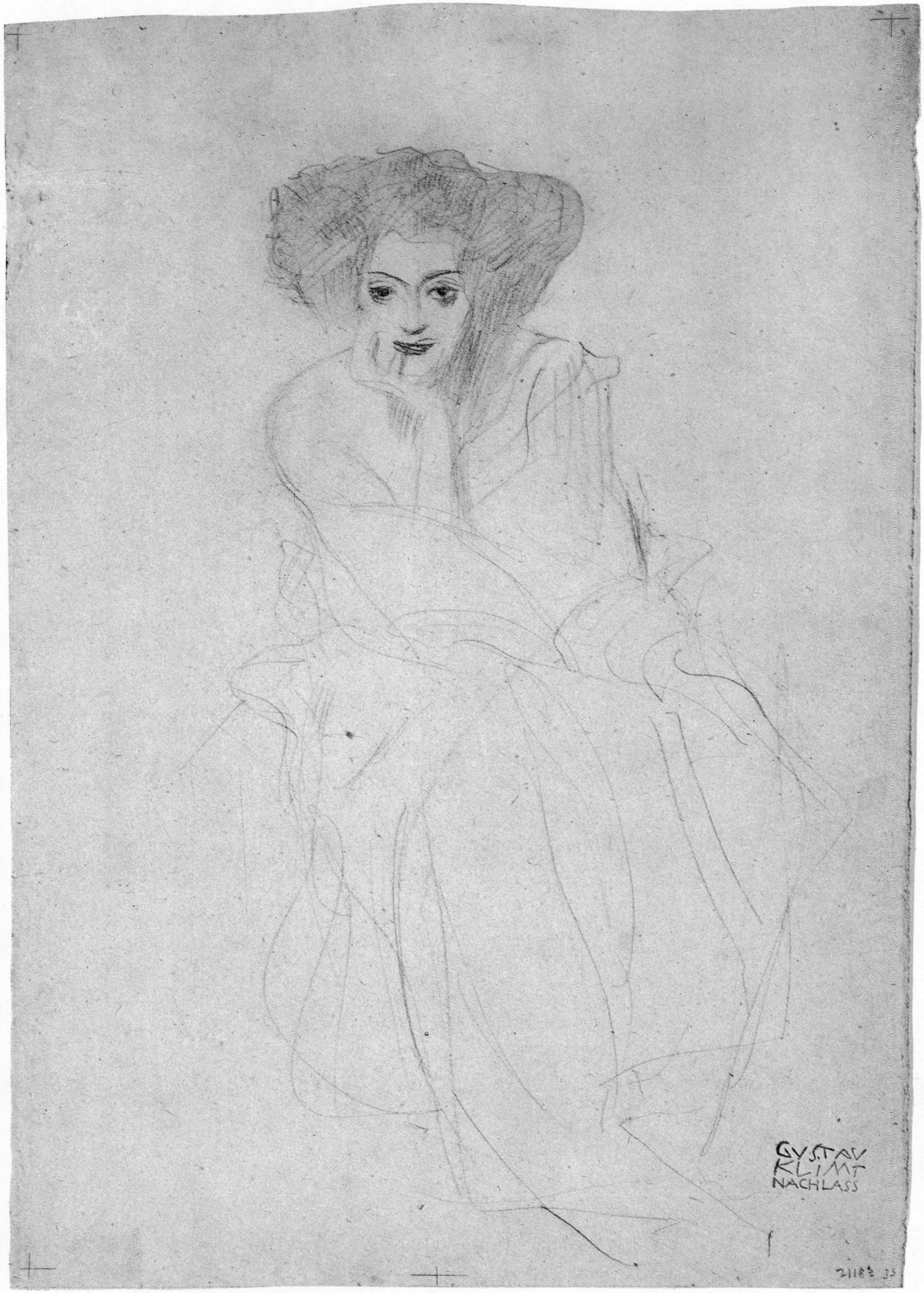

13. *Seated woman with chin resting on right hand*, 1897.

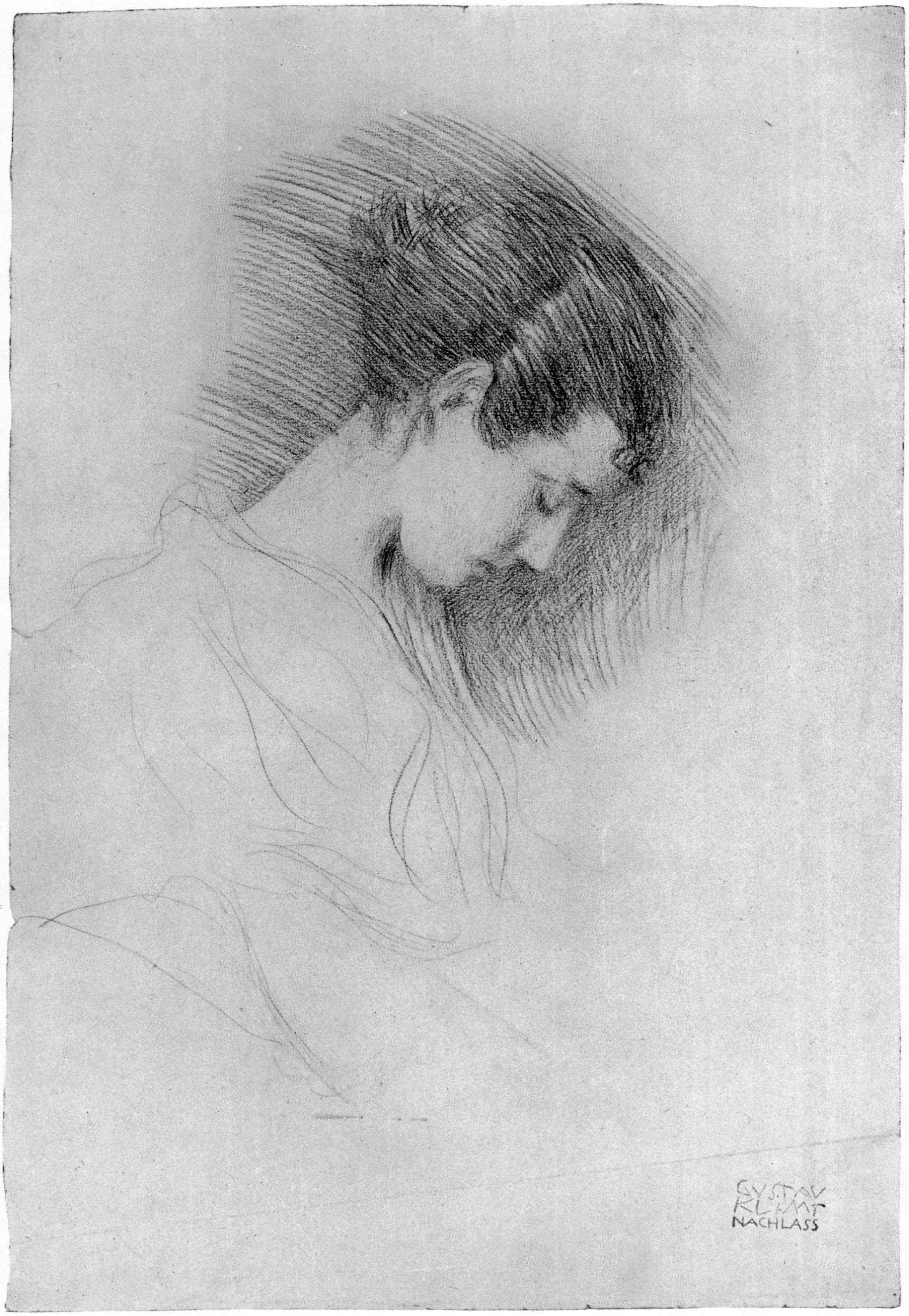

14. *Portrait study of a young woman in profile with tilted head,* 1897–98.

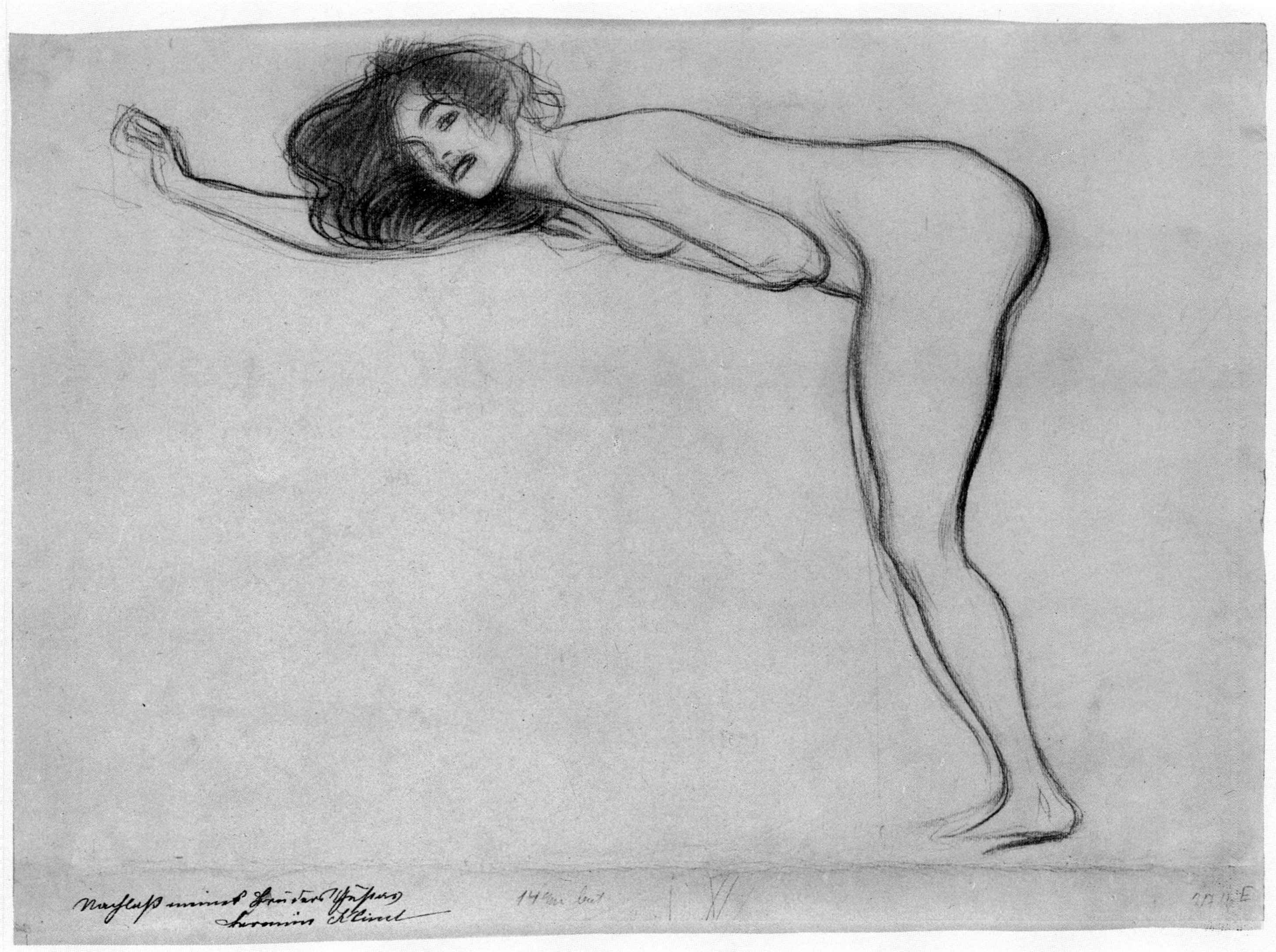

15 *Nude, bending forwards*, 1898.

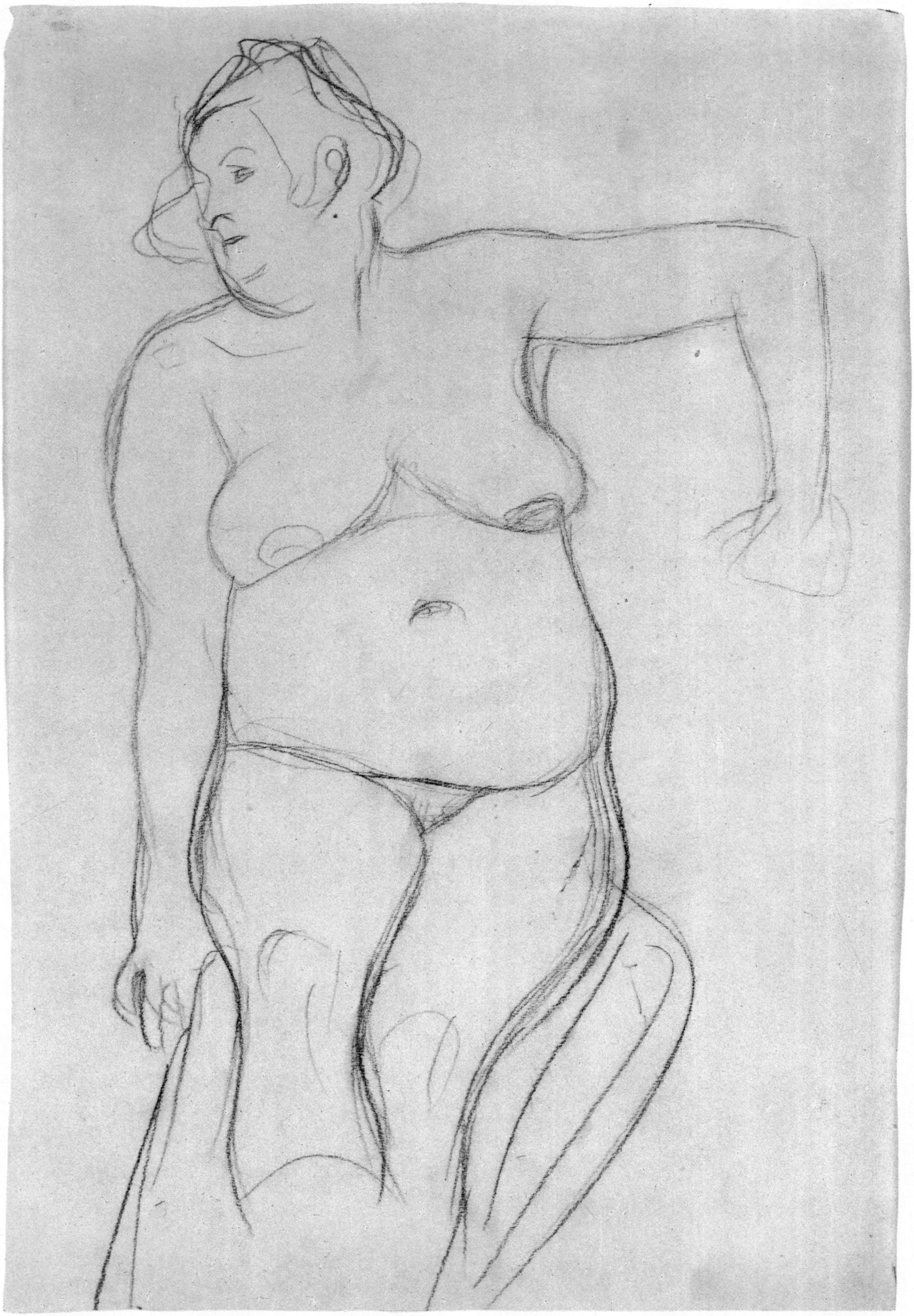

16. *Seated nude, fat woman*, 1899–1900.

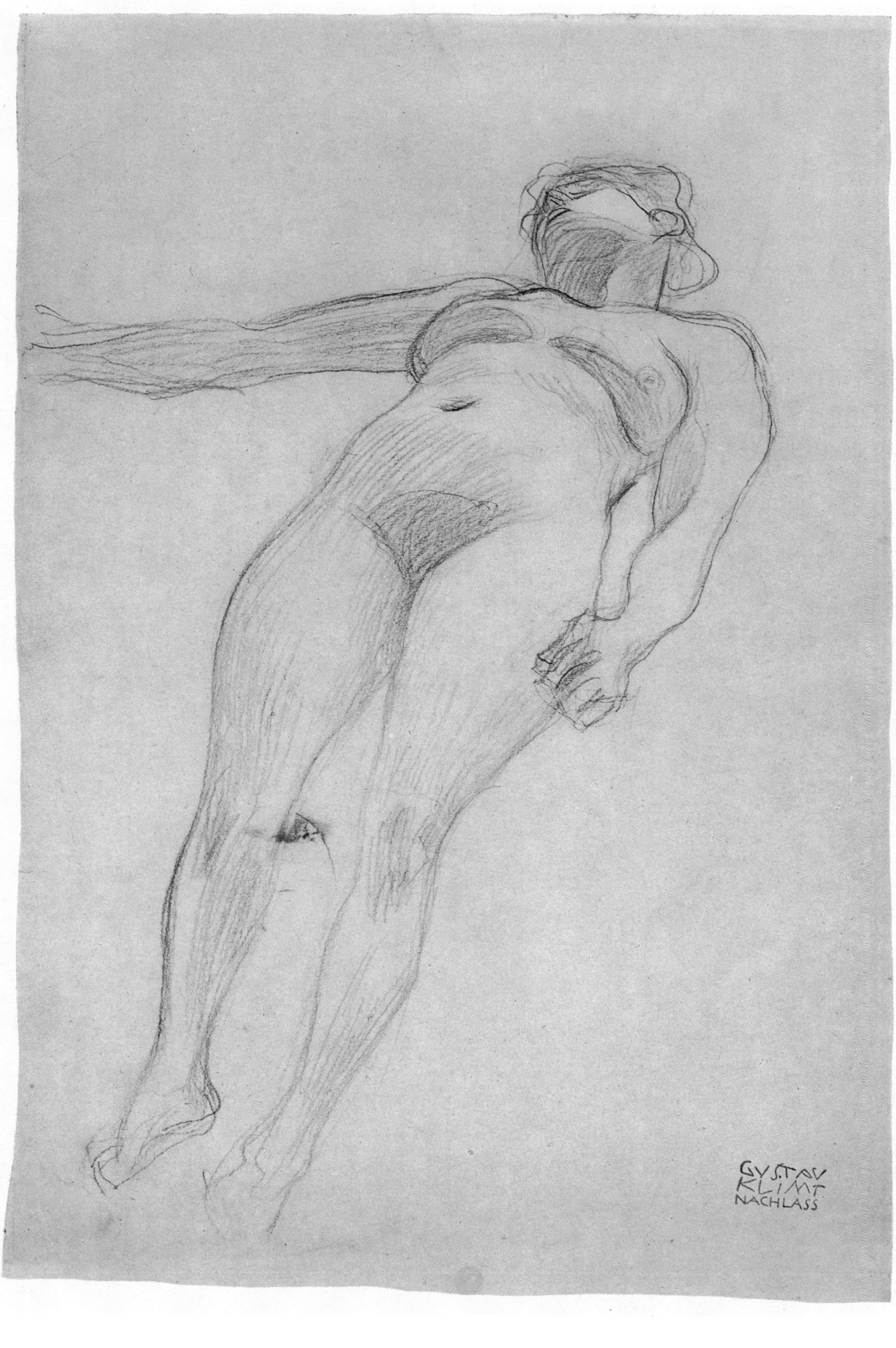

17. *Nude with right arm extended*, 1900.

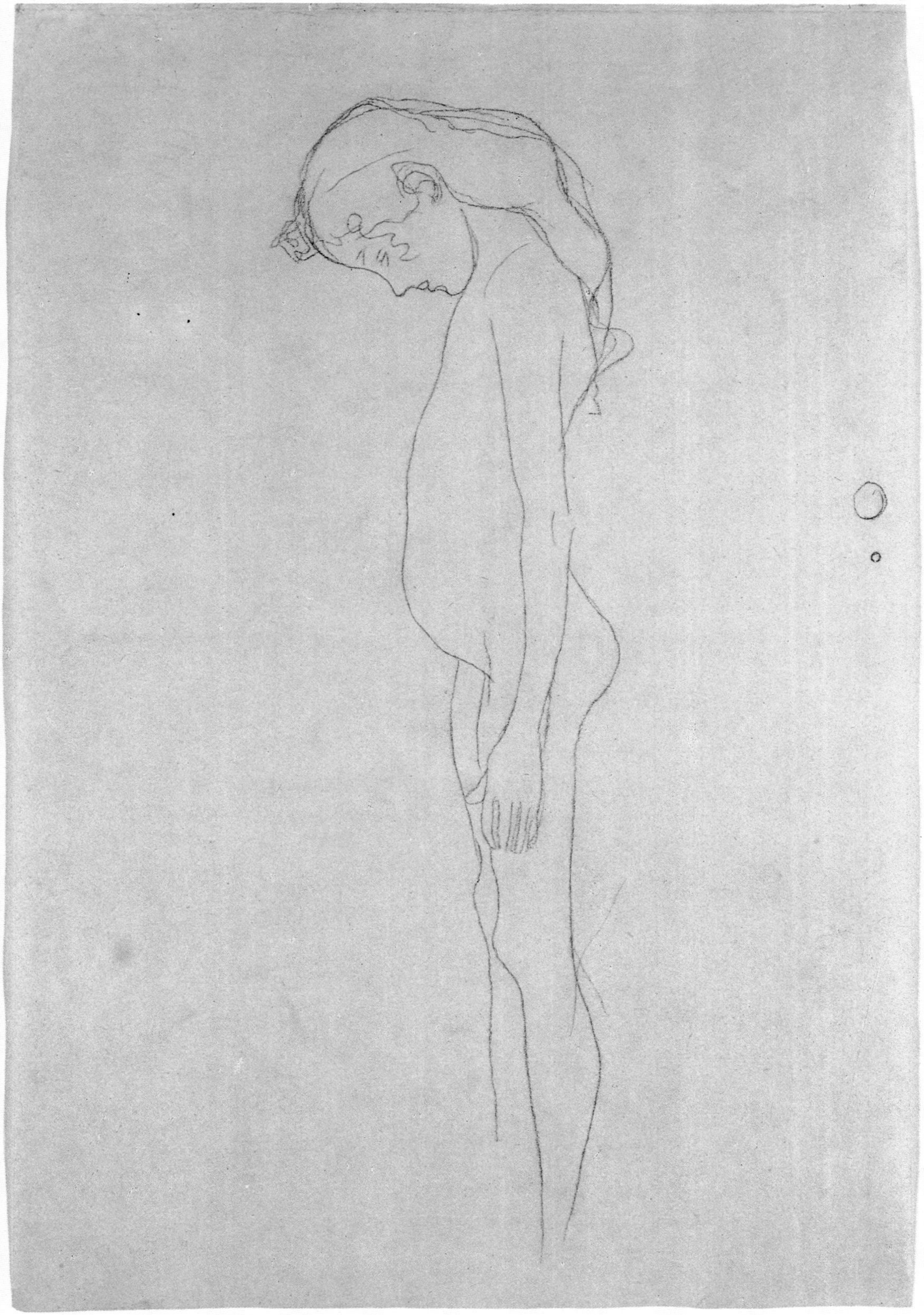

18. *Nude: young girl standing, looking downwards*, *c.* 1901.

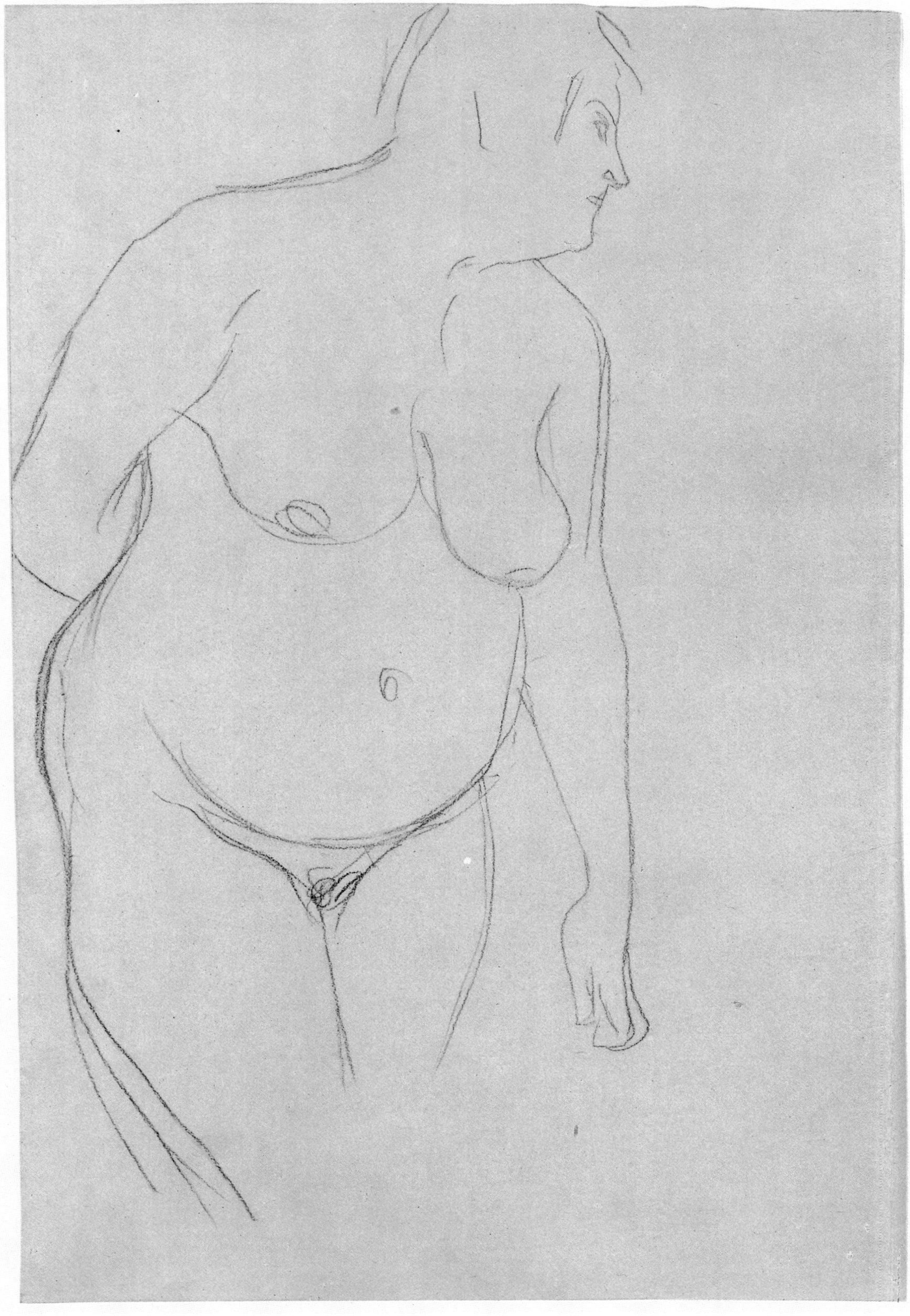

19. *Nude: fat woman, standing*, c. 1901.

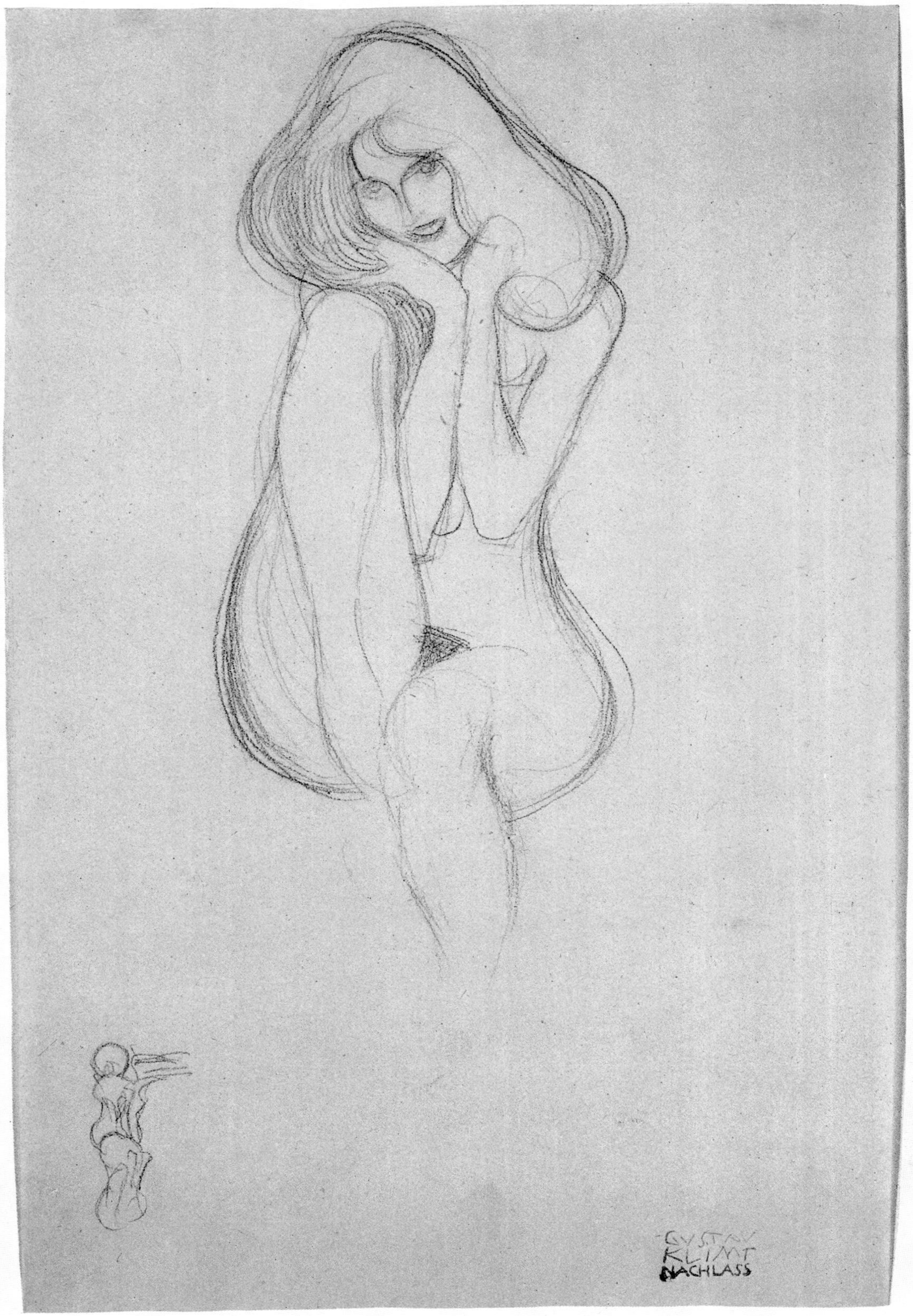

20. *Seated nude with right leg raised,* c. 1901.

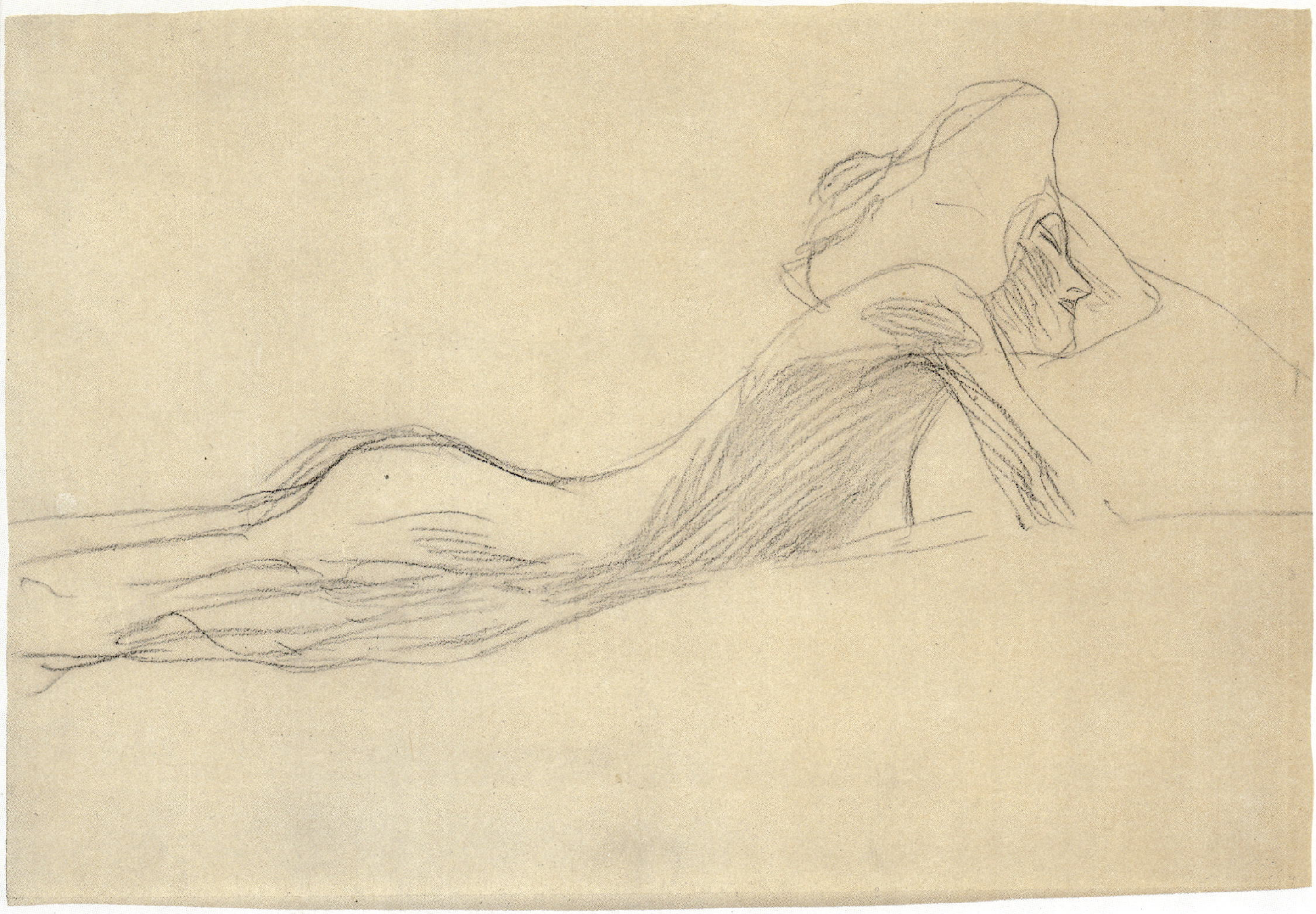

21. *Nude, prone*, *c.* 1901.

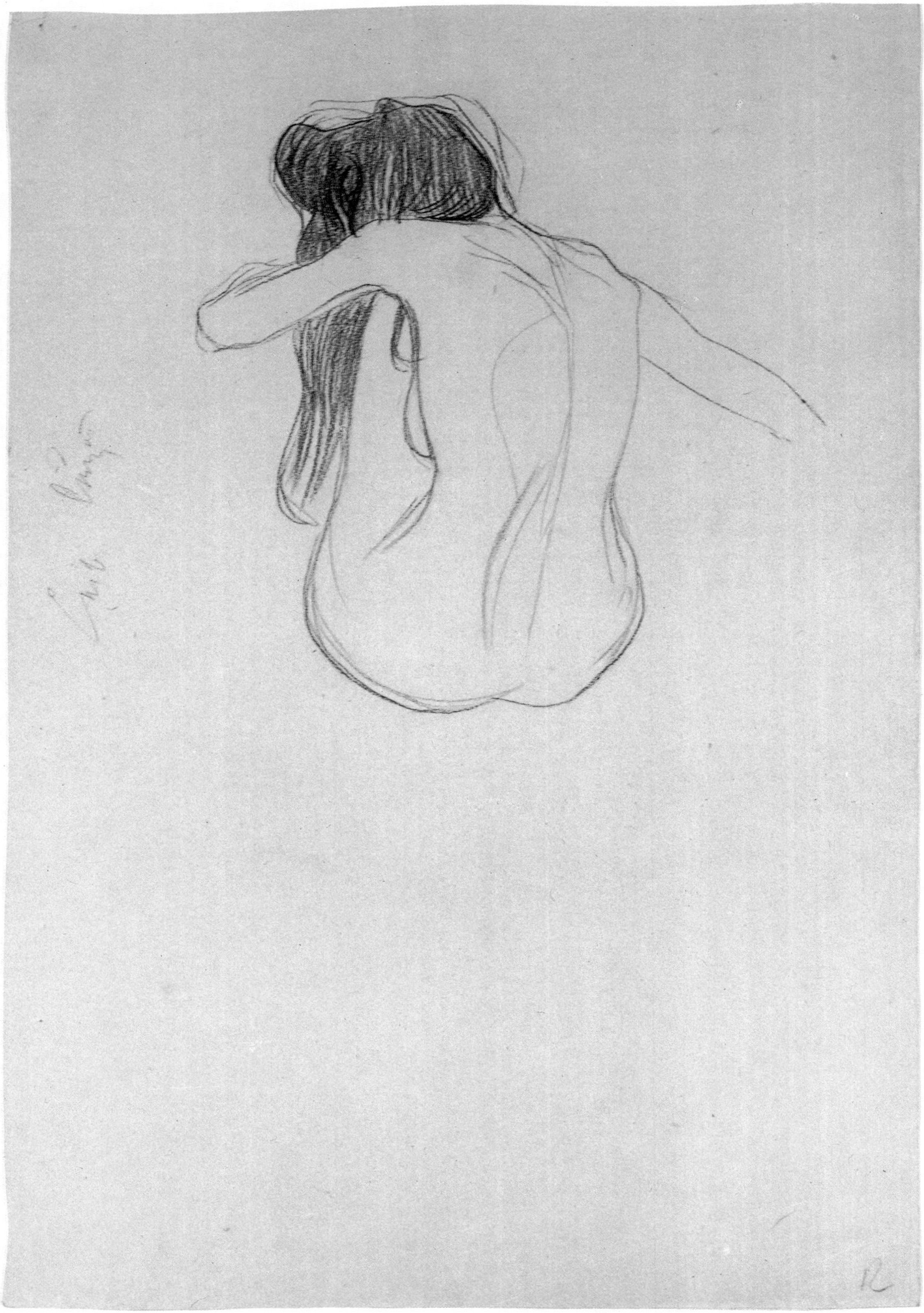

22. *Seated nude,*
back view, *c.* 1901.

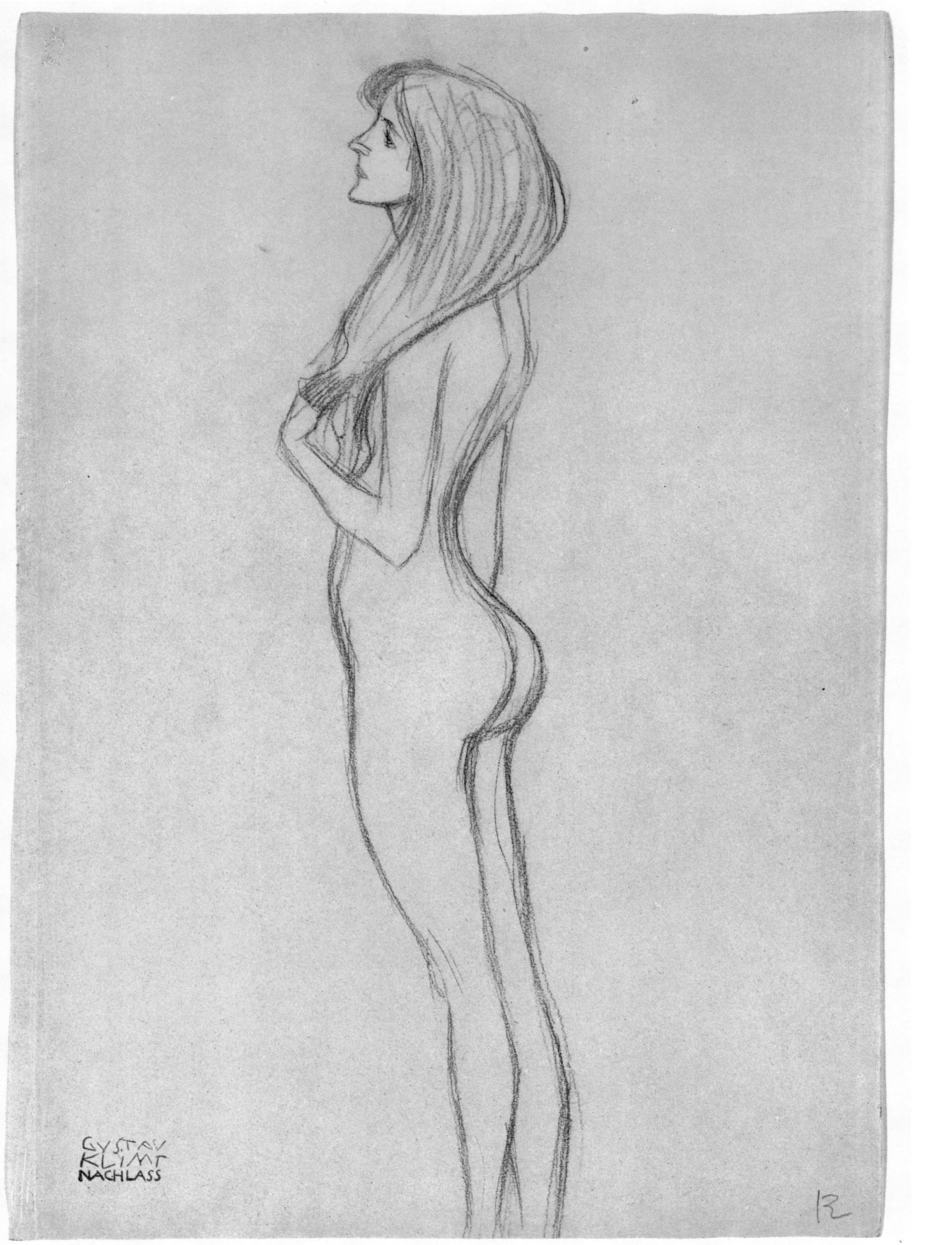

23. *Standing nude in profile*, 1901.

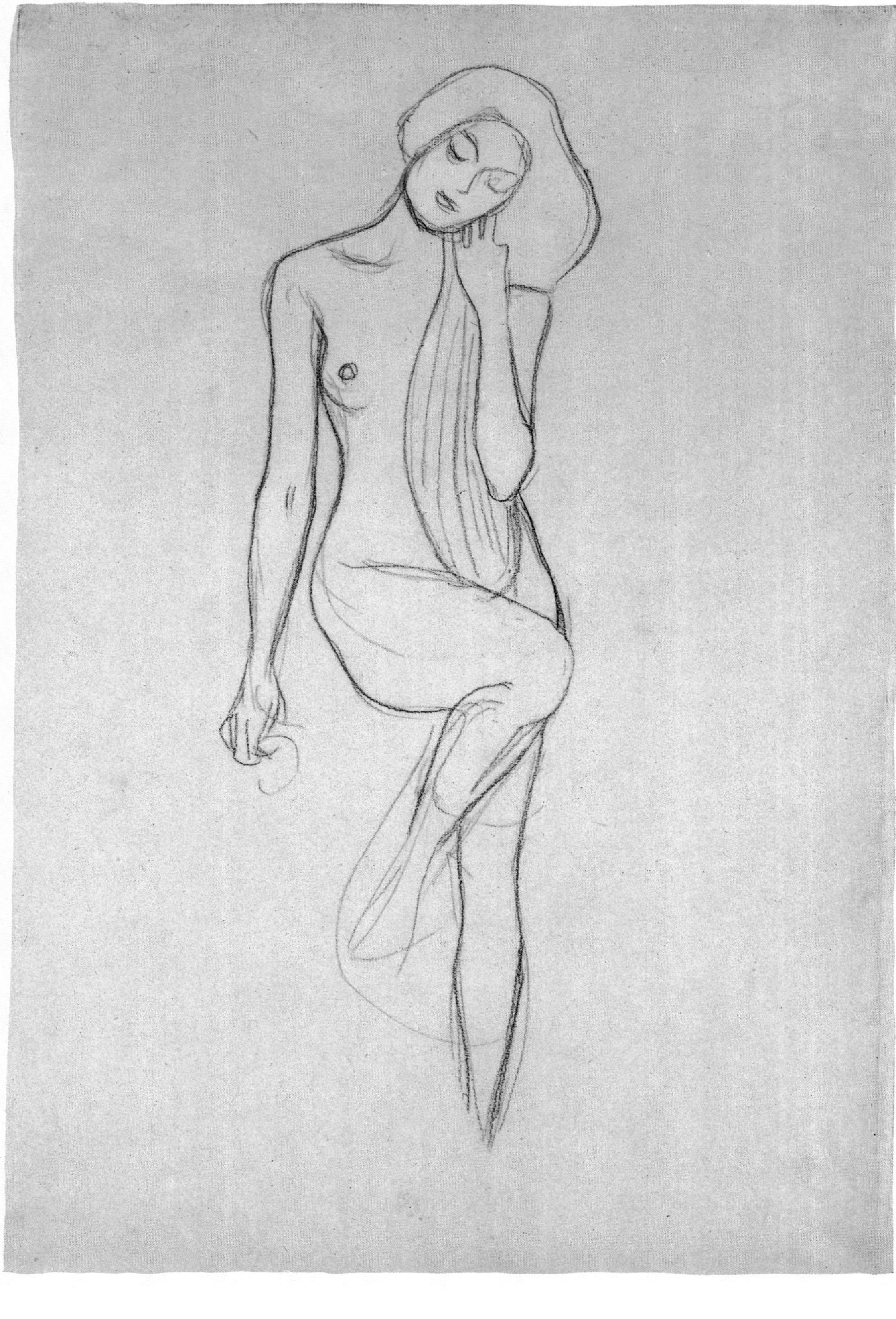

24. *Standing nude with right leg raised,* 1901.

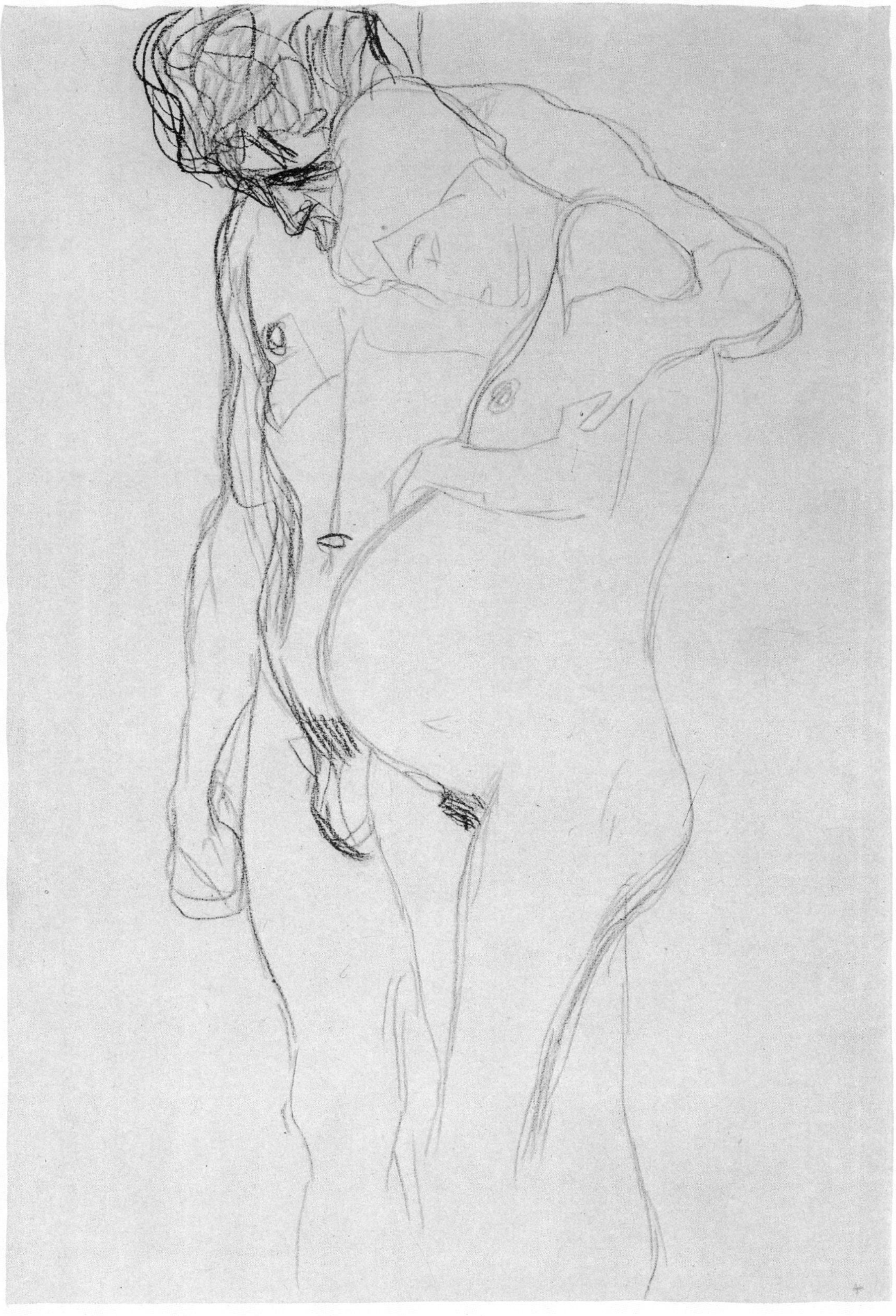

25. *Nudes: male and pregnant female*, 1902.

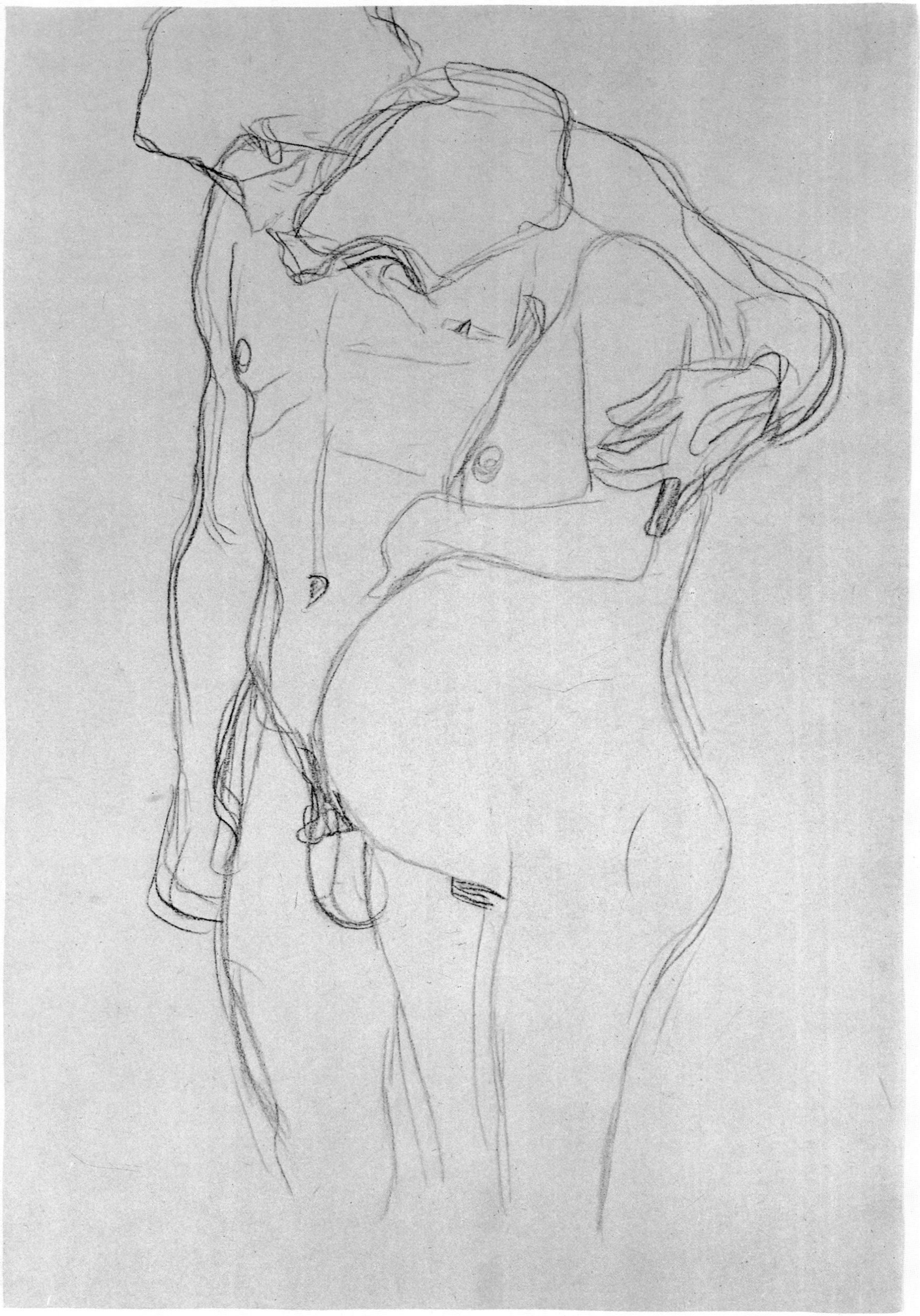

26. *Nudes: male and pregnant female*, 1902.

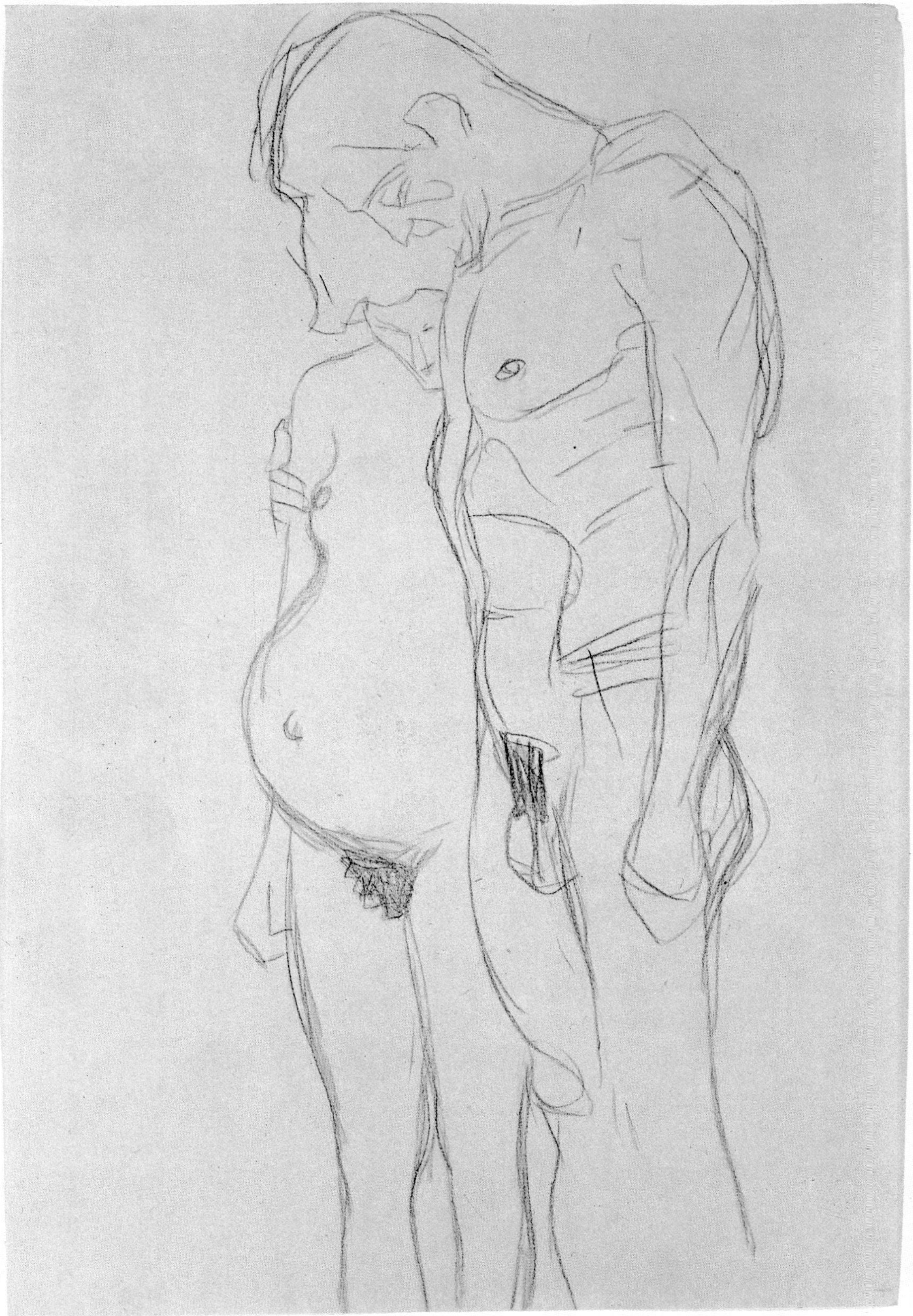

27. *Nudes: male and pregnant female*, 1902.

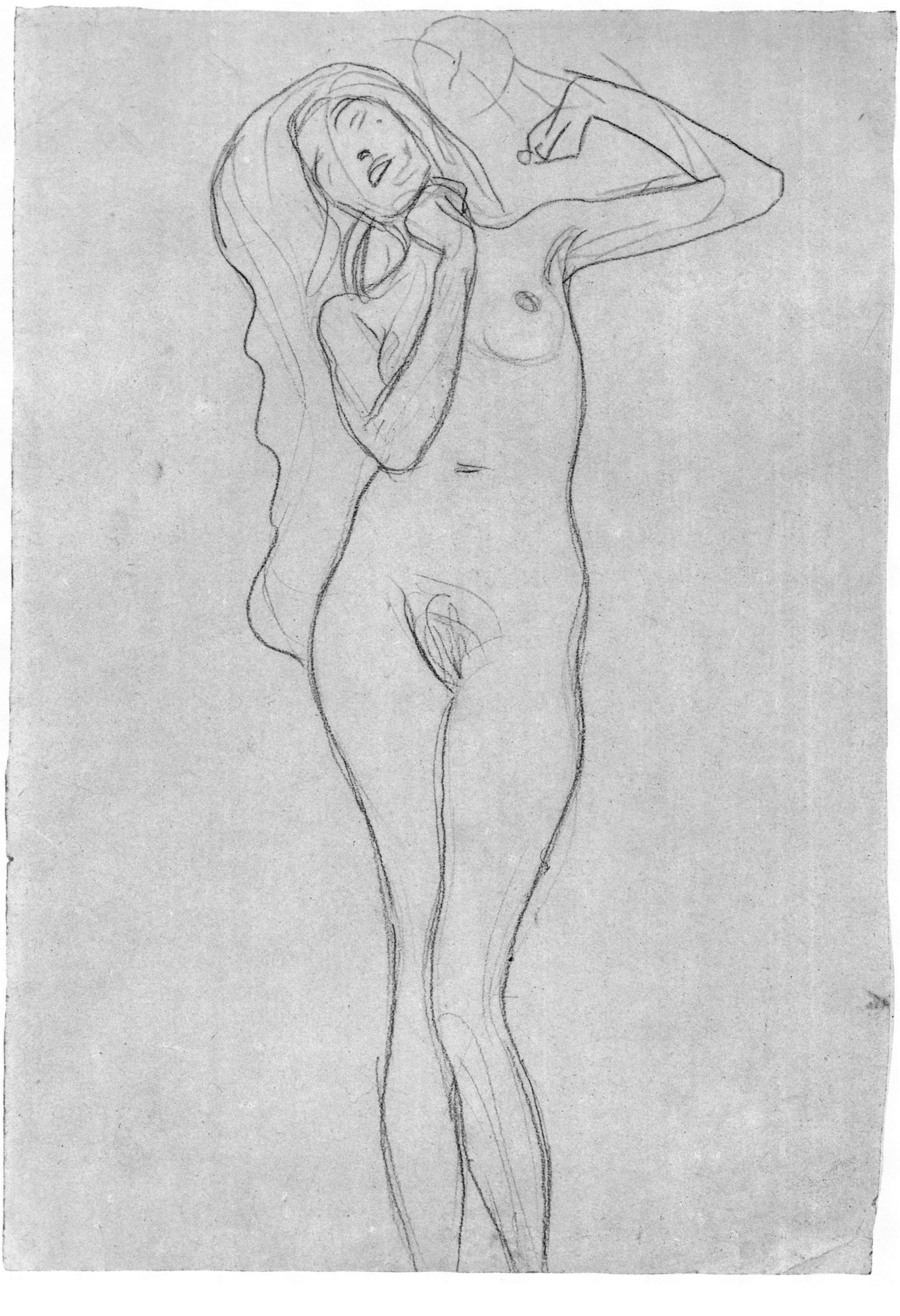

28. *Standing nude with raised arms, c.* 1902.

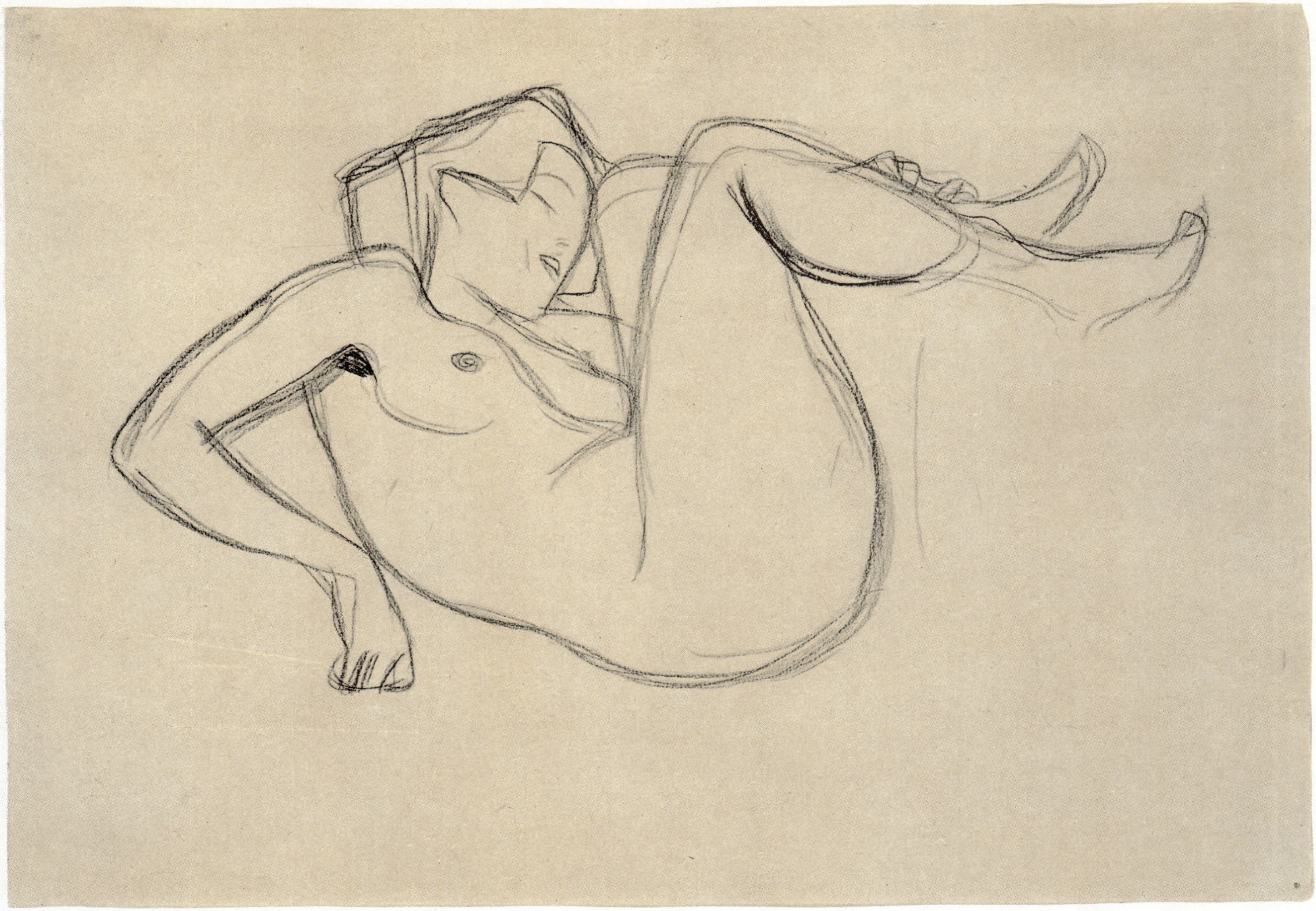

29. *Nude, supine*, 1903.

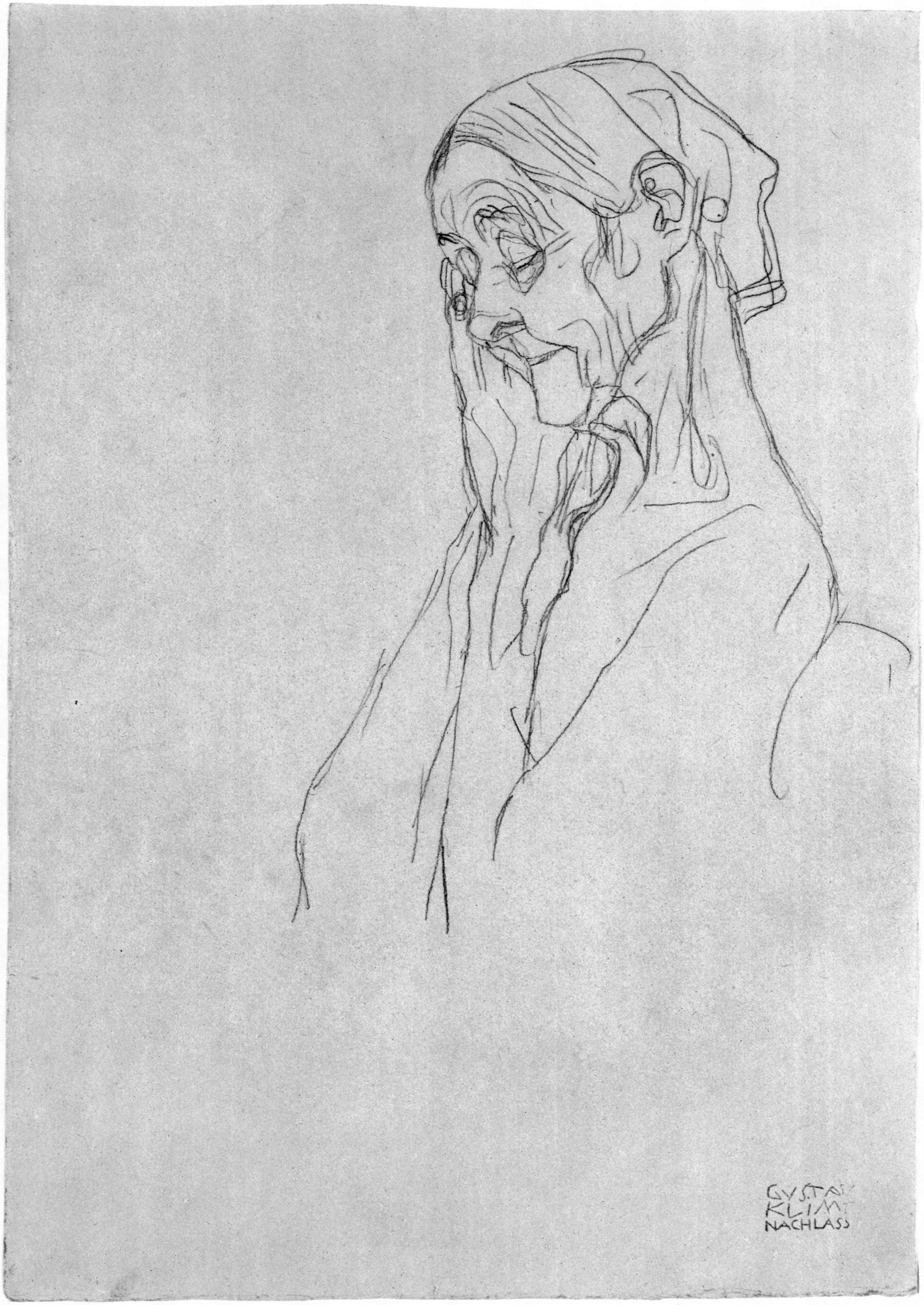

30. *Portrait study of an old woman with hands to her face*, 1903.

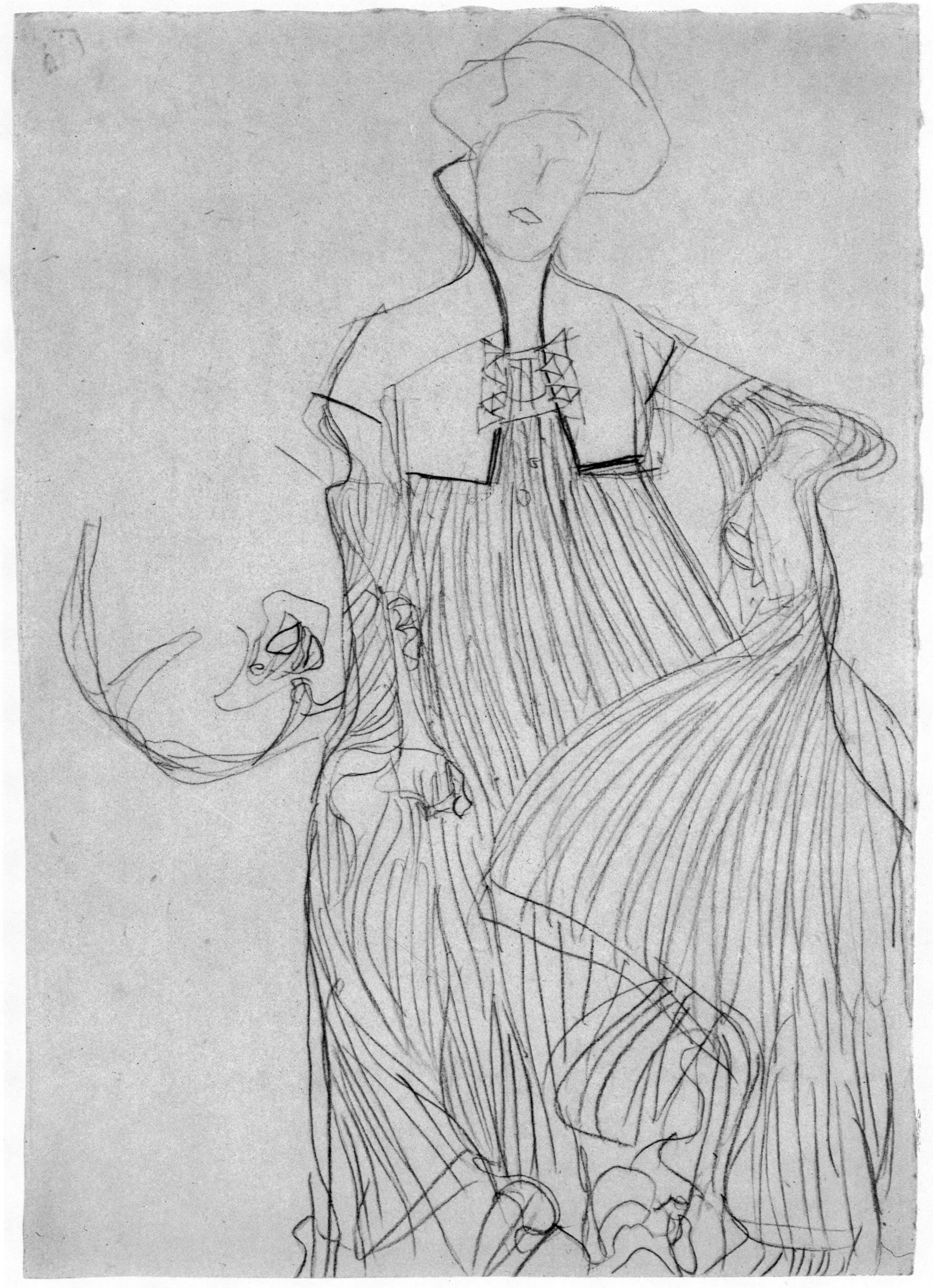

31. *Seated lady*, 1903.

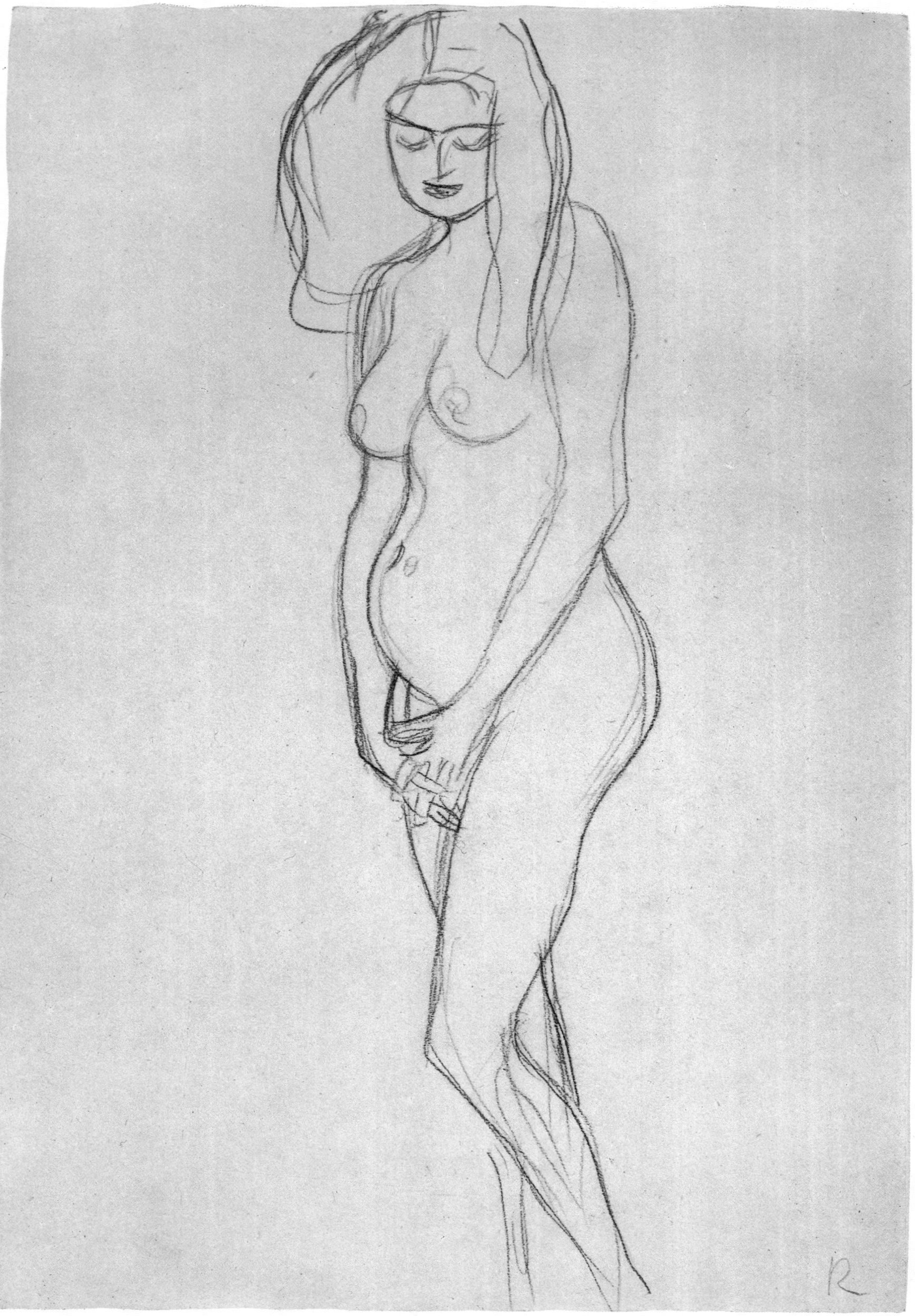

32. *Standing nude looking downwards*, 1903.

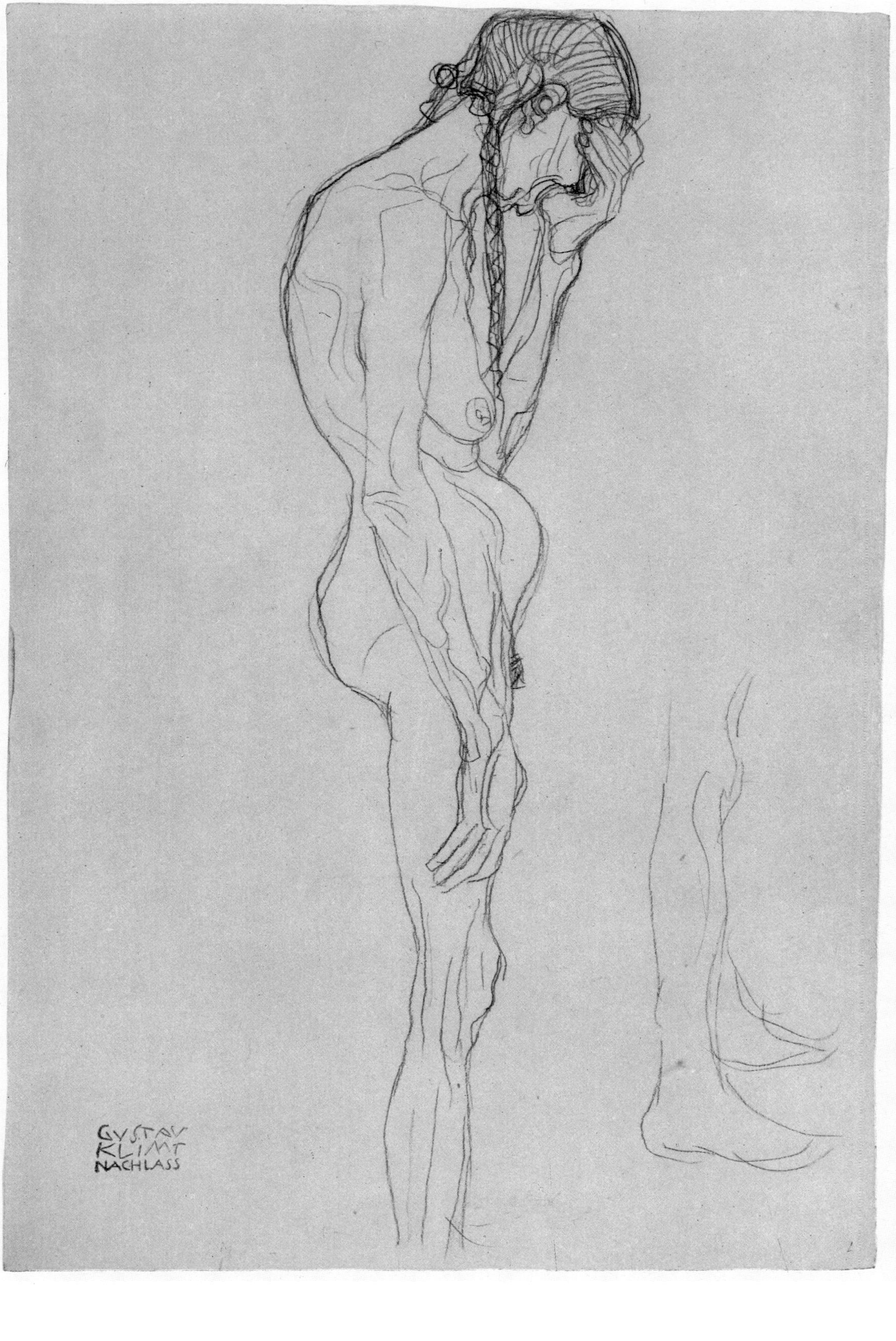

33. *Nude: old woman standing in profile, and study of legs*, 1903.

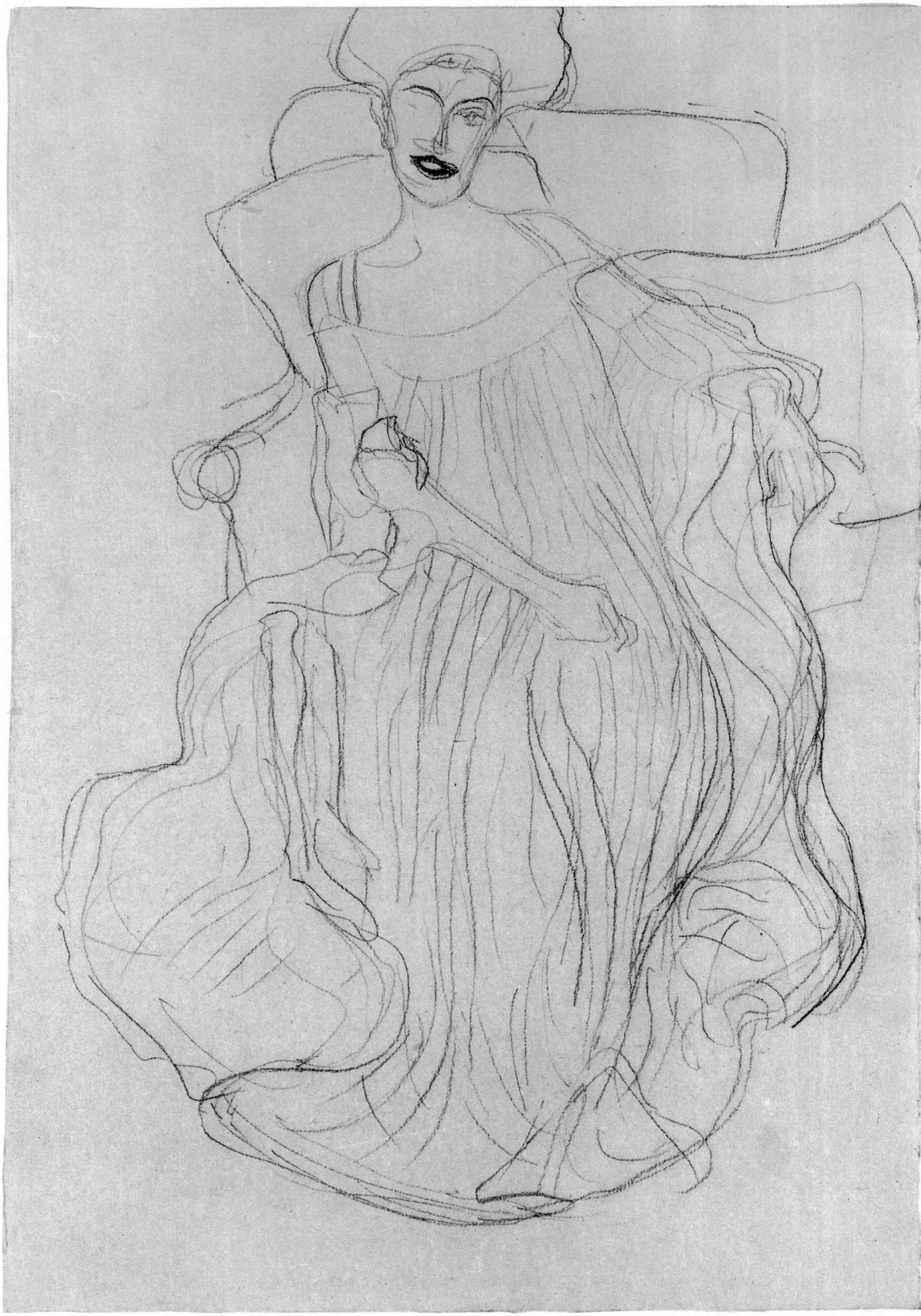

34. *Lady seated in an armchair*, 1903–04.

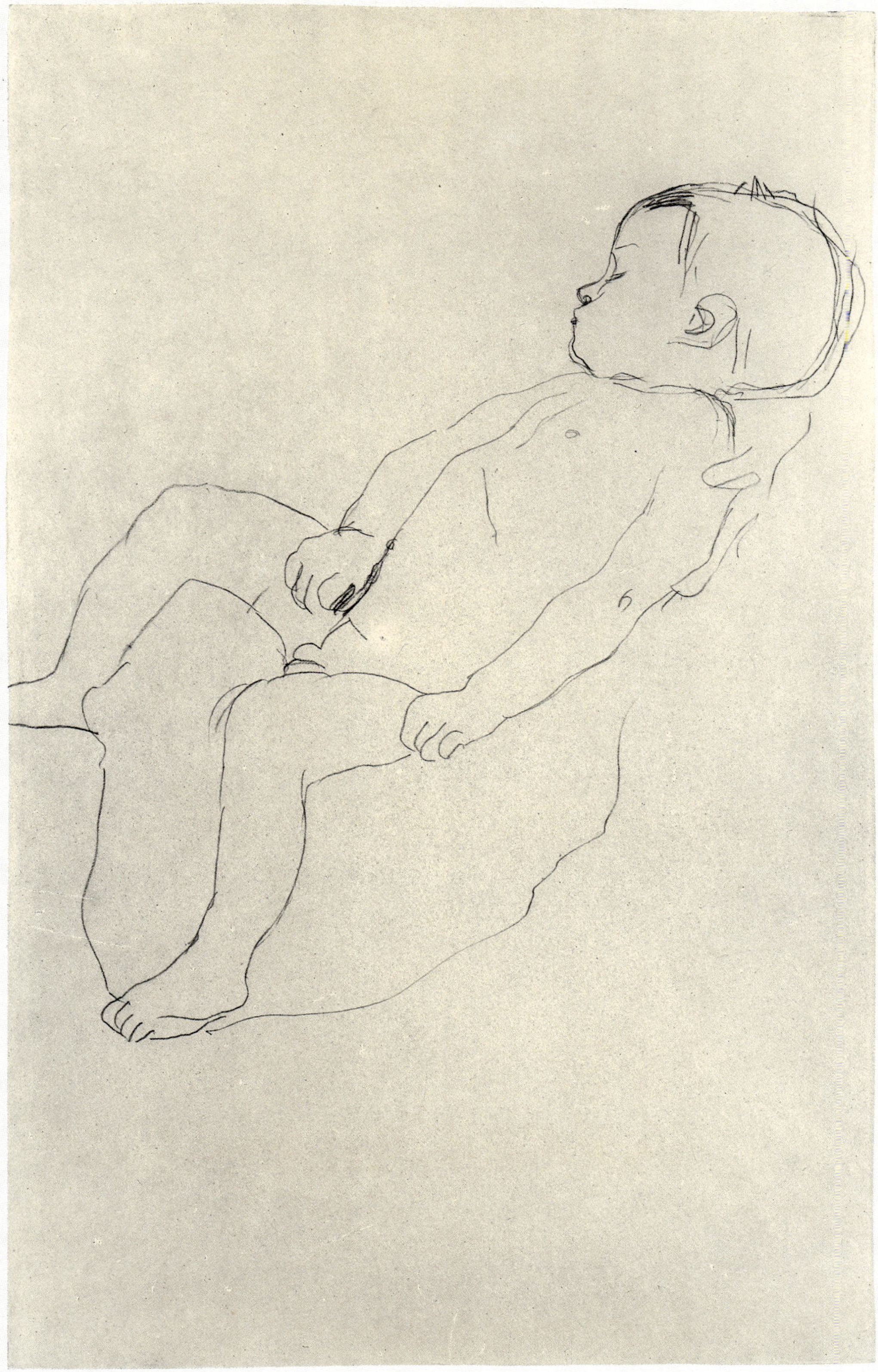

35. *Sleeping infant*, 1904.

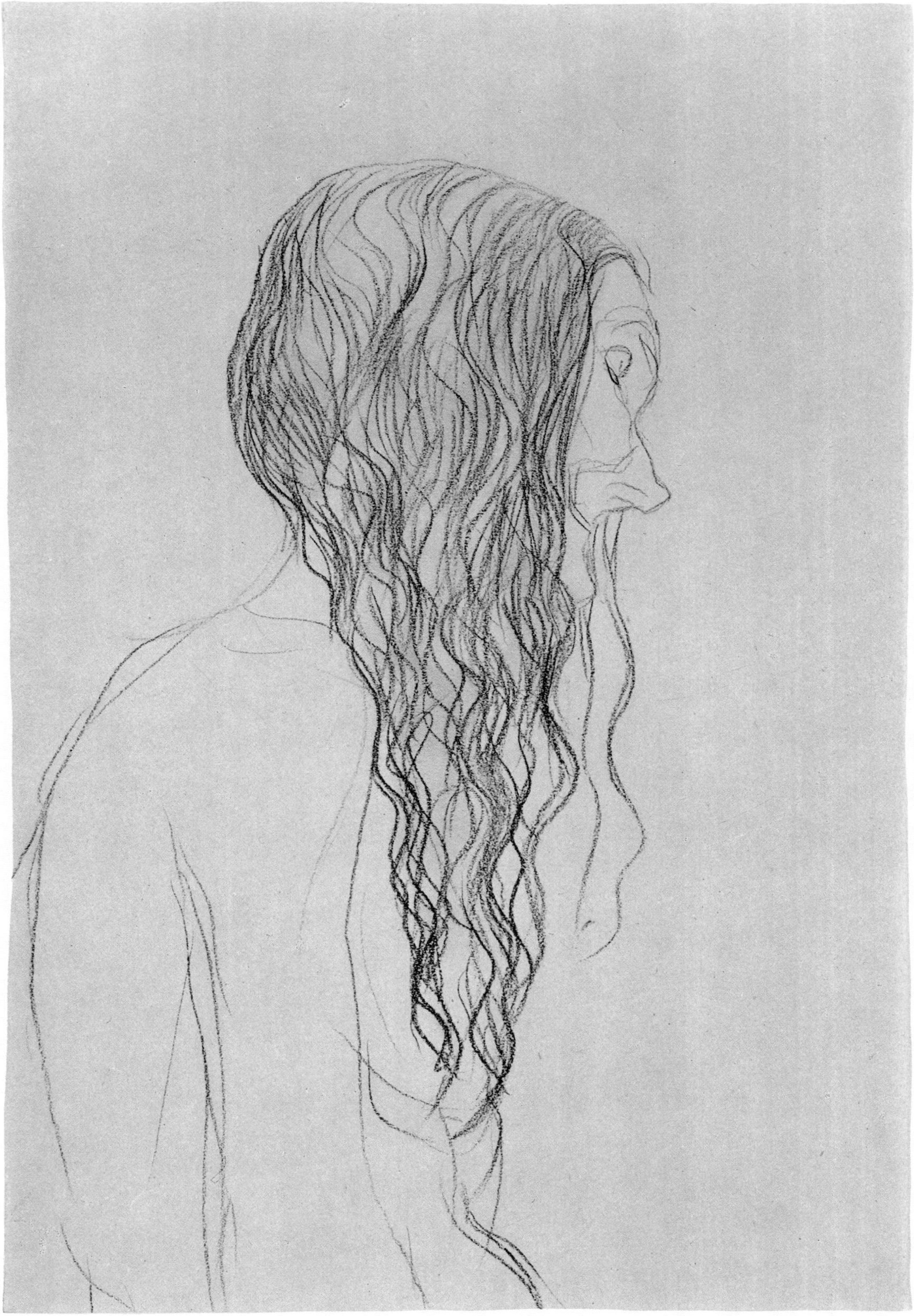

36. *Study of an old woman in profile*, 1904.

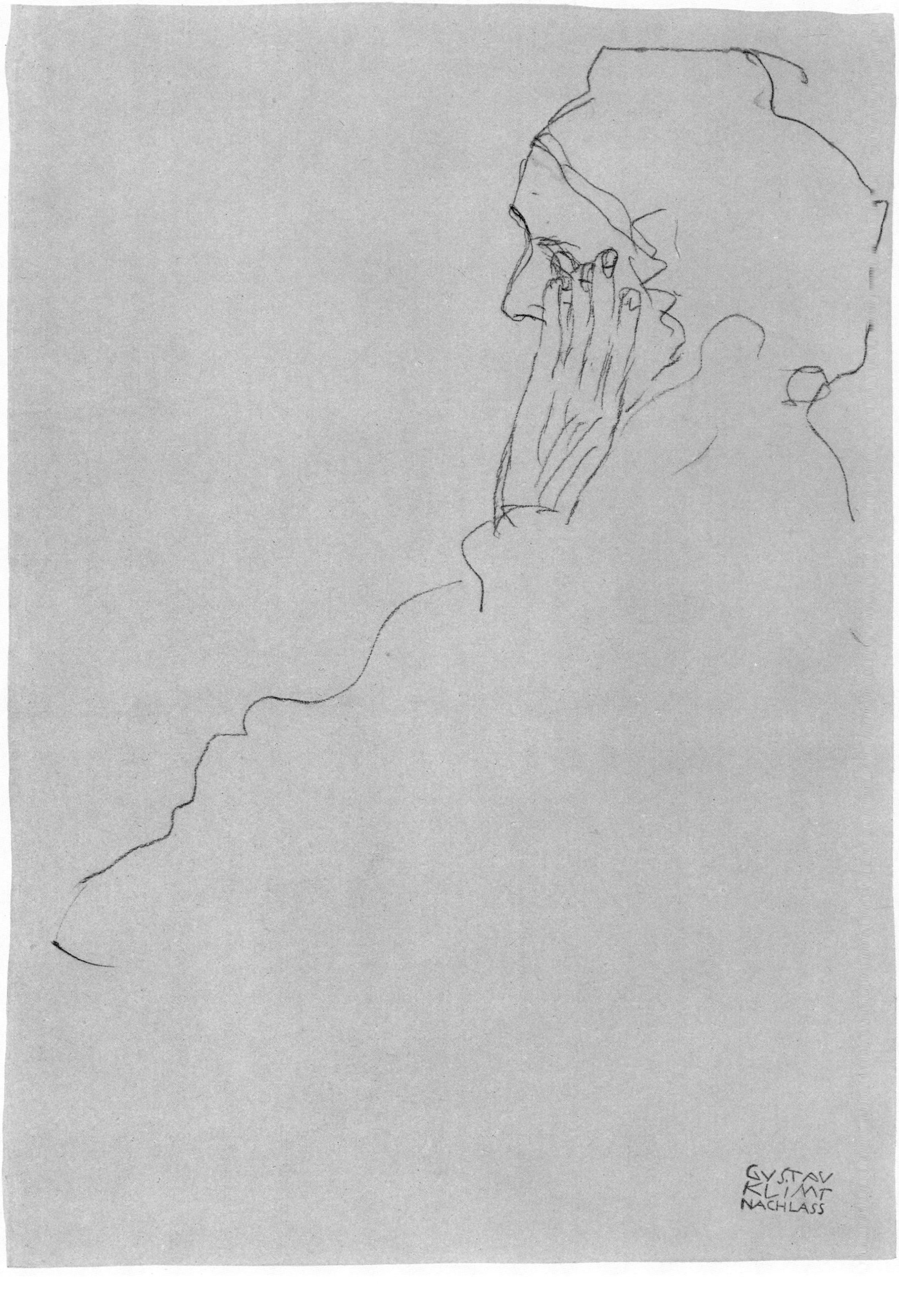

37. *Old woman, seated, with left hand to her face*, 1904.

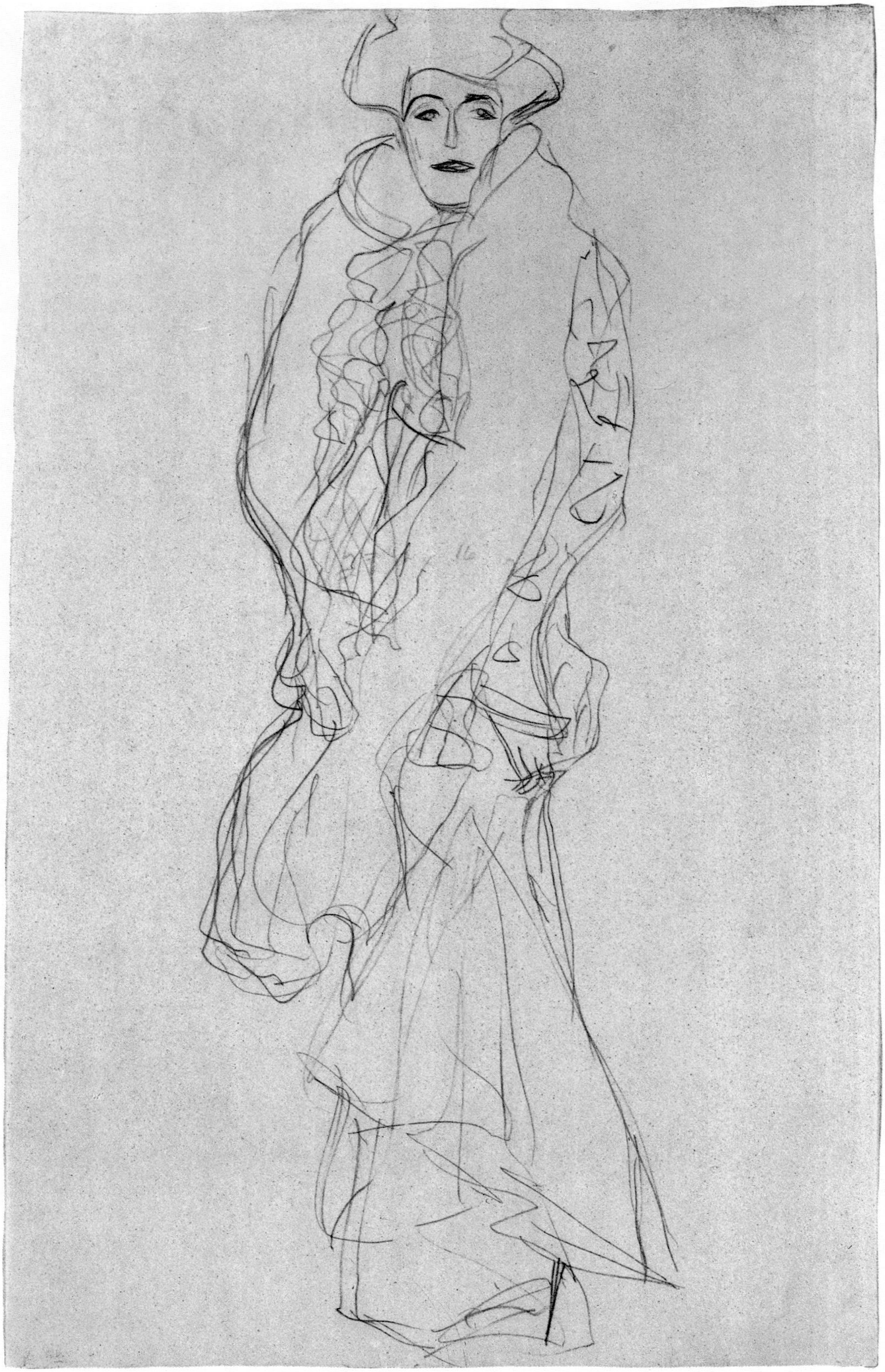

38. *Standing lady*, 1904–05.

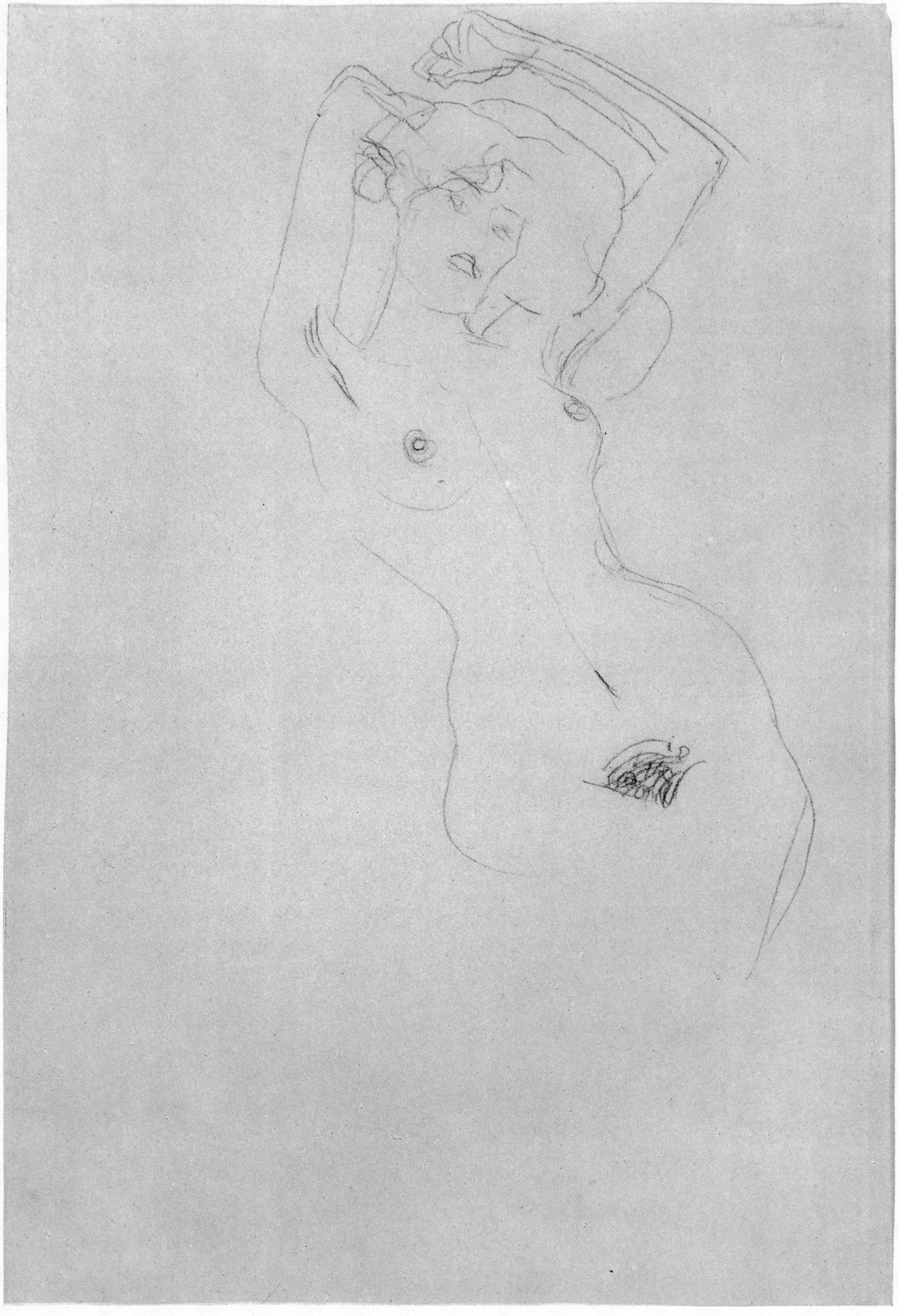

39. *Nude with raised arms*, 1905–06.

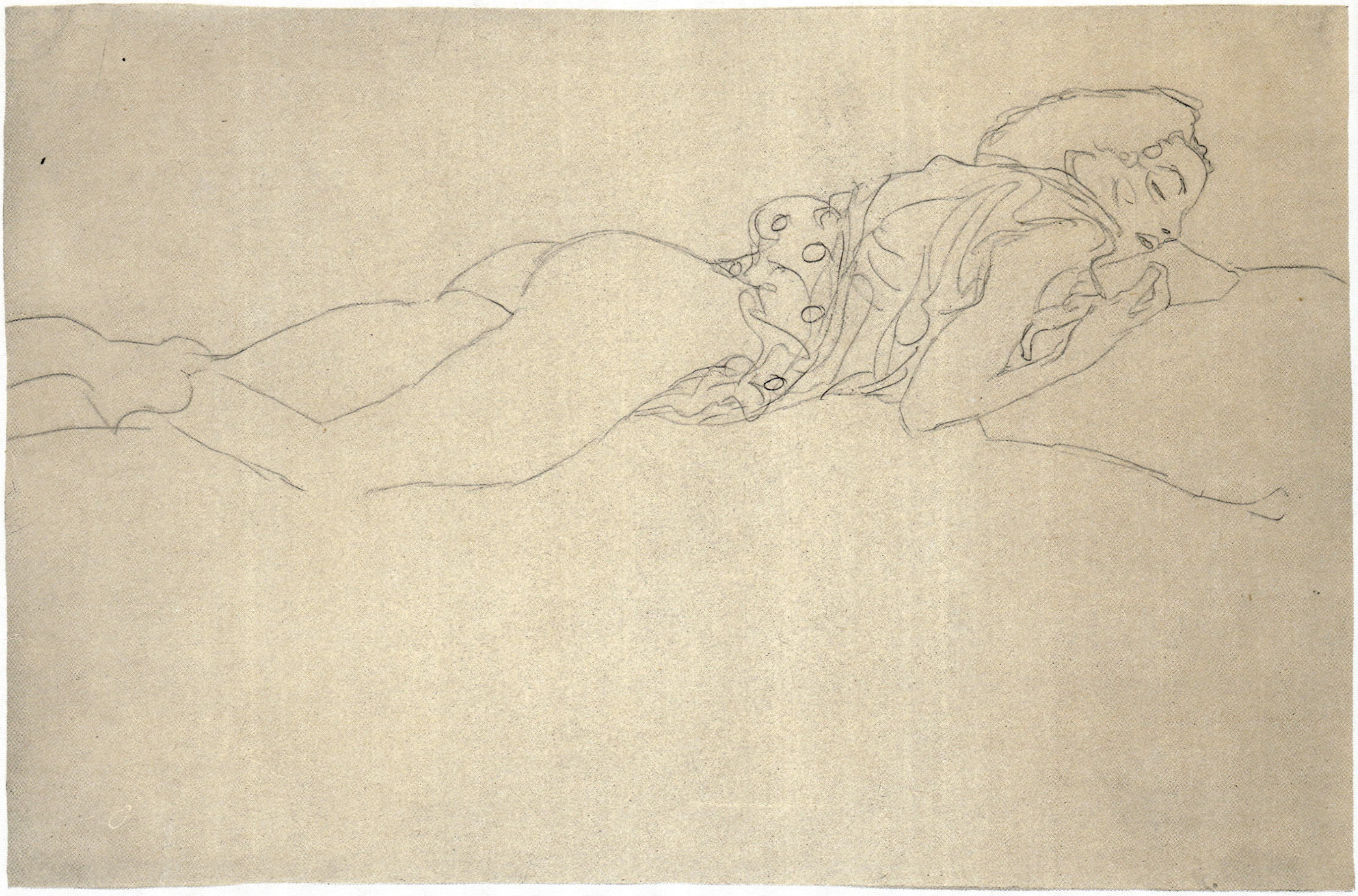

40. *Prone figure, semi-nude*, 1905–06.

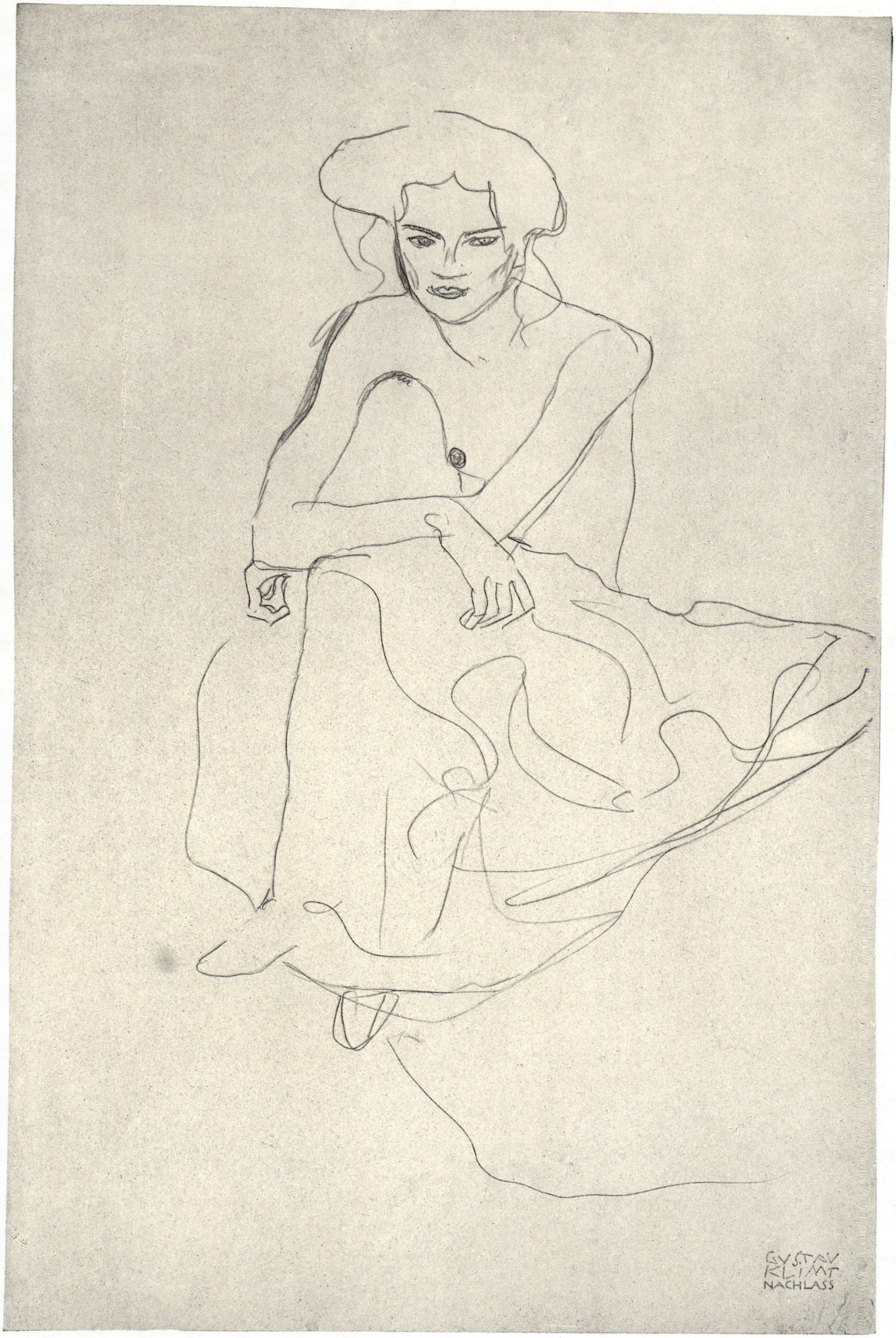

41. *Seated figure, semi-nude, with arms resting on her legs,* 1906–07.

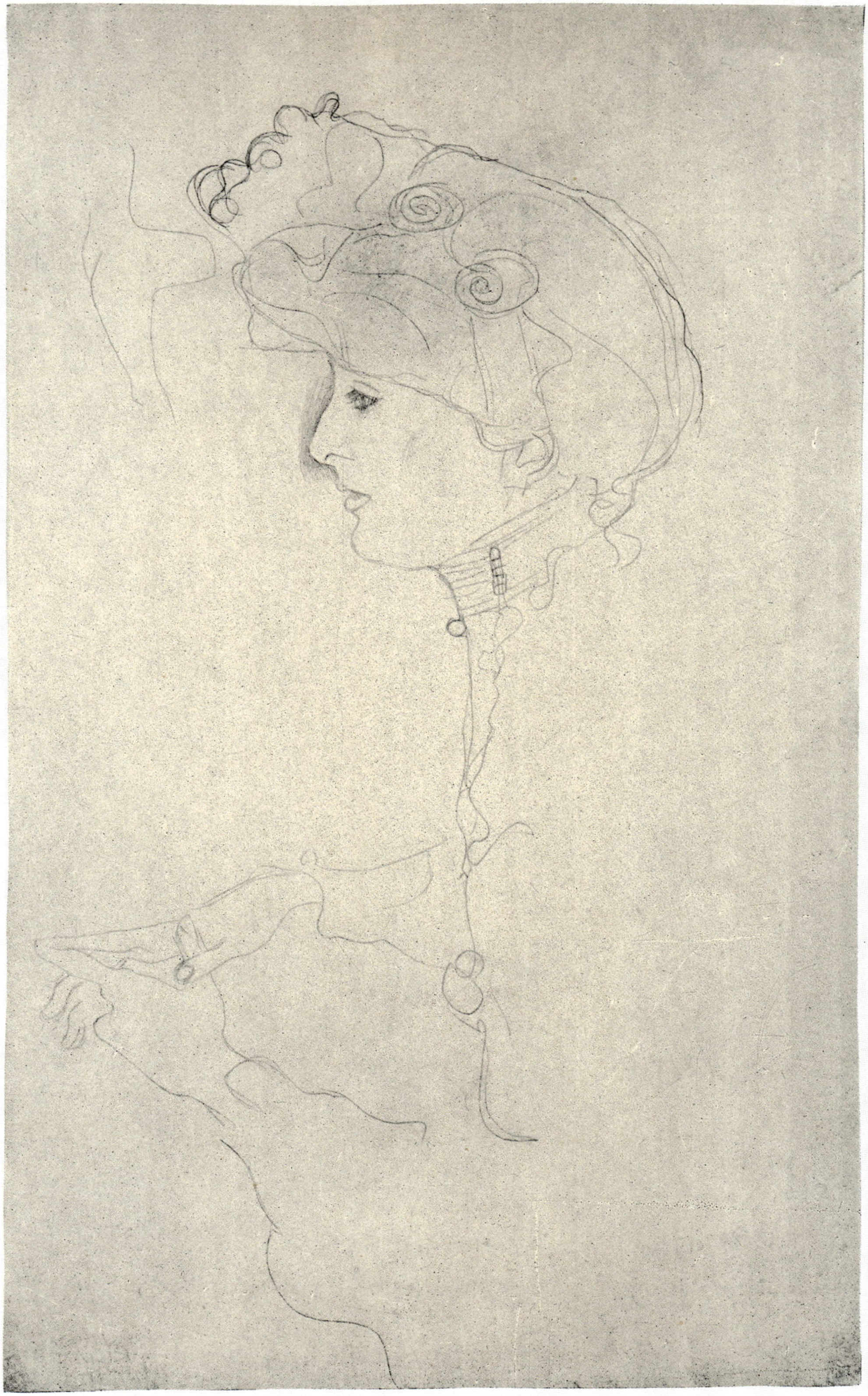

42. *Portrait study of a lady in profile with a high-collared blouse, c.* 1906–07.

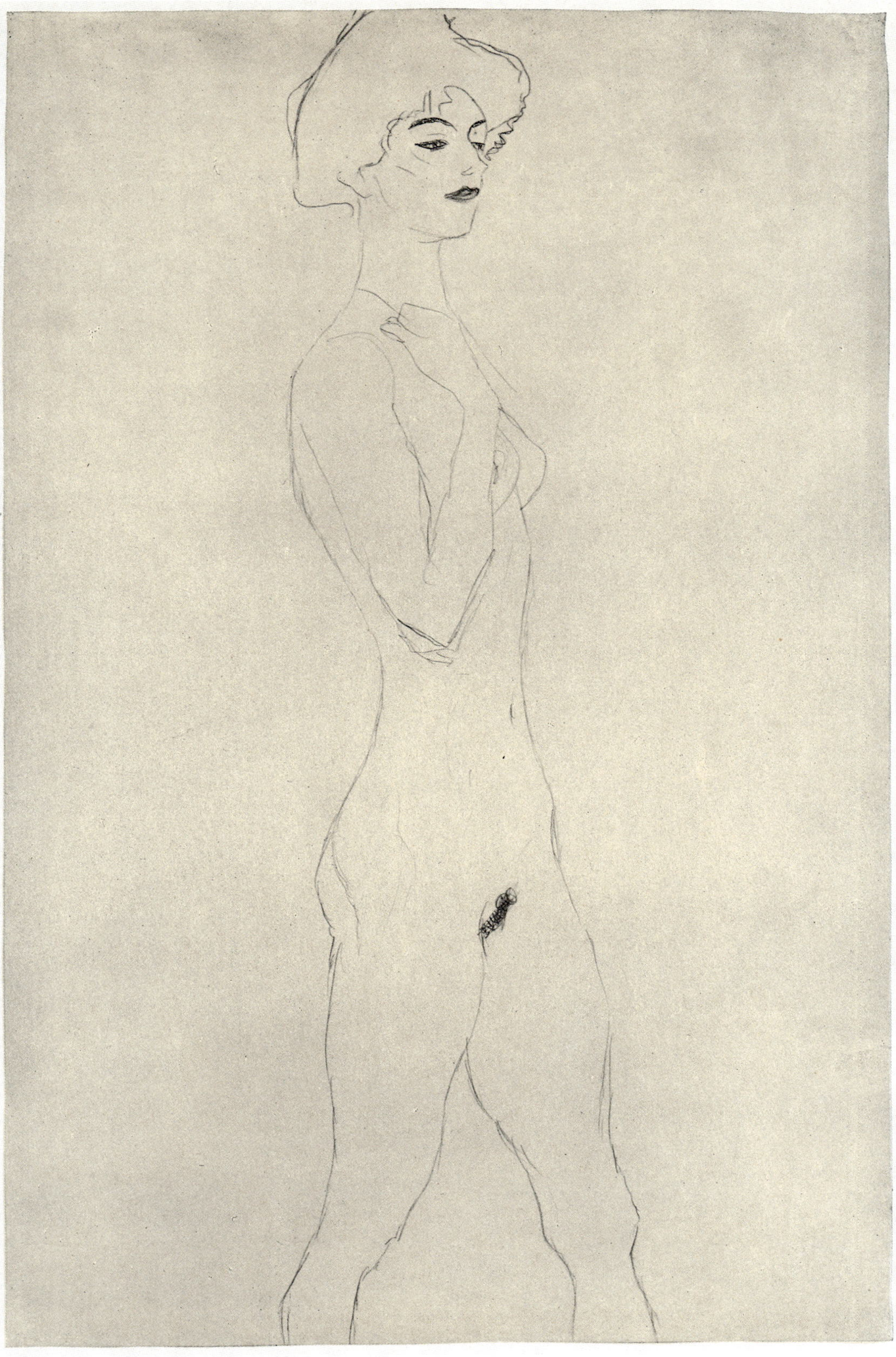

43. *Standing nude with red lips*, 1906–07.

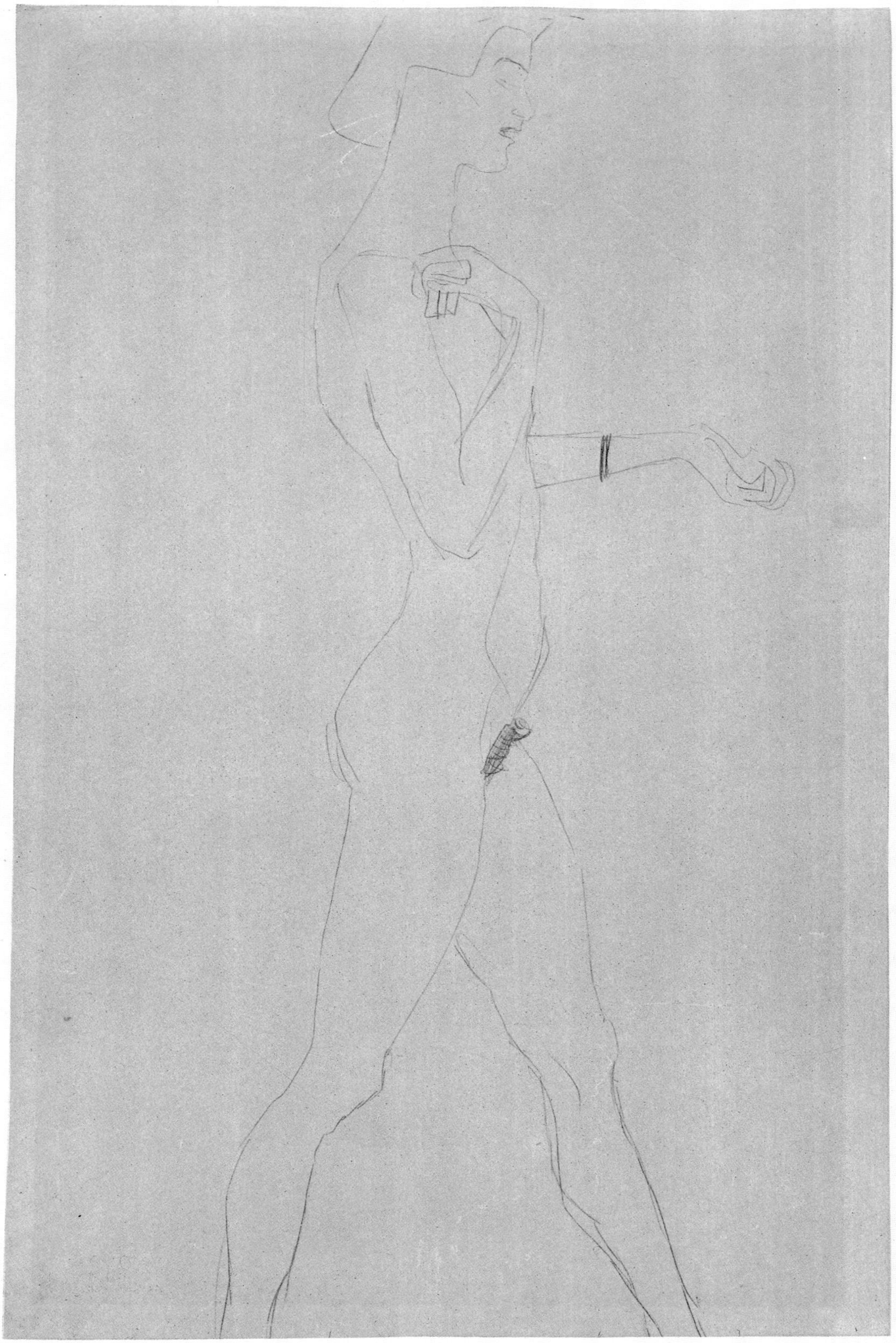

44. *Standing nude in profile*, 1906–07.

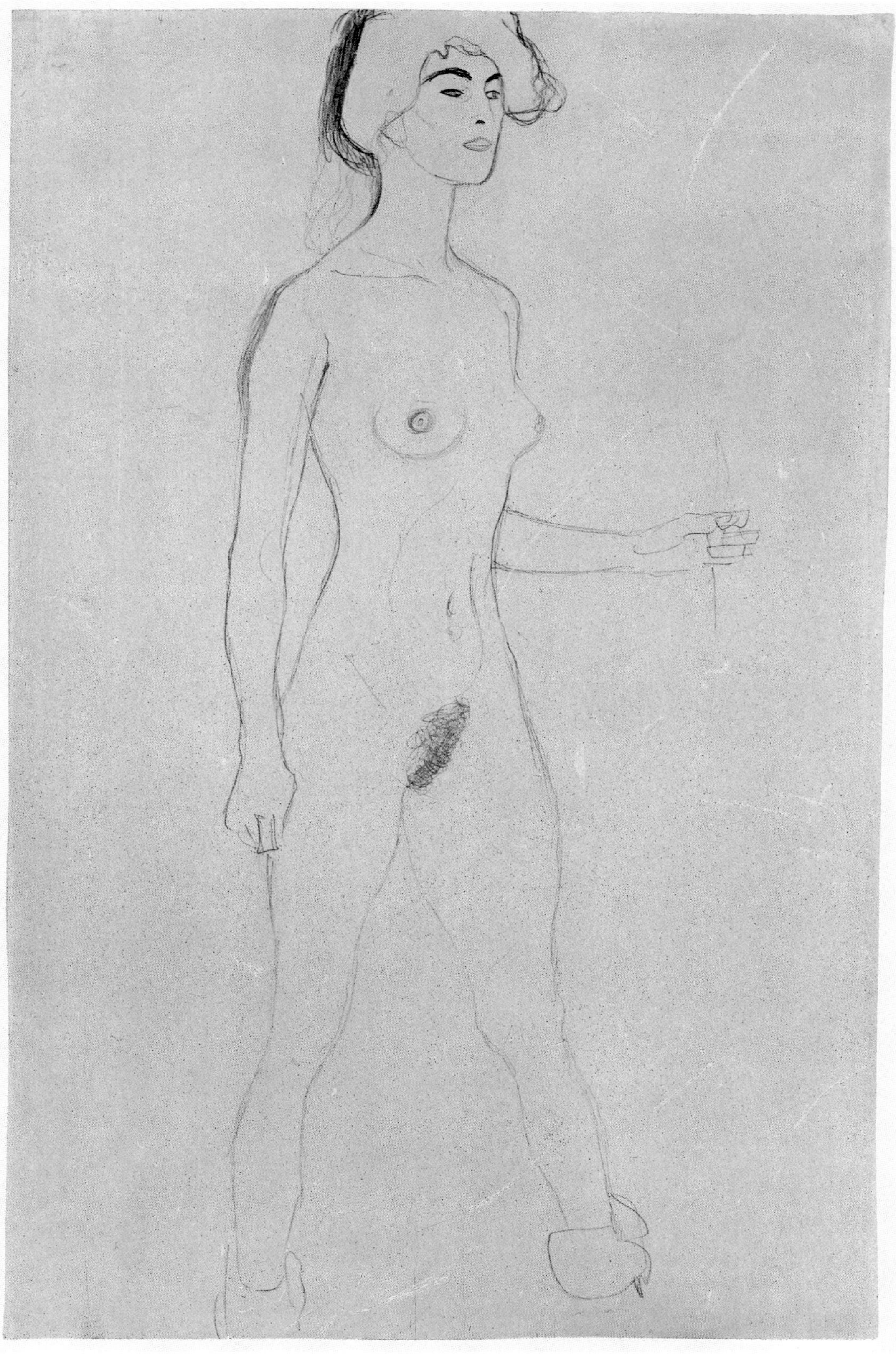

45. *Standing nude*, *c.* 1907.

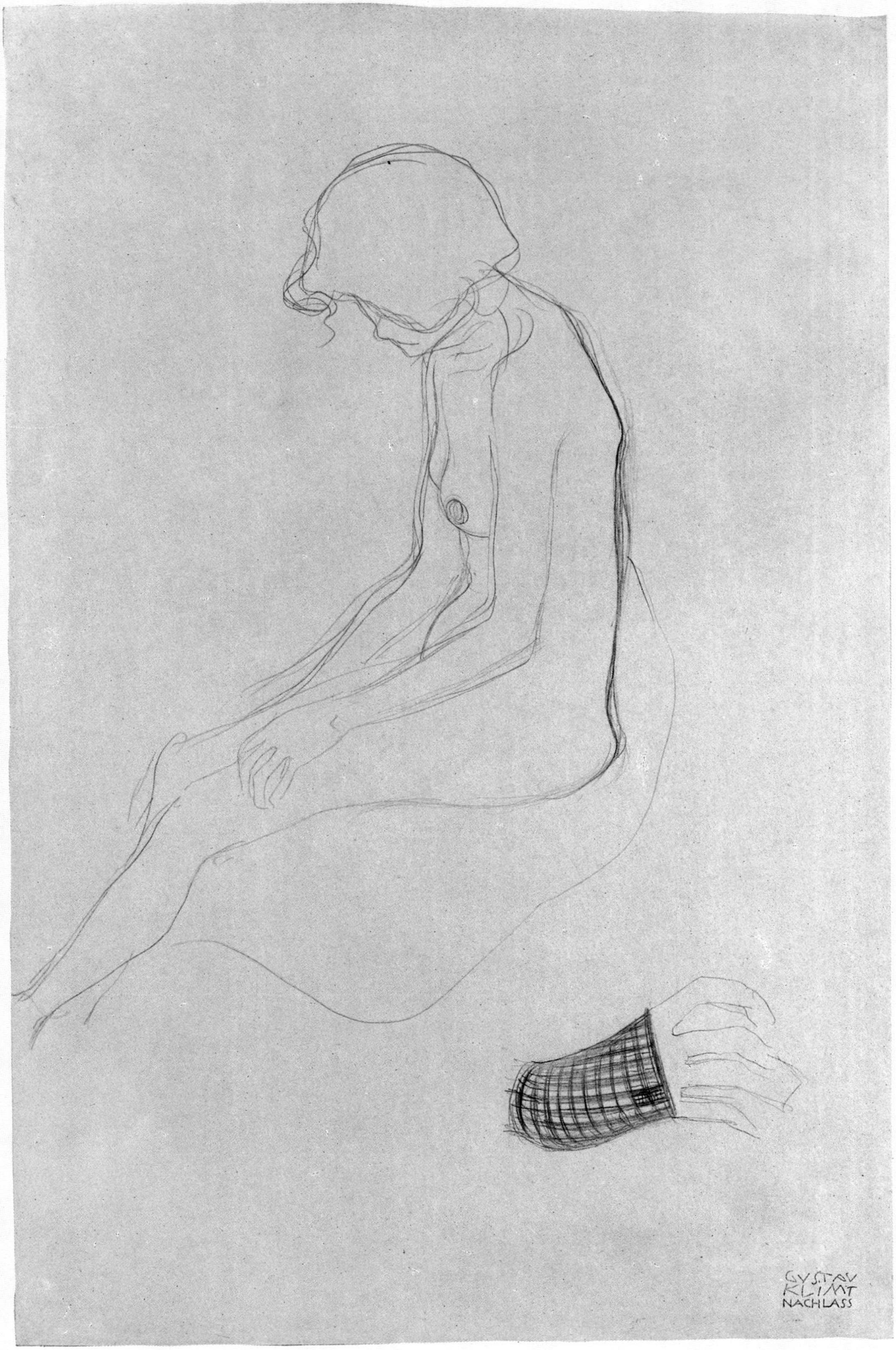

46. *Seated nude looking downwards to the left, and study of a hand*, 1907–08.

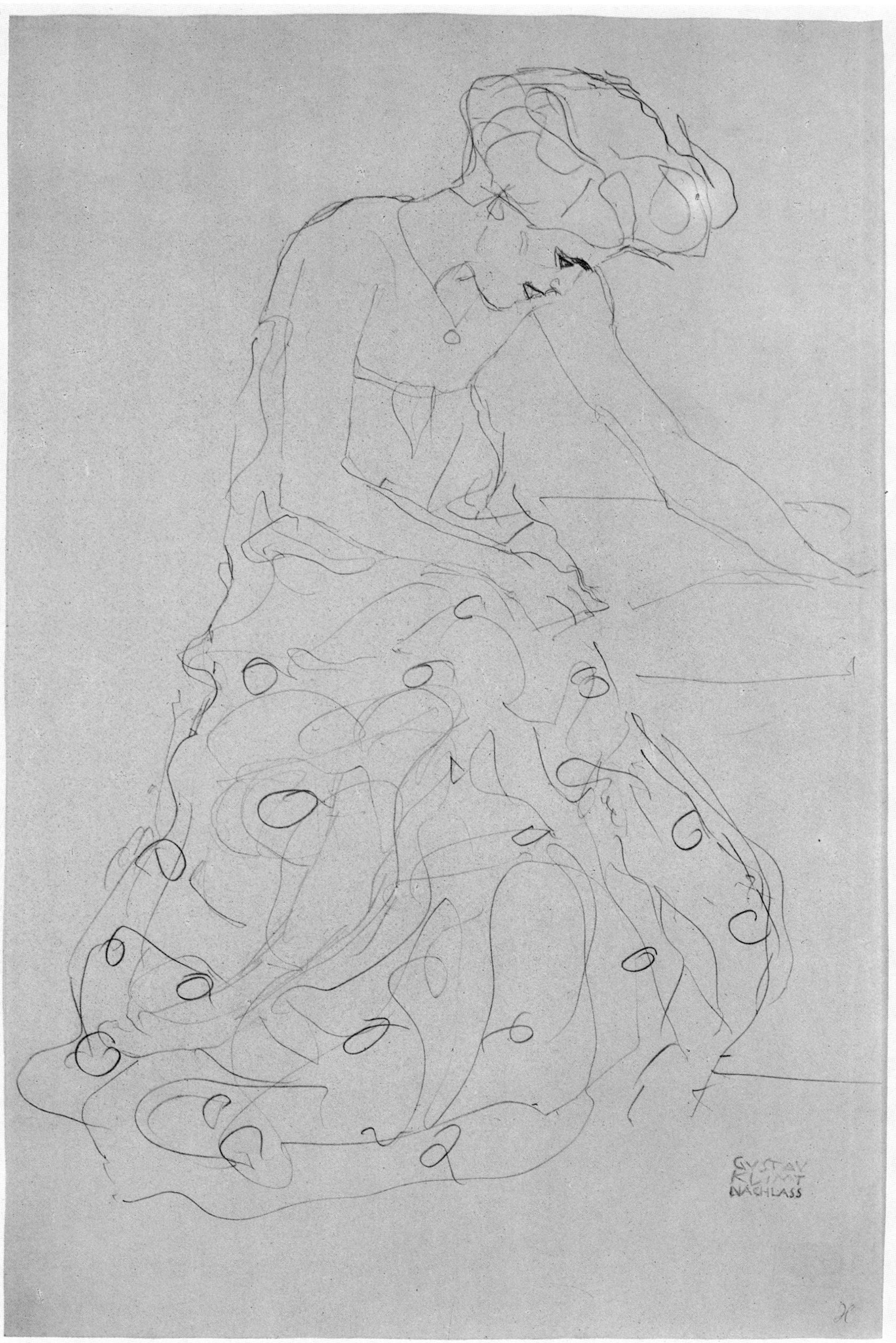

47. *Seated woman*, 1907–08.

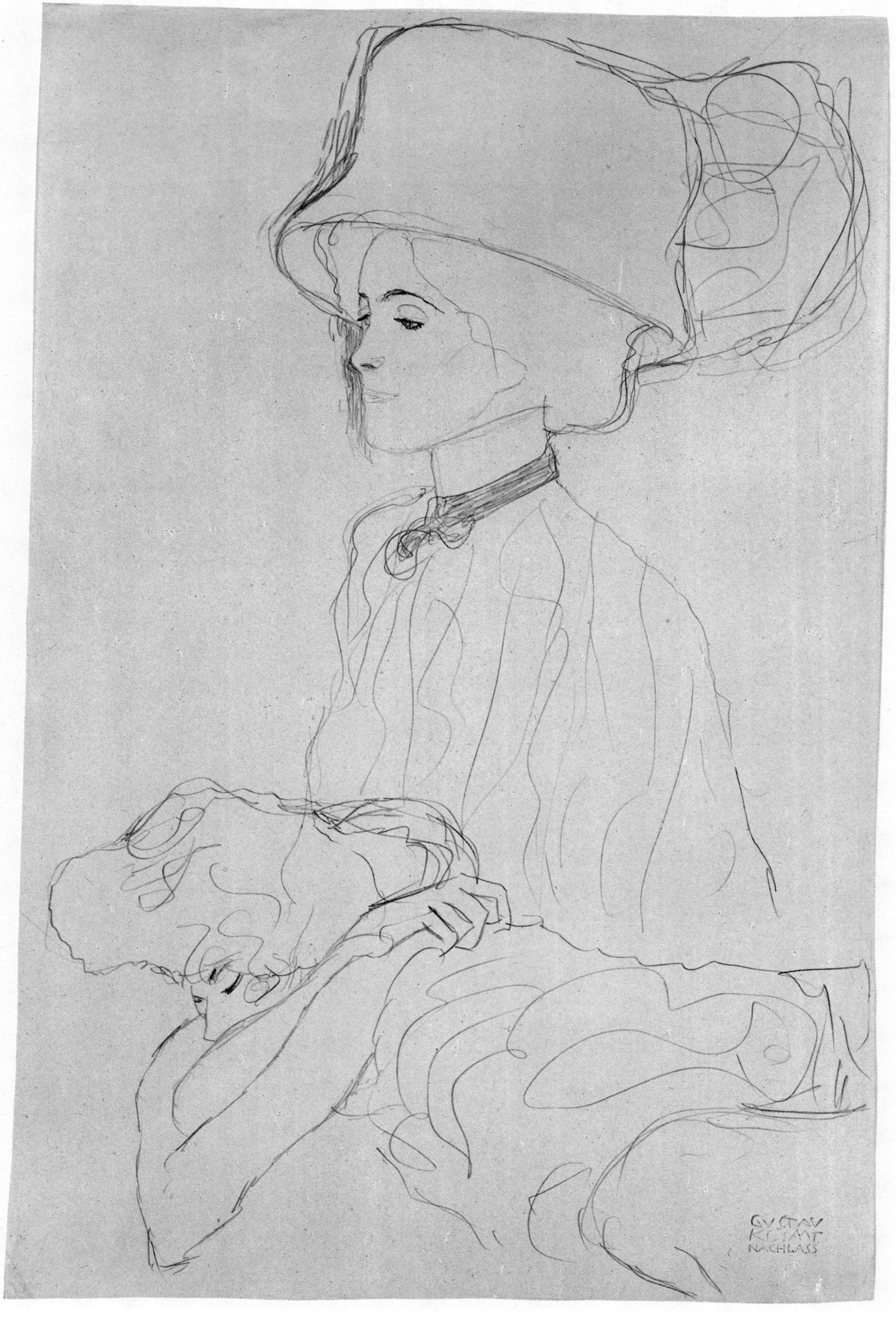

48. *Portrait of a lady with a tall hat, and lying female figure*, 1907–08.

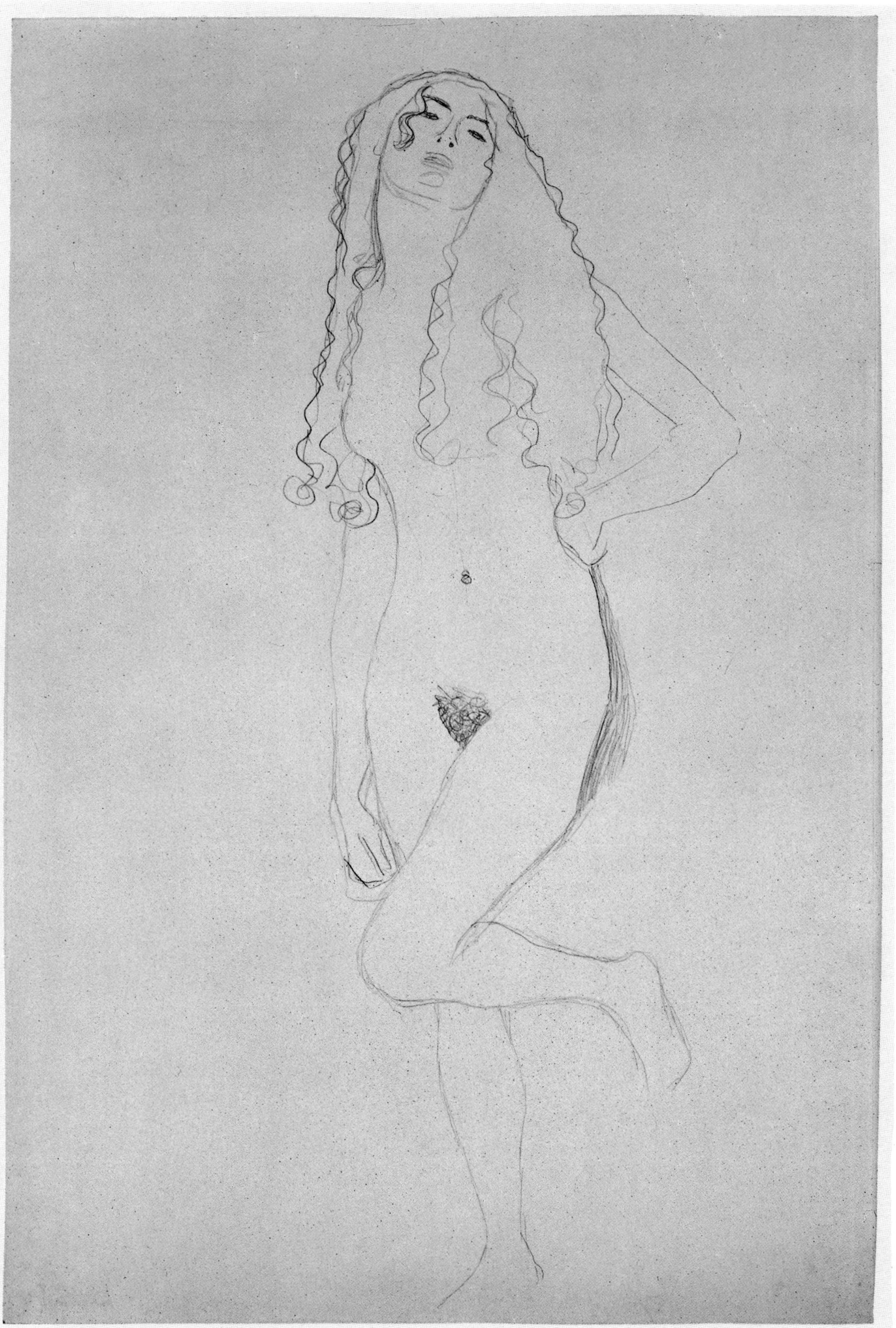

49. *Standing nude with left arm raised,* 1907–08.

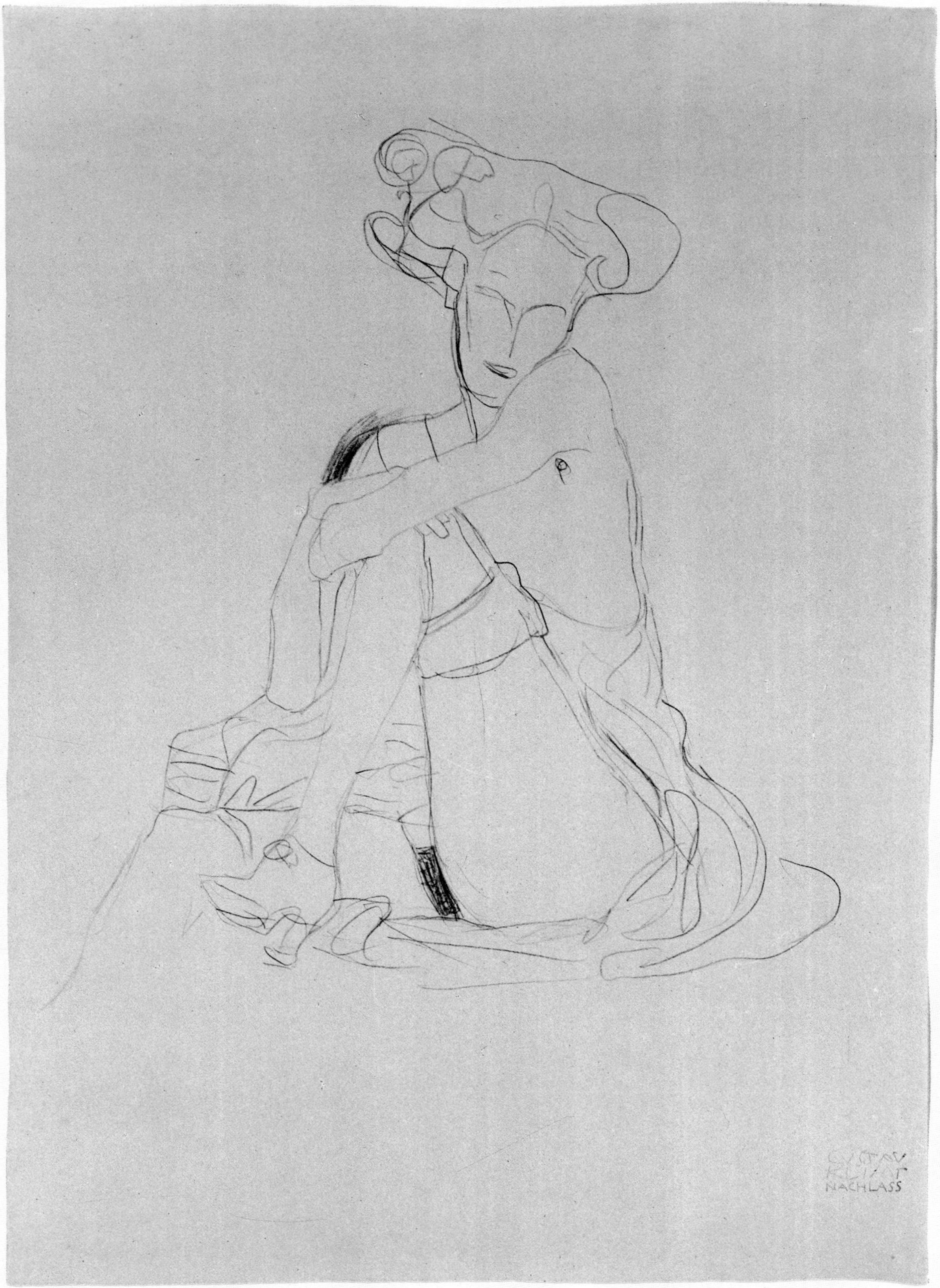

50. *Seated figure, semi-nude*, *c.* 1908.

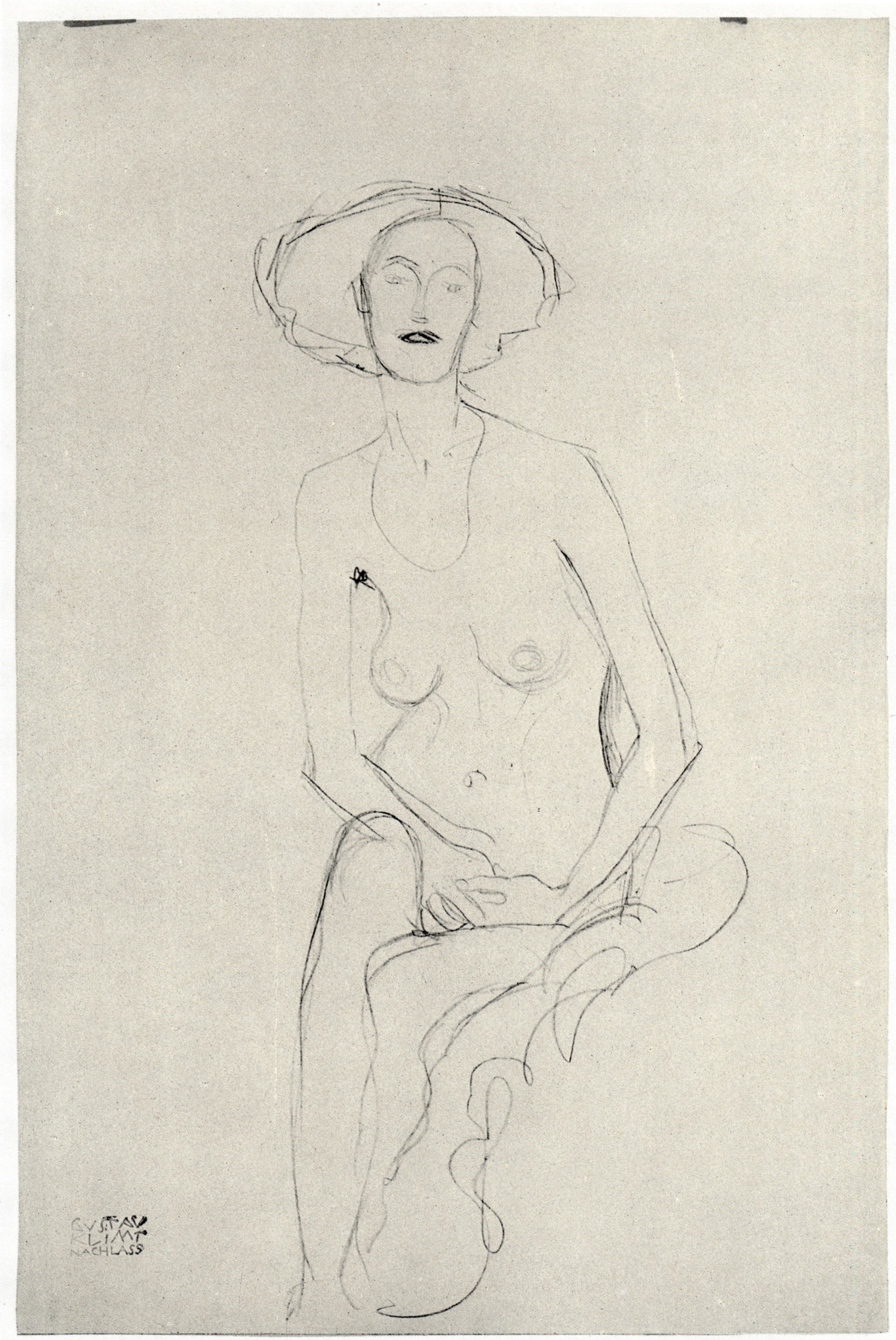

51. *Seated nude with hands in her lap*, 1908.

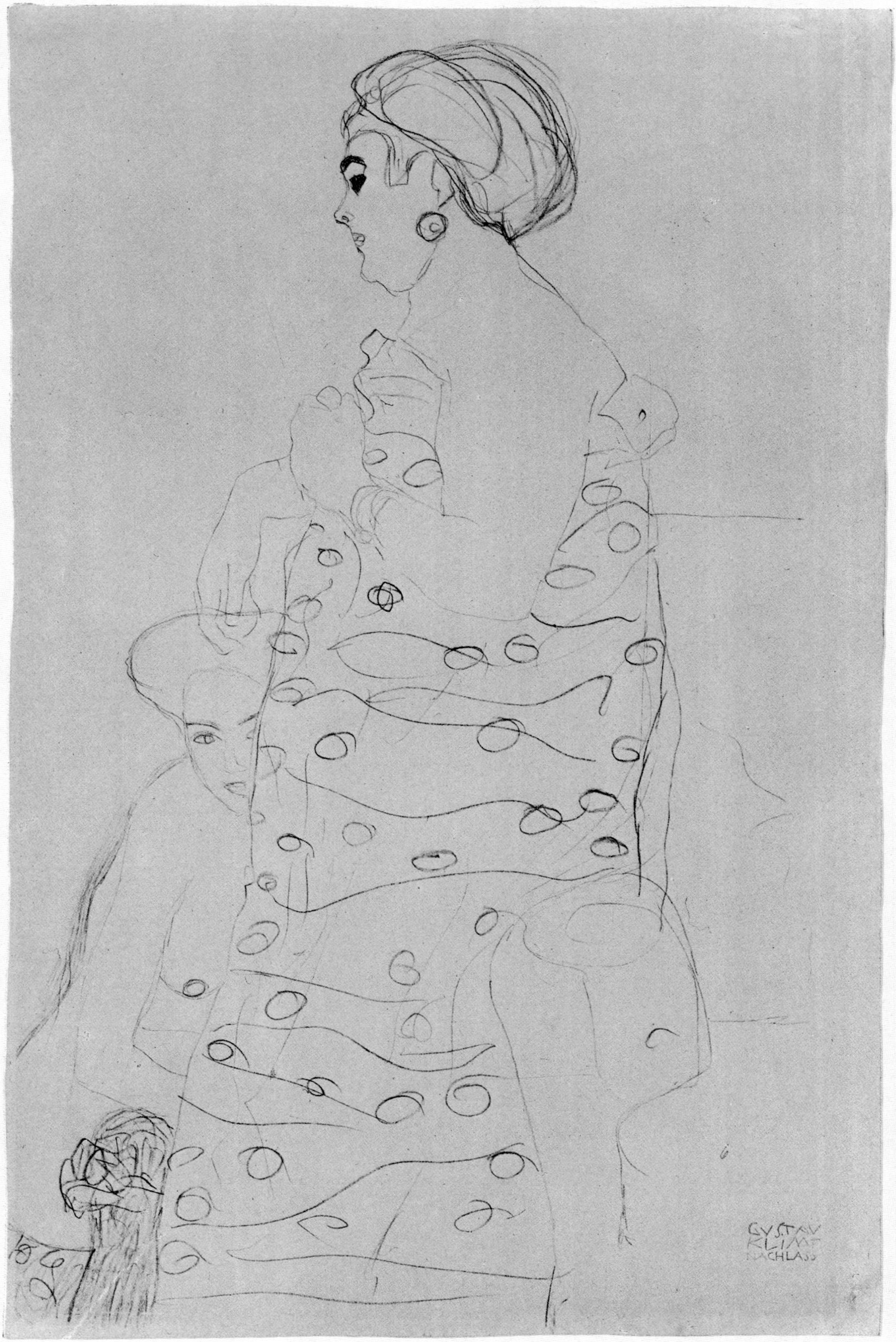

52. *Standing woman, with a nude woman crouching behind her*, 1908.

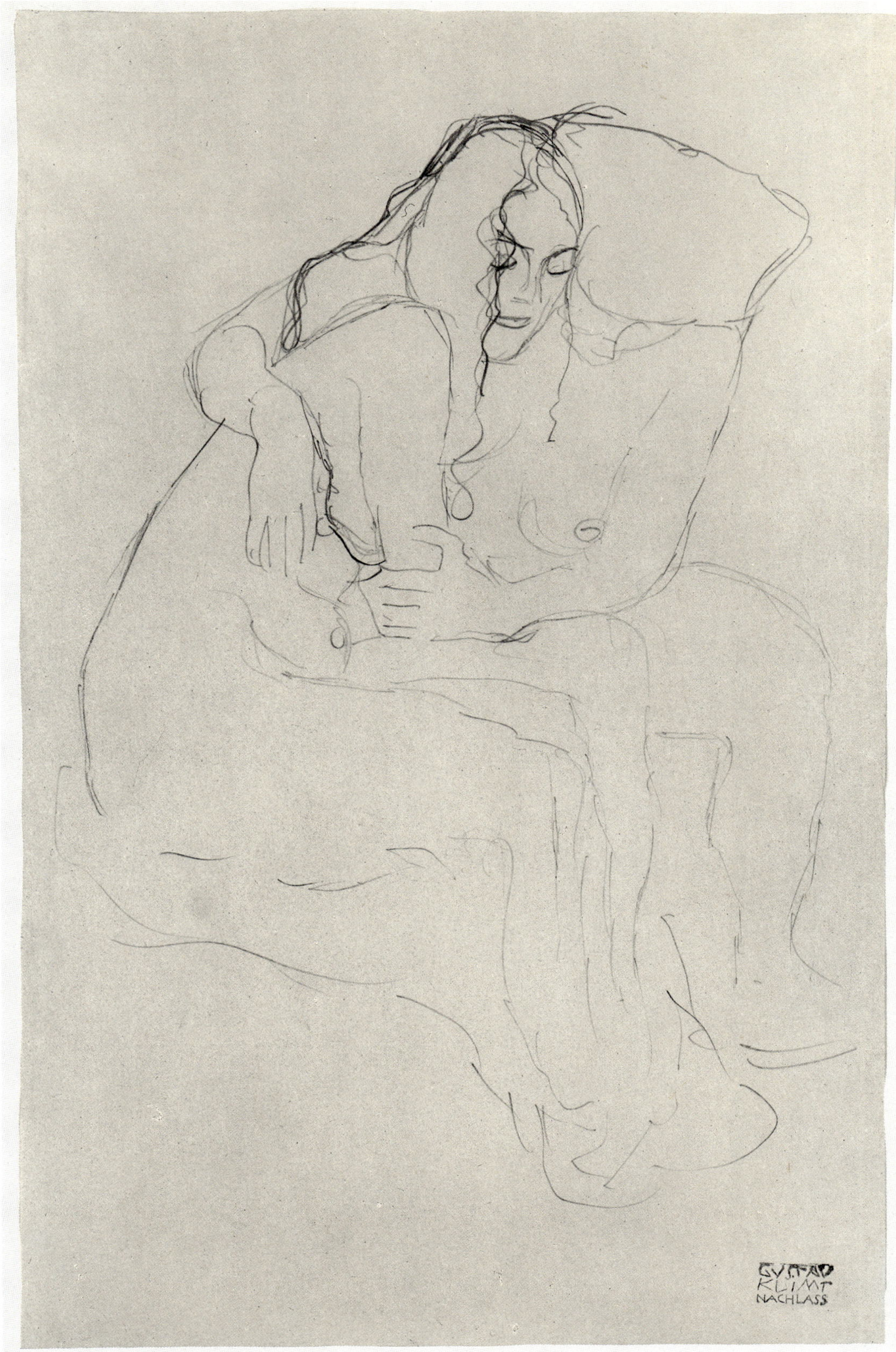

53. *Two female nudes embracing*, 1909–10.

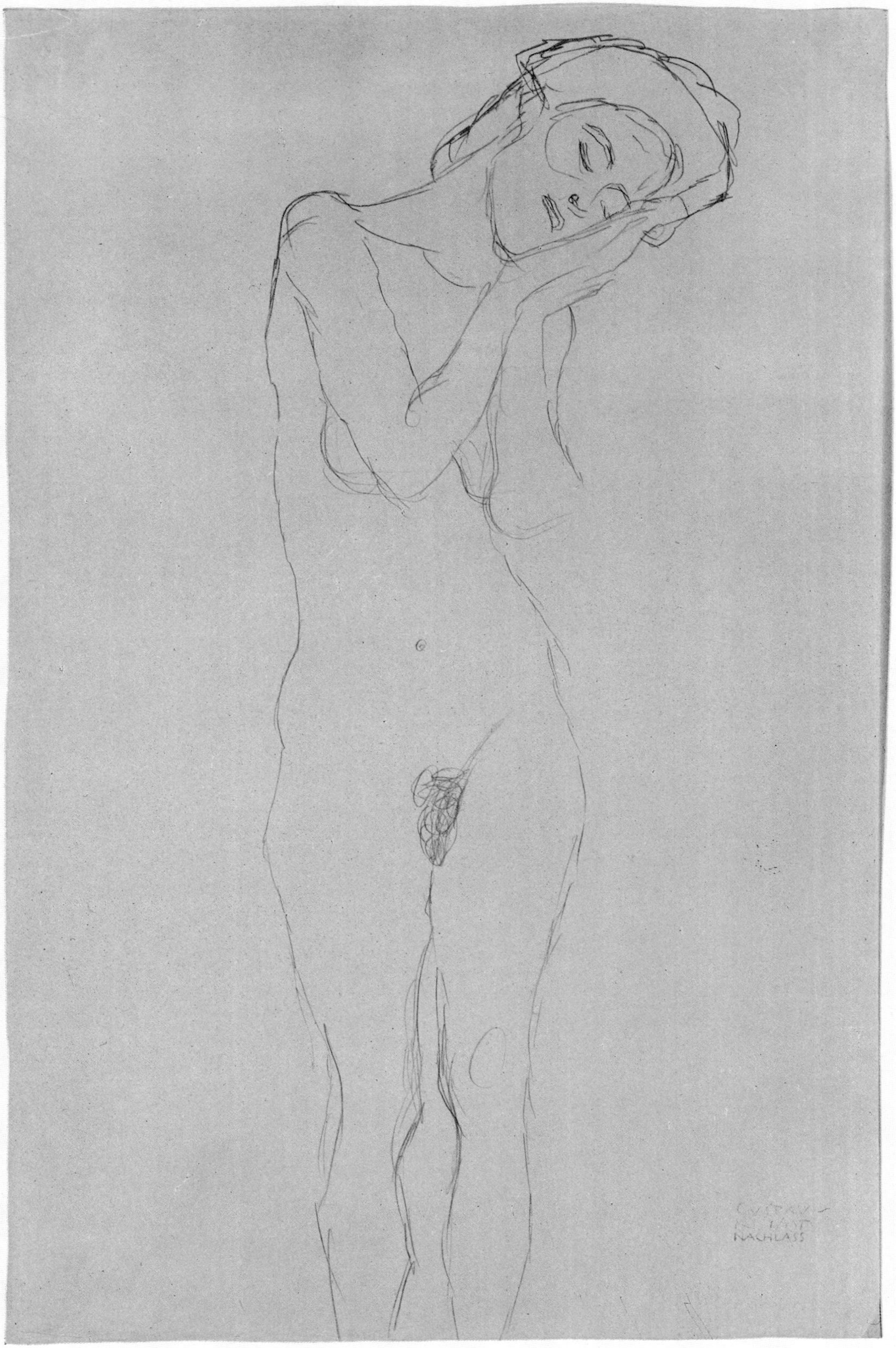

54. *Standing nude with head bent to the left and leaning on her hands*, c. 1910.

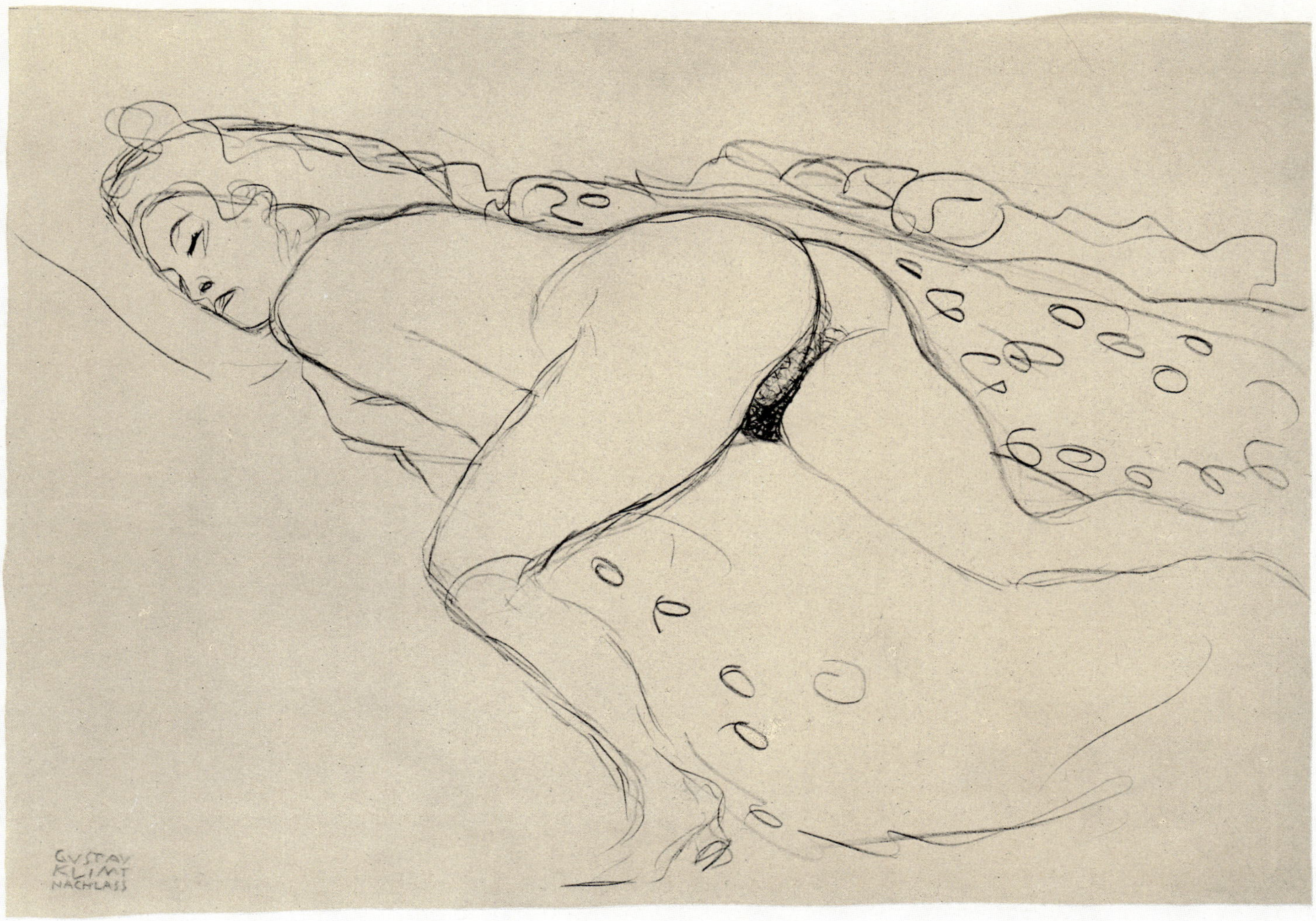

55. *Prone nude*, 1910.

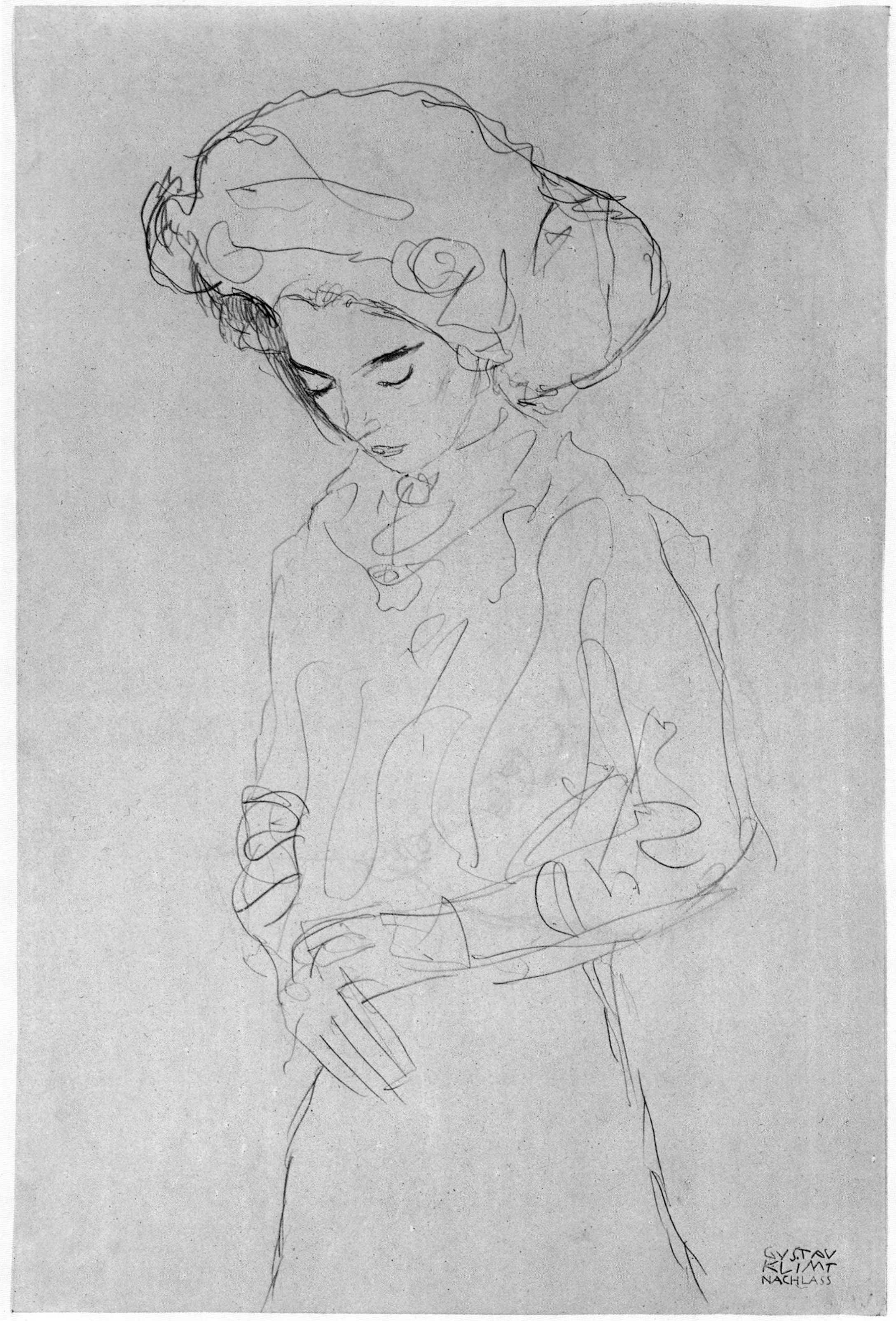

56. *Portrait study of a young woman looking downwards*, *c.* 1910–12.

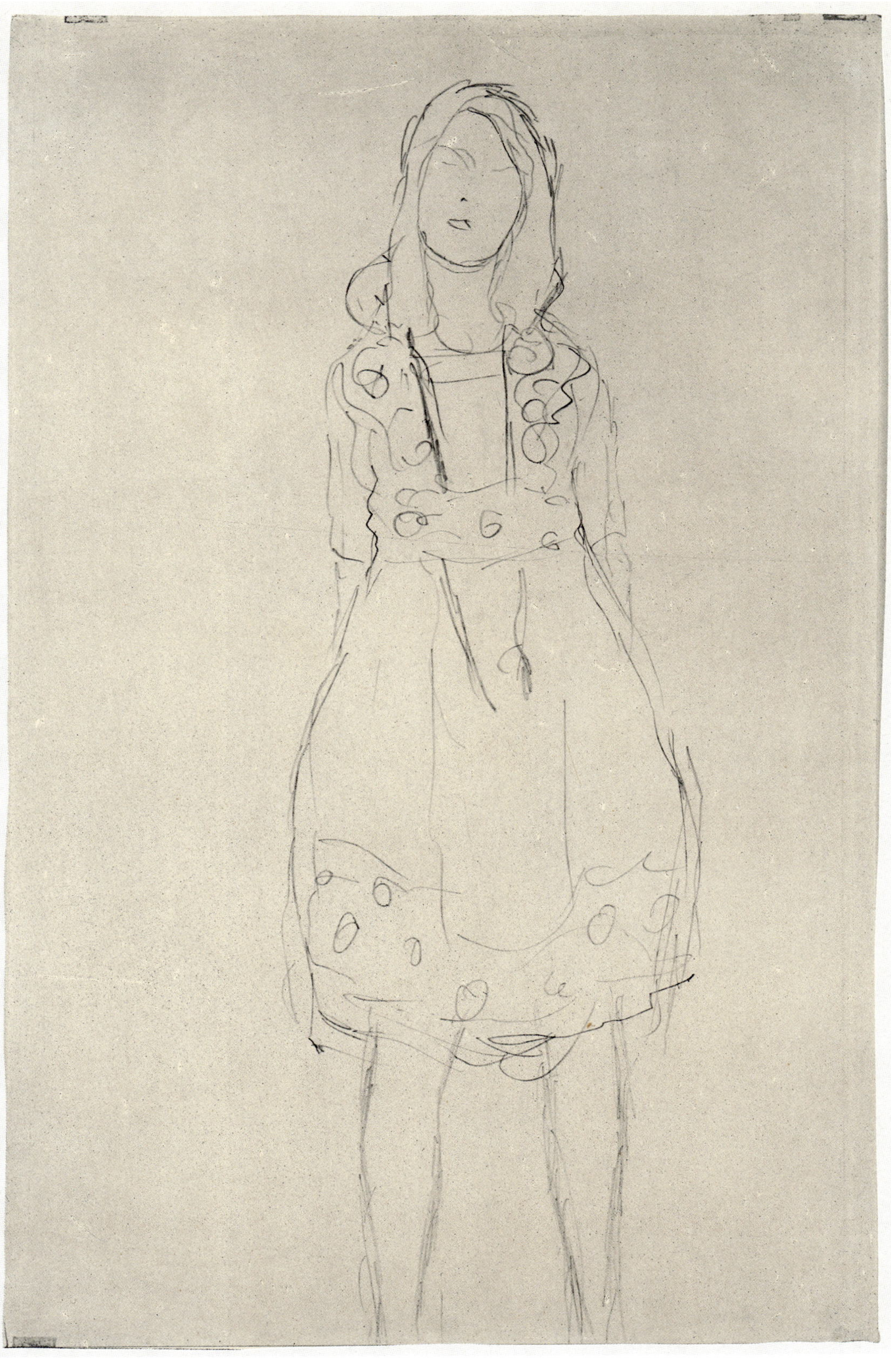

57. *Young girl with apron*, 1912.

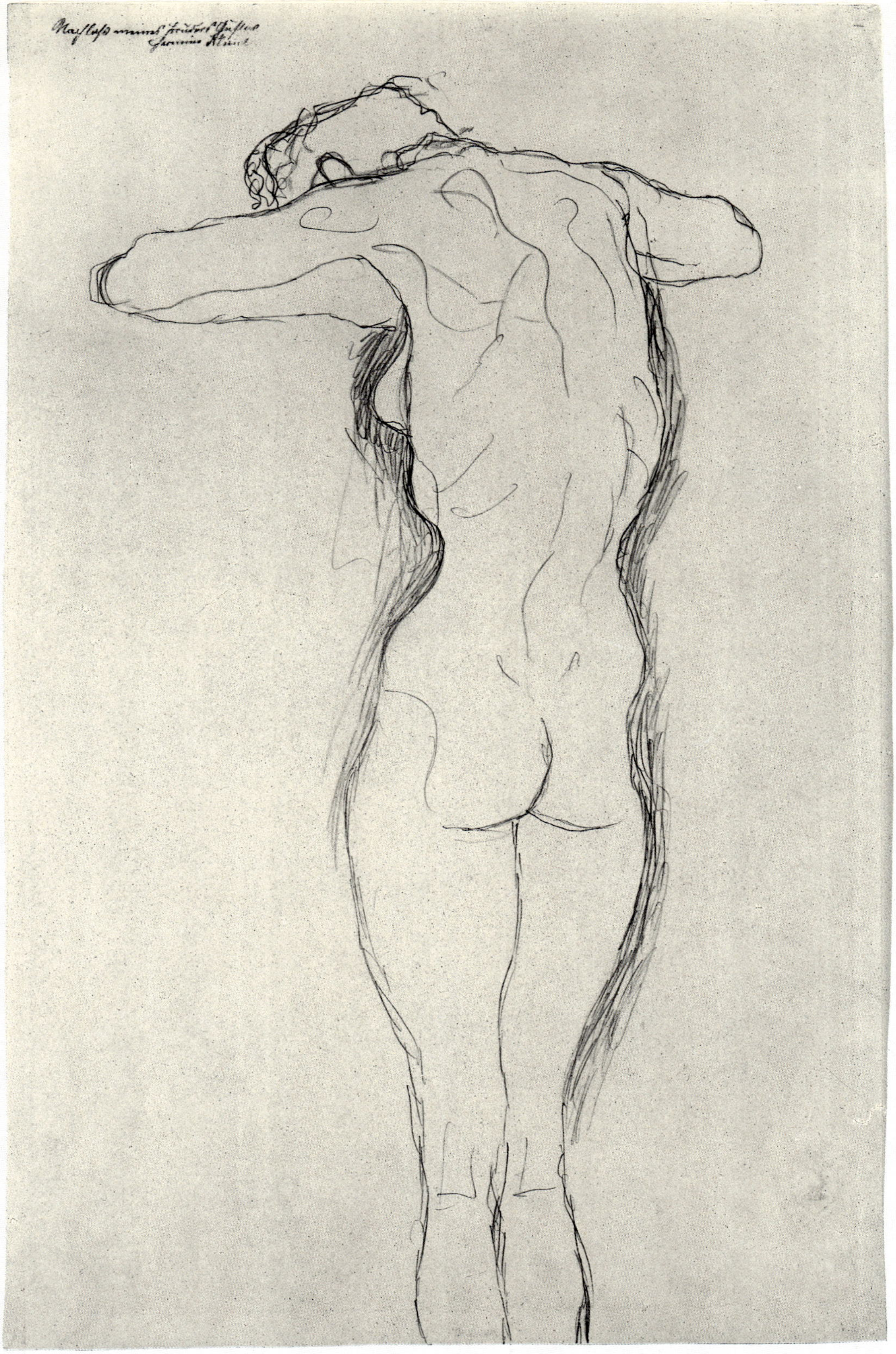

58. *Standing nude, back view,*
1912–13.

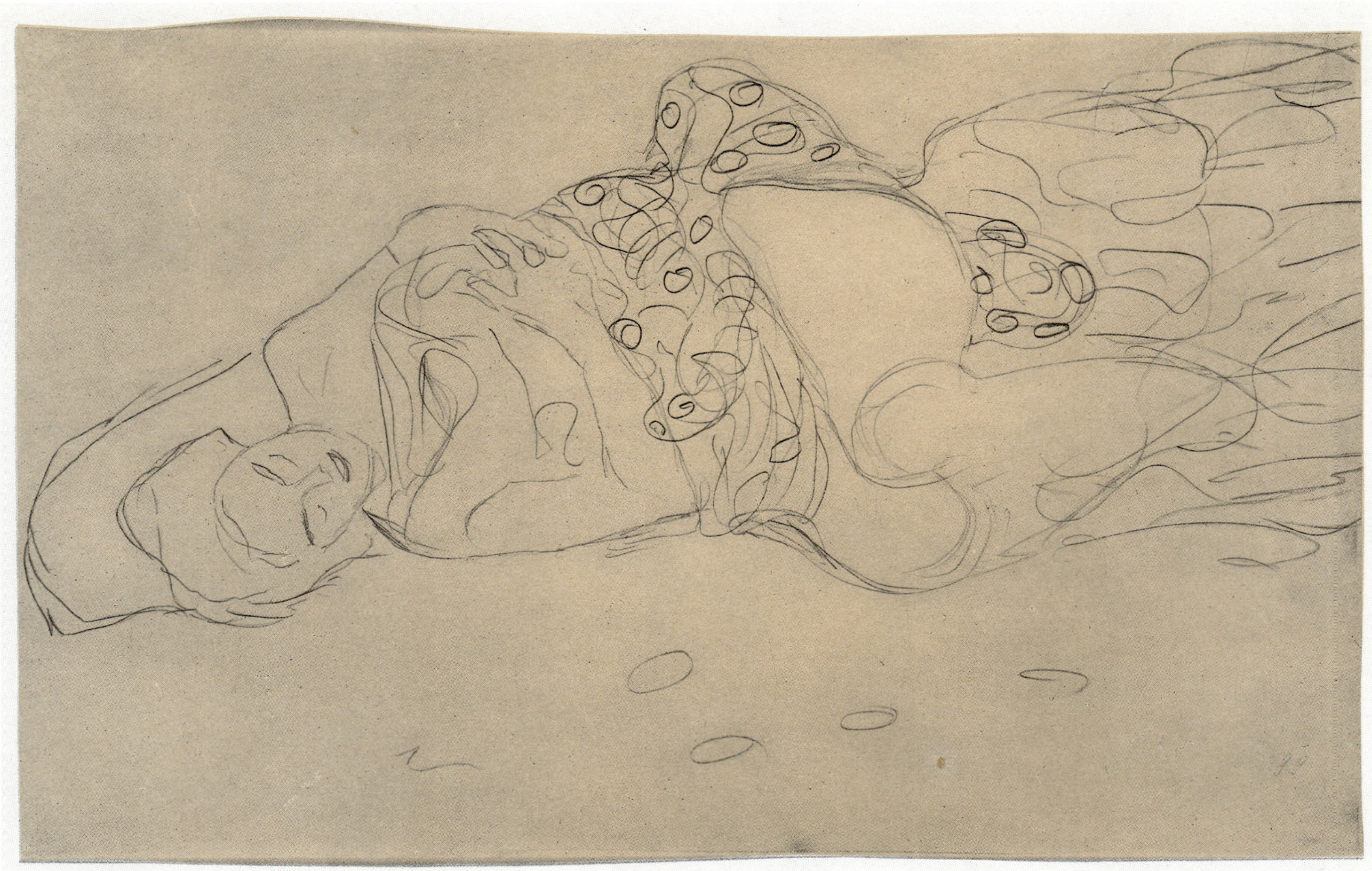

59. *Woman reclining*, 1912–13.

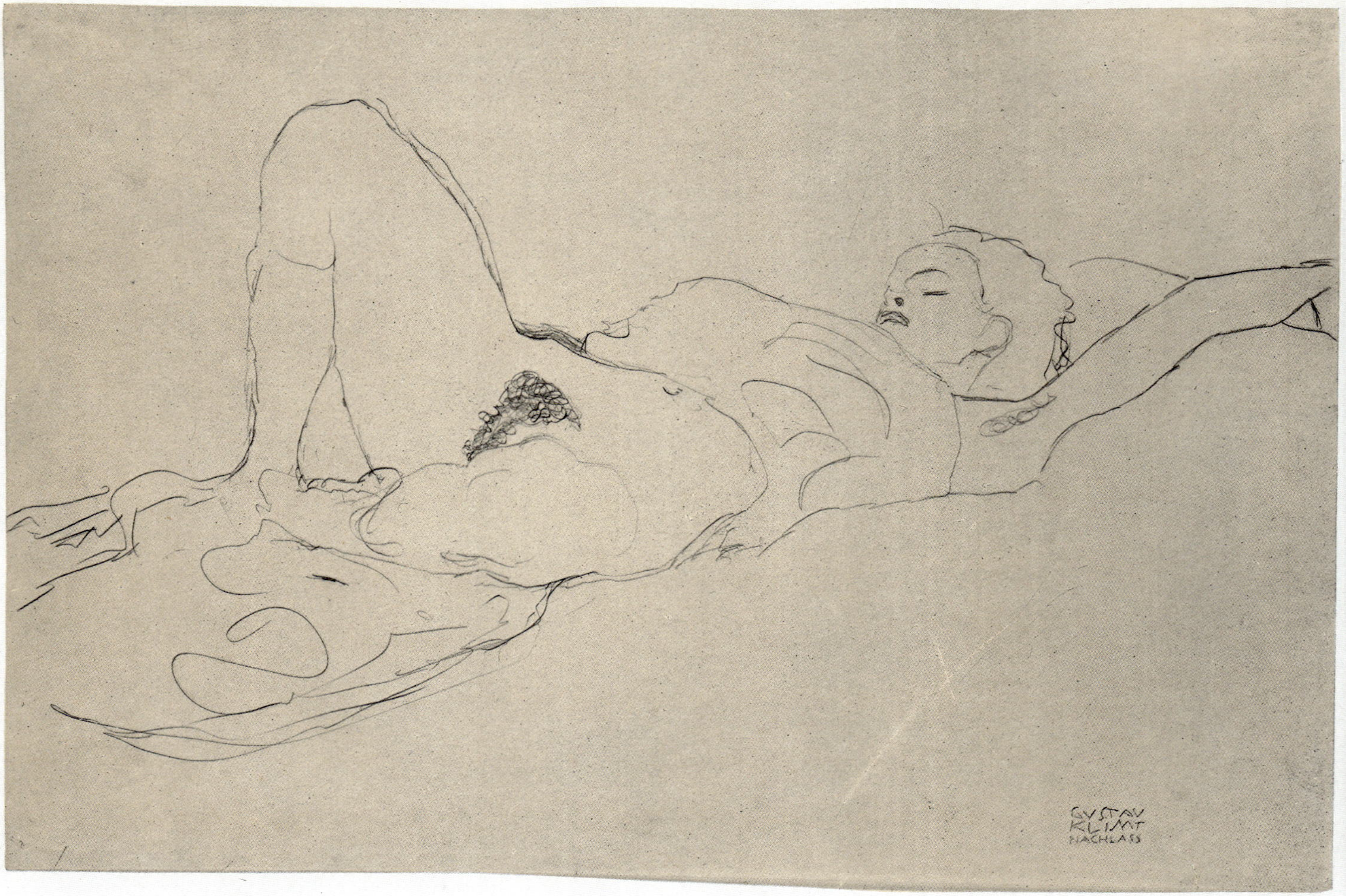

60. *Woman reclining, semi-nude*, 1912–13.

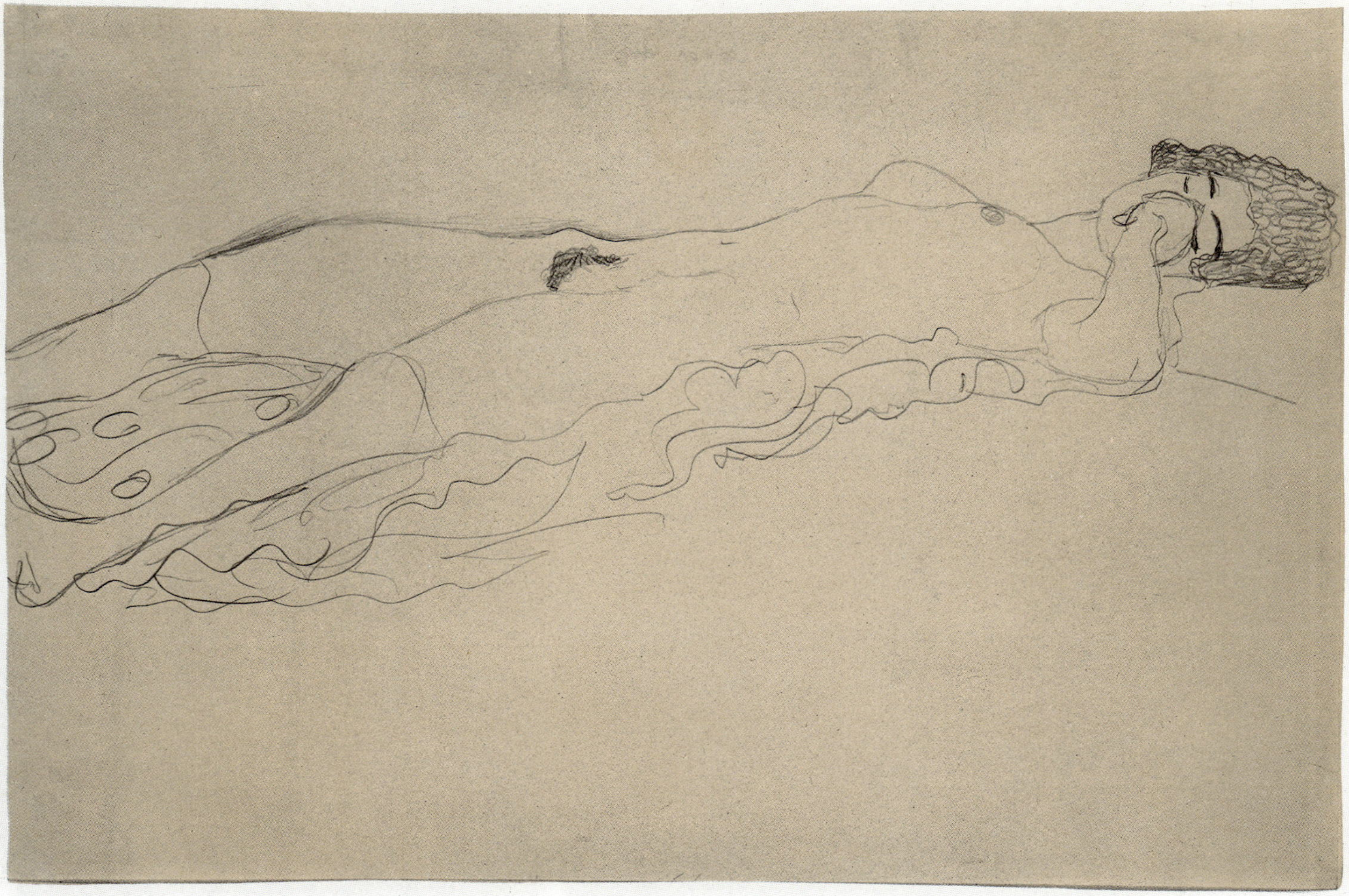

61. *Reclining nude with left hand on her face*, 1912–13.

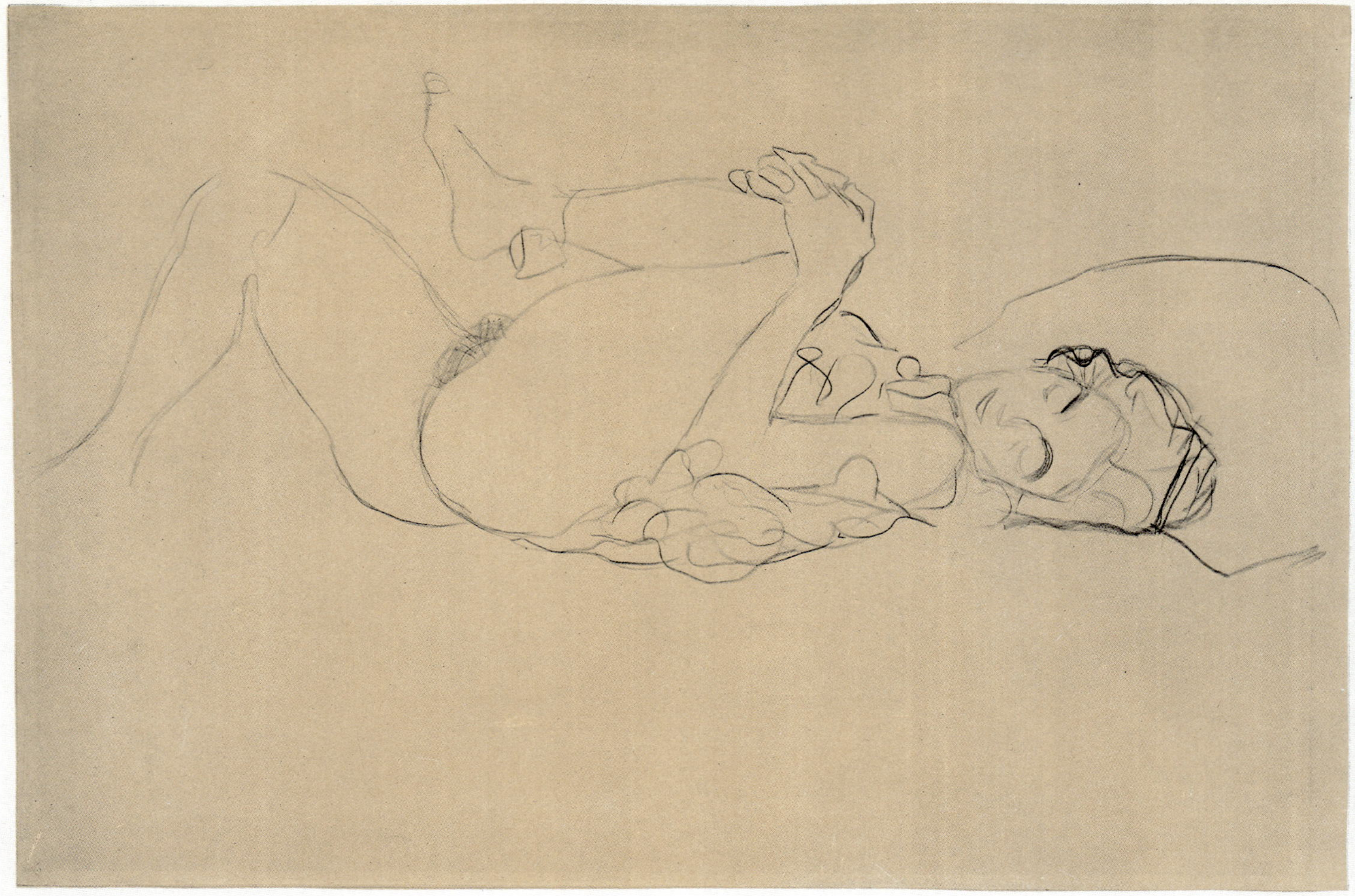

62. *Reclining nude with left leg raised*, 1913.

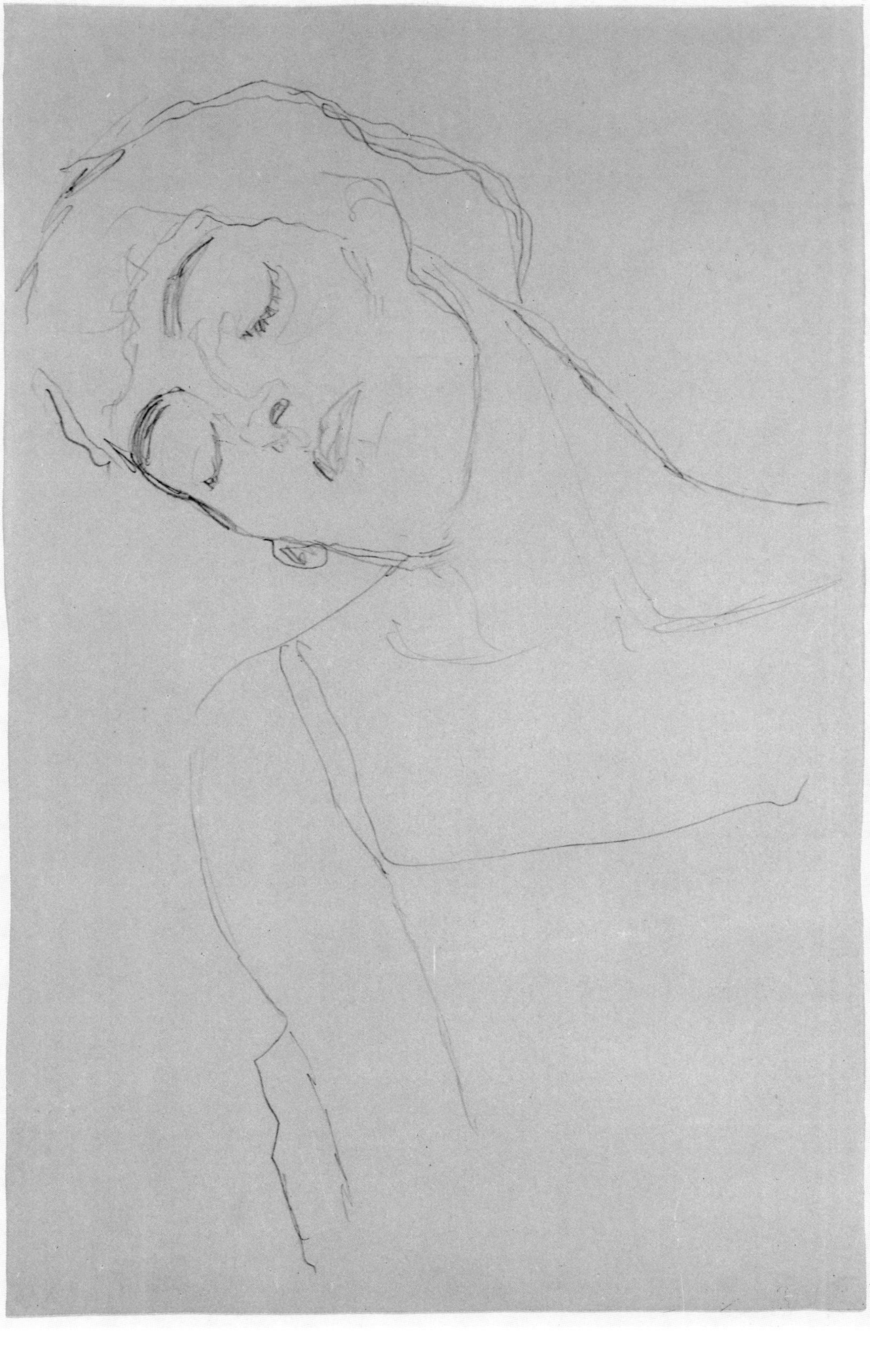

63. *Portrait study of a lady with head tilted and eyes closed*, 1913.

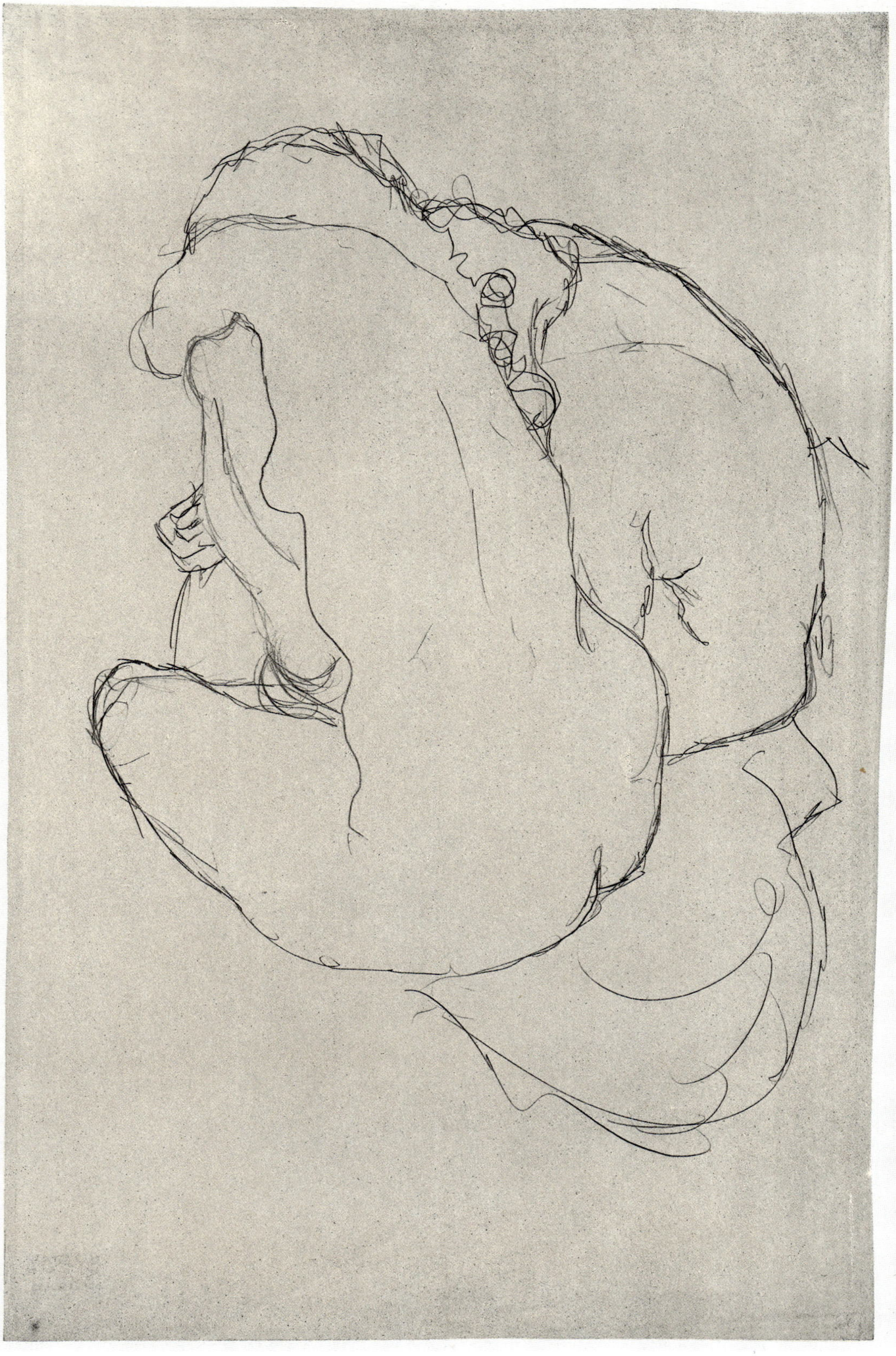

64. *Two seated nudes, back view*, 1913.

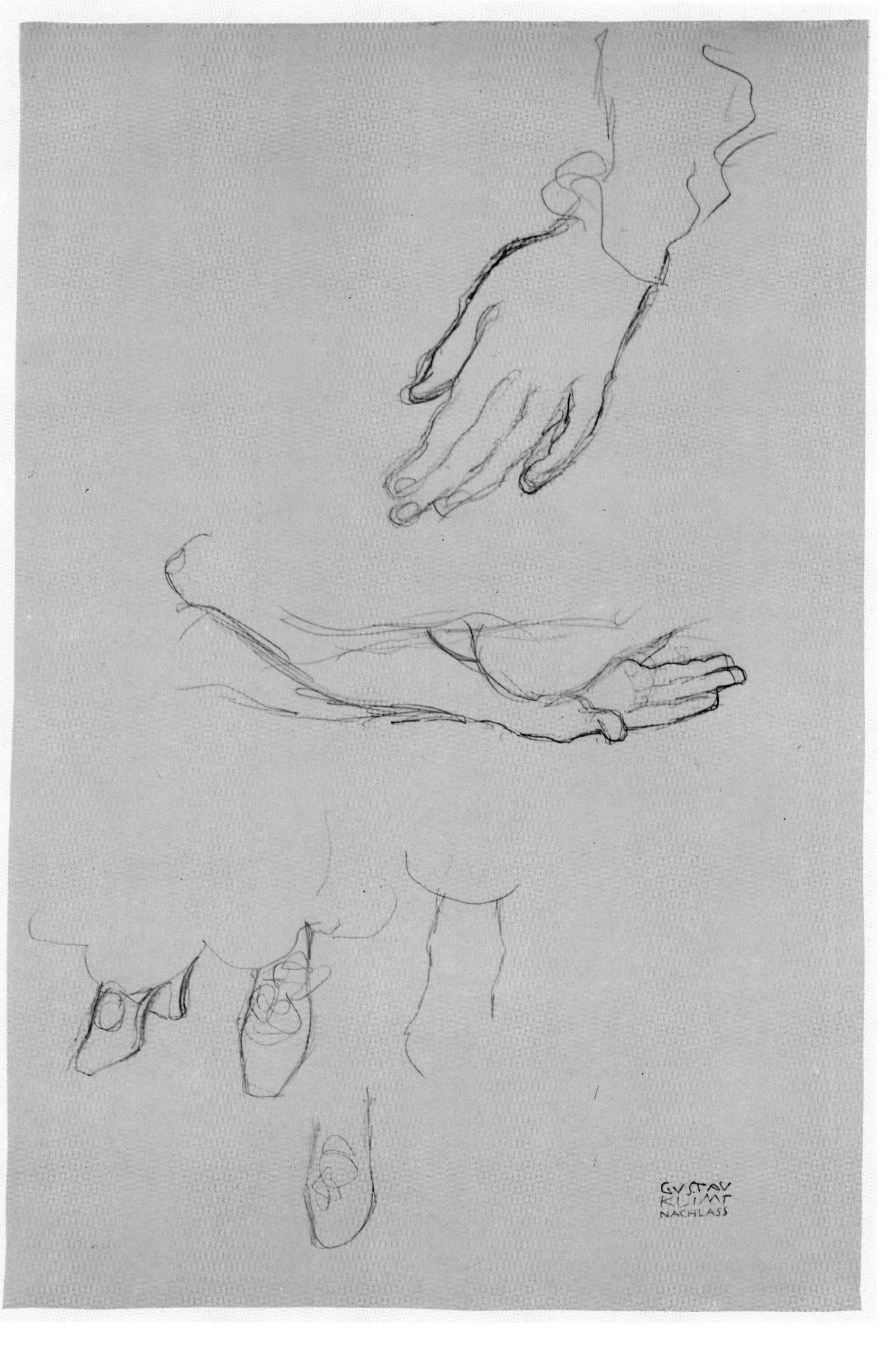

65. *Studies of hands and shoes*, *c*. 1914.

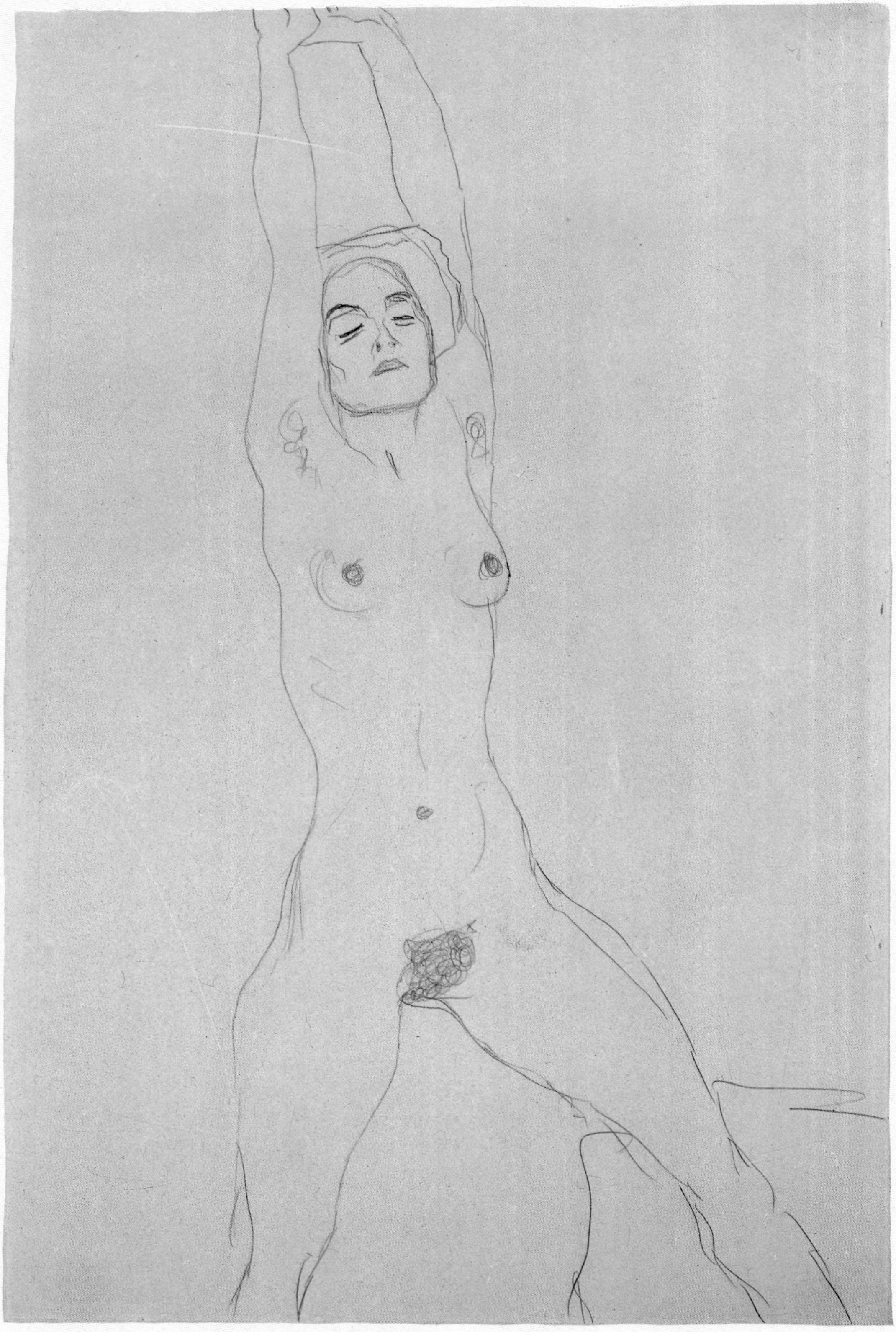

66. *Nude with arms raised above the head*, 1914.

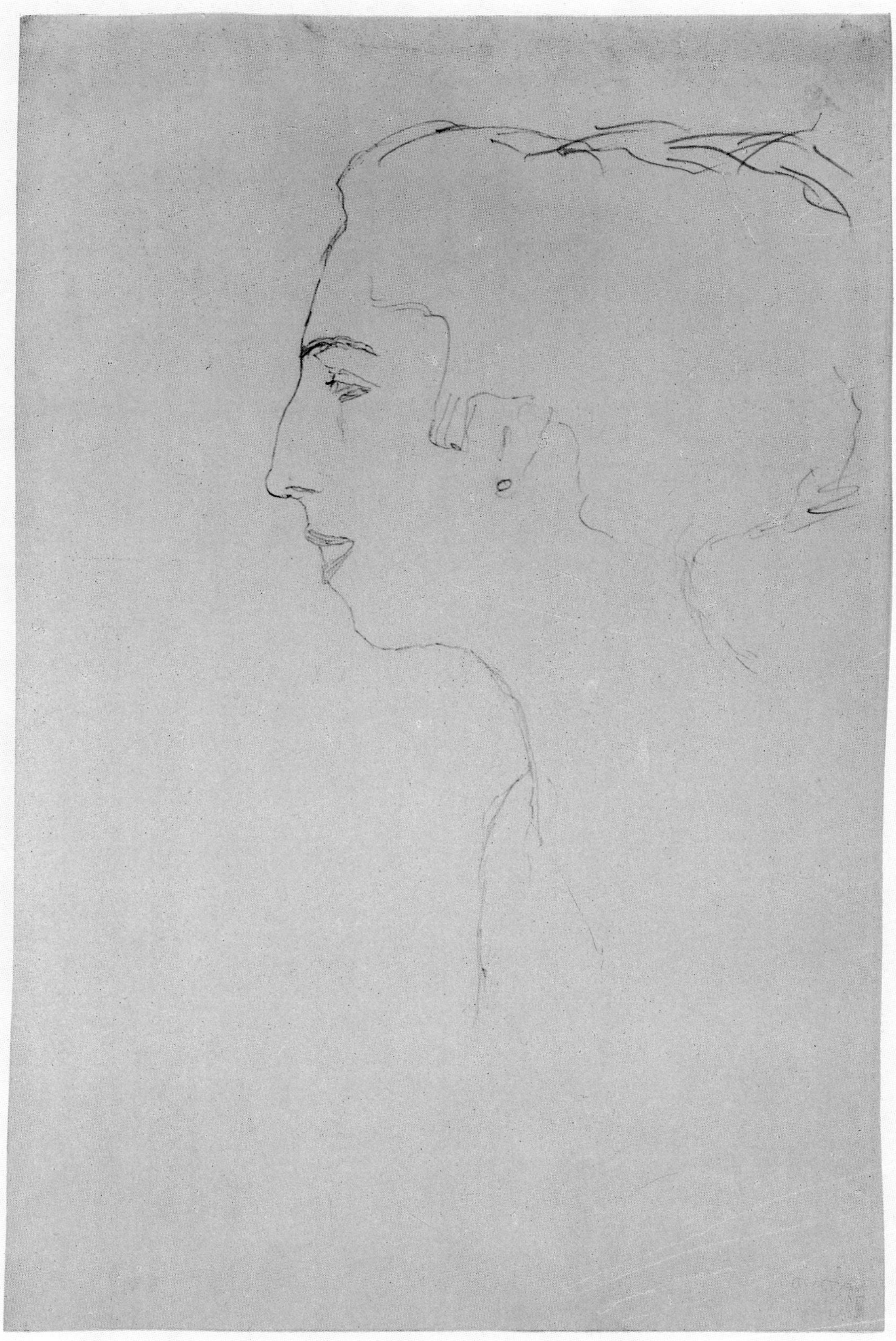

67. *Portrait study of a woman in profile*, 1914.

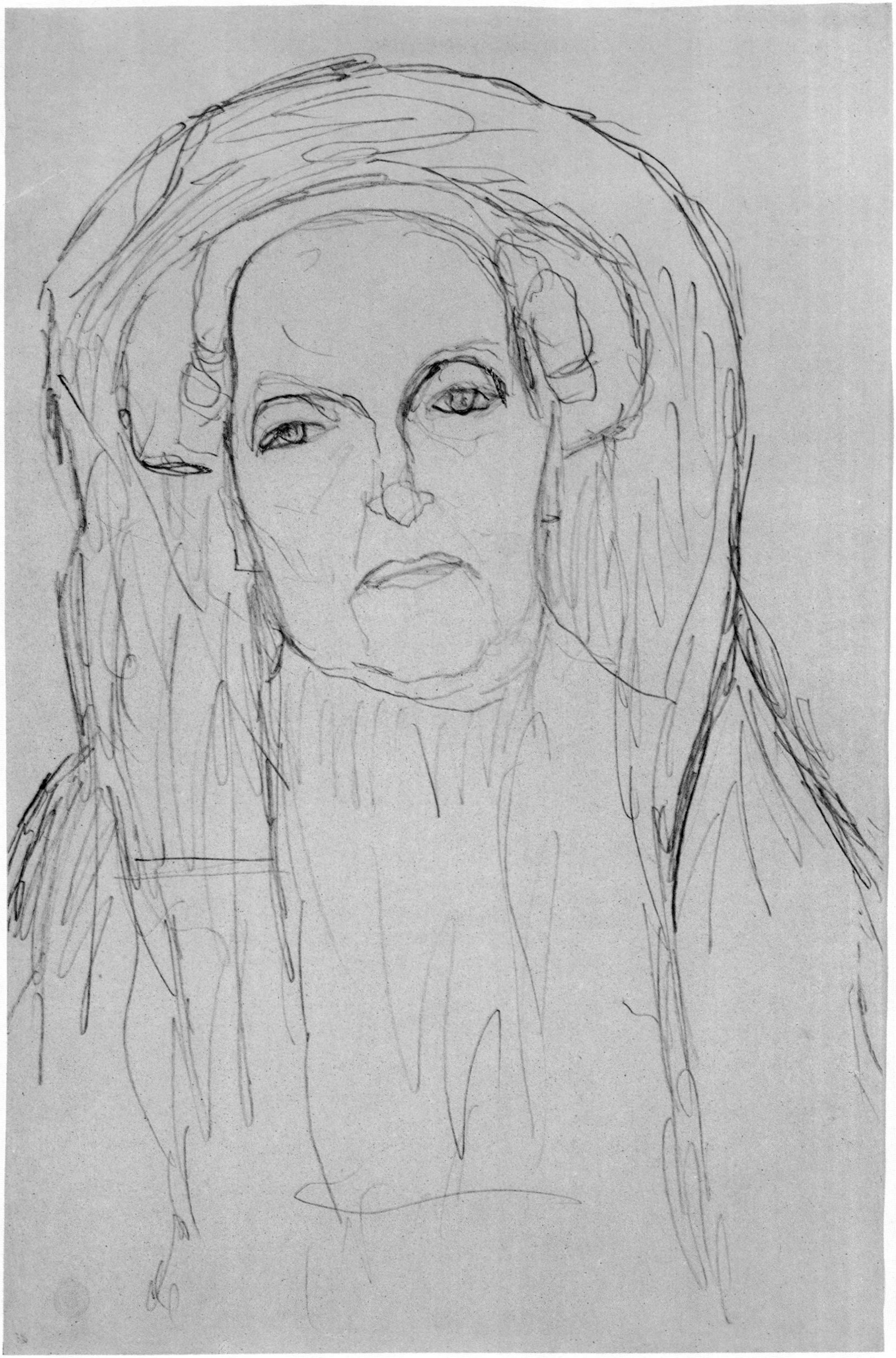

68. *Portrait study of an old lady*, 1914.

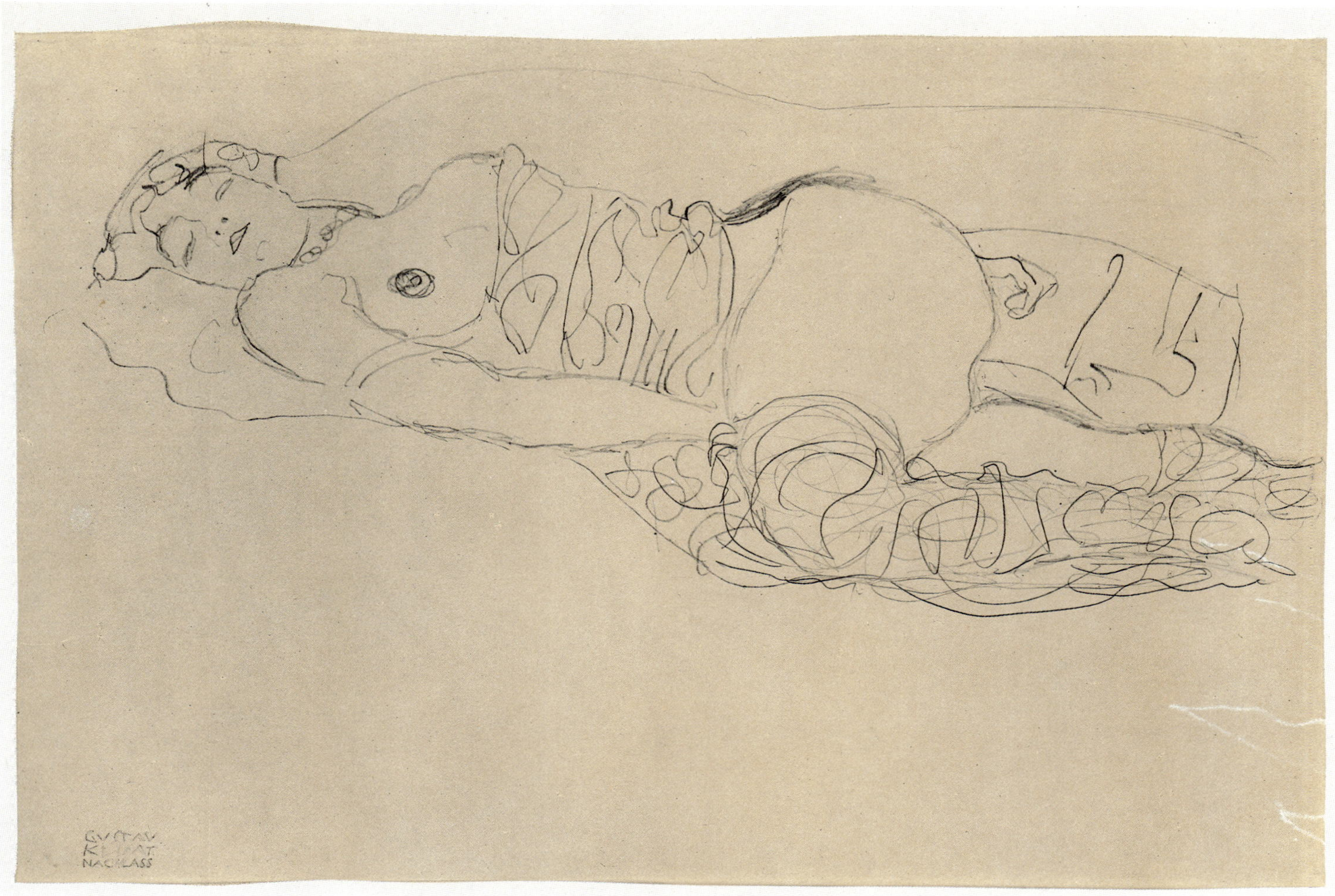

69. *Semi-nude figure reclining*, 1914.

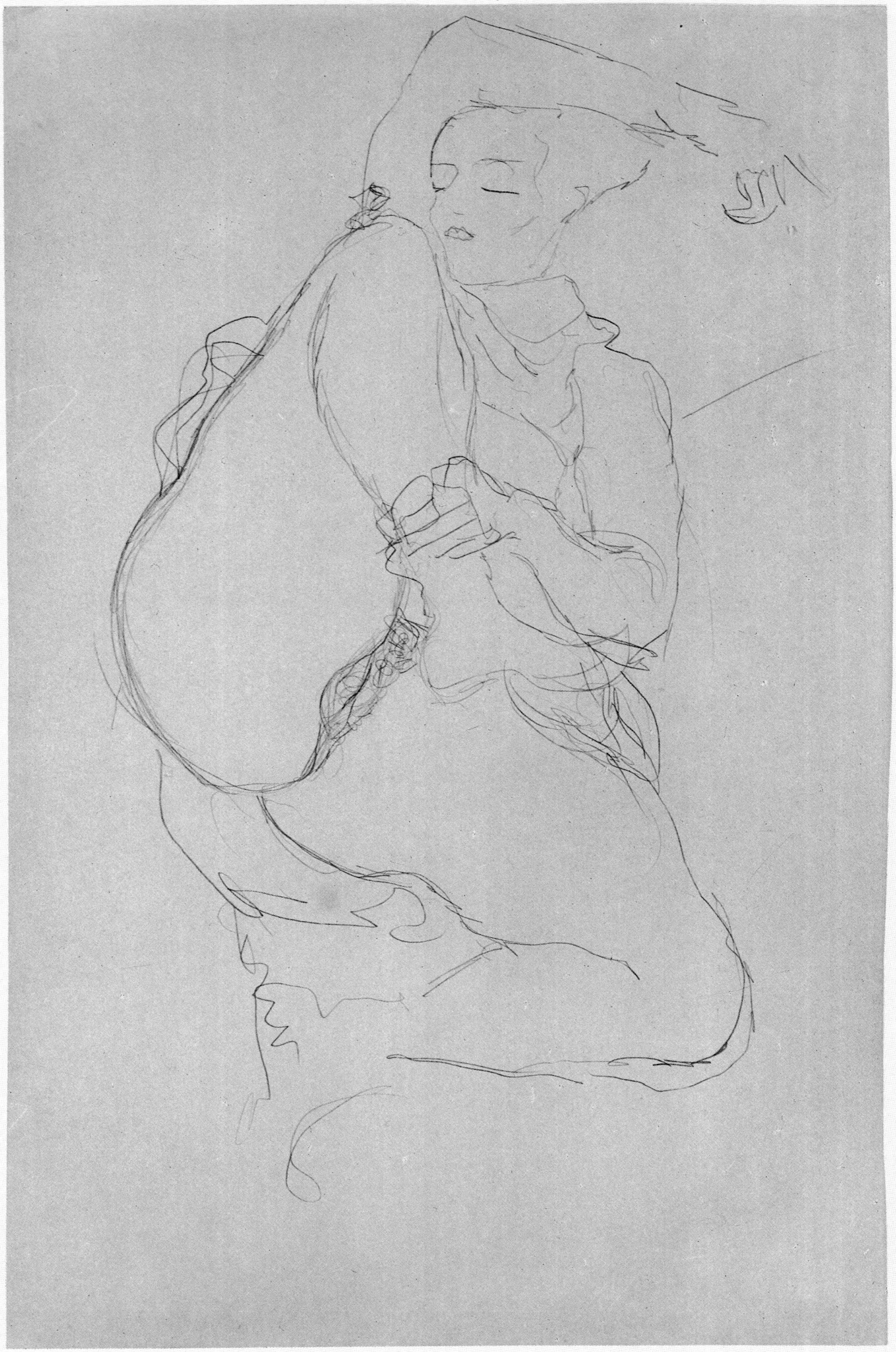

70. *Semi-nude figure reclining*,
1914–15.

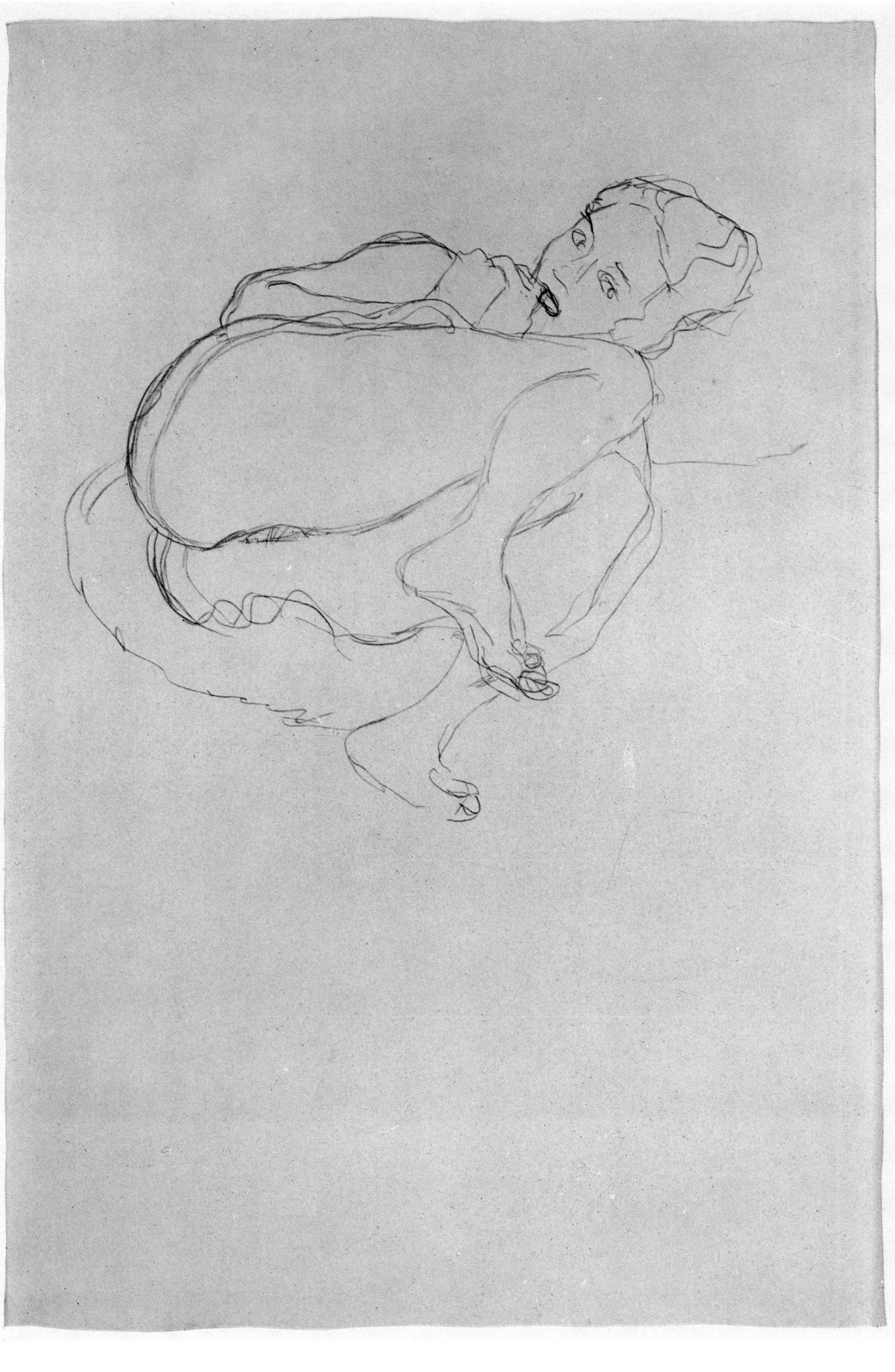

71. *Semi-nude figure reclining with legs drawn up,* 1914–15.

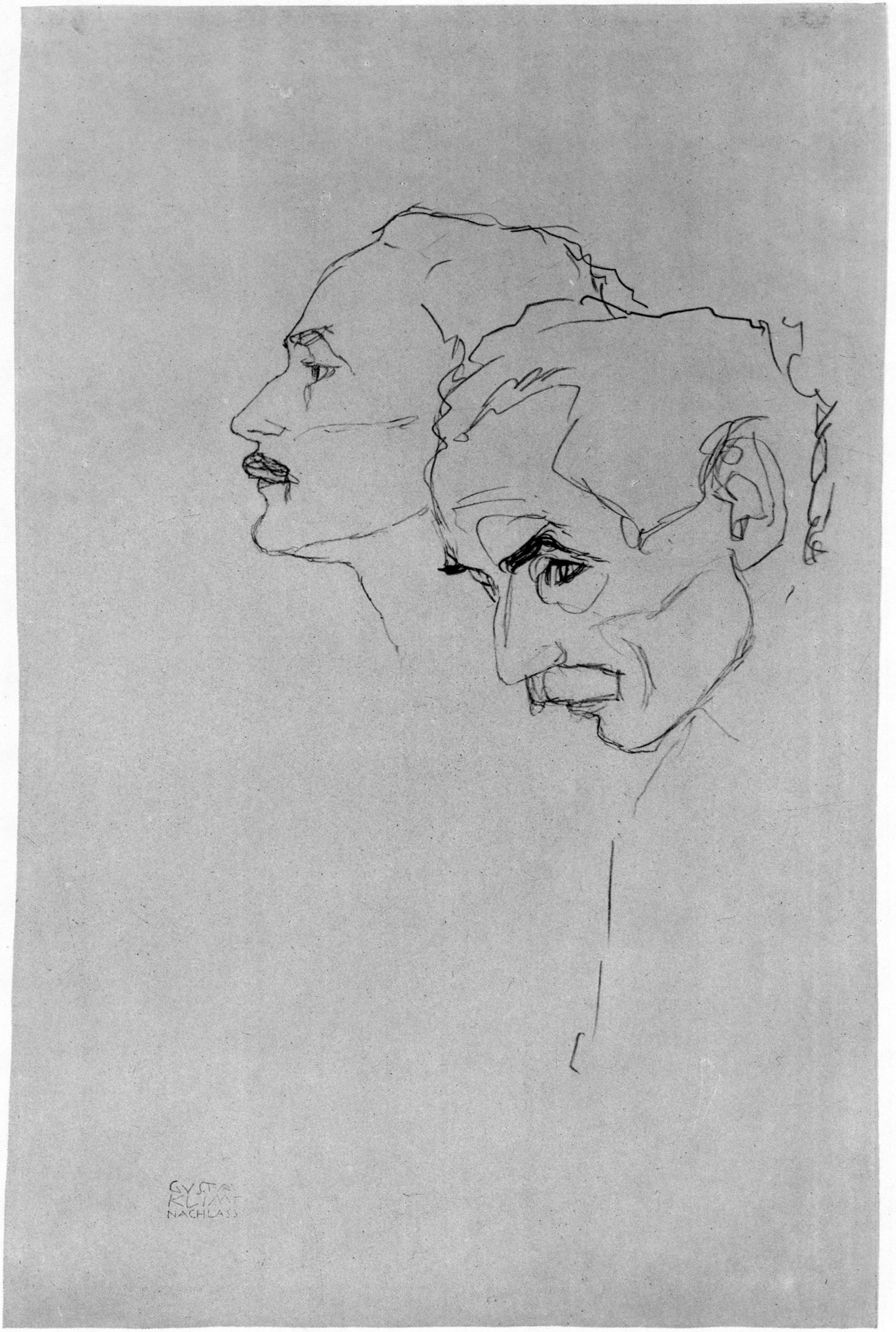

72. *Two male heads in profile*, 1914–15.

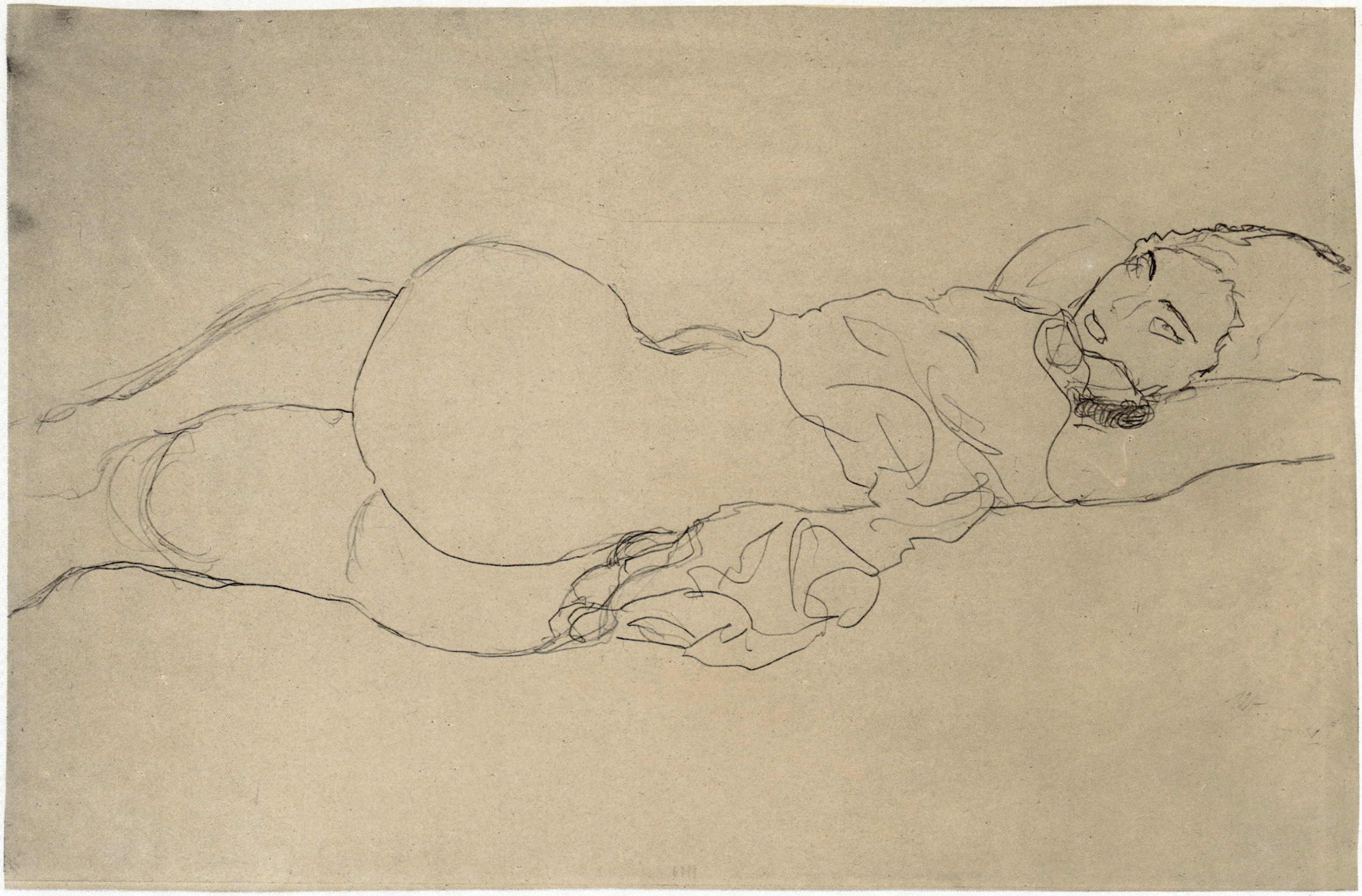

73. *Reclining nude*, *c*. 1914–18.

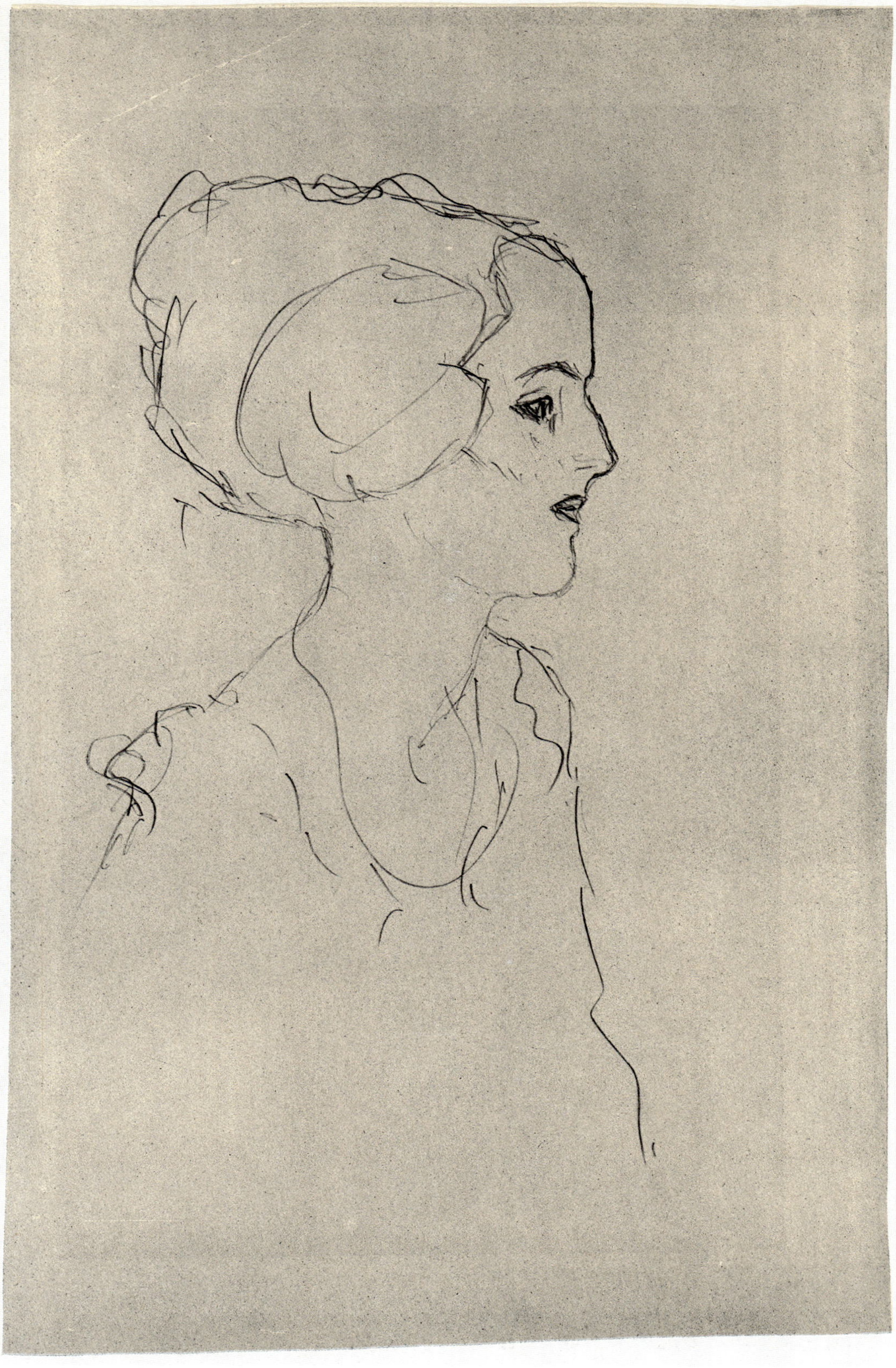

74. *Portrait study of a young woman in profile, c.* 1915.

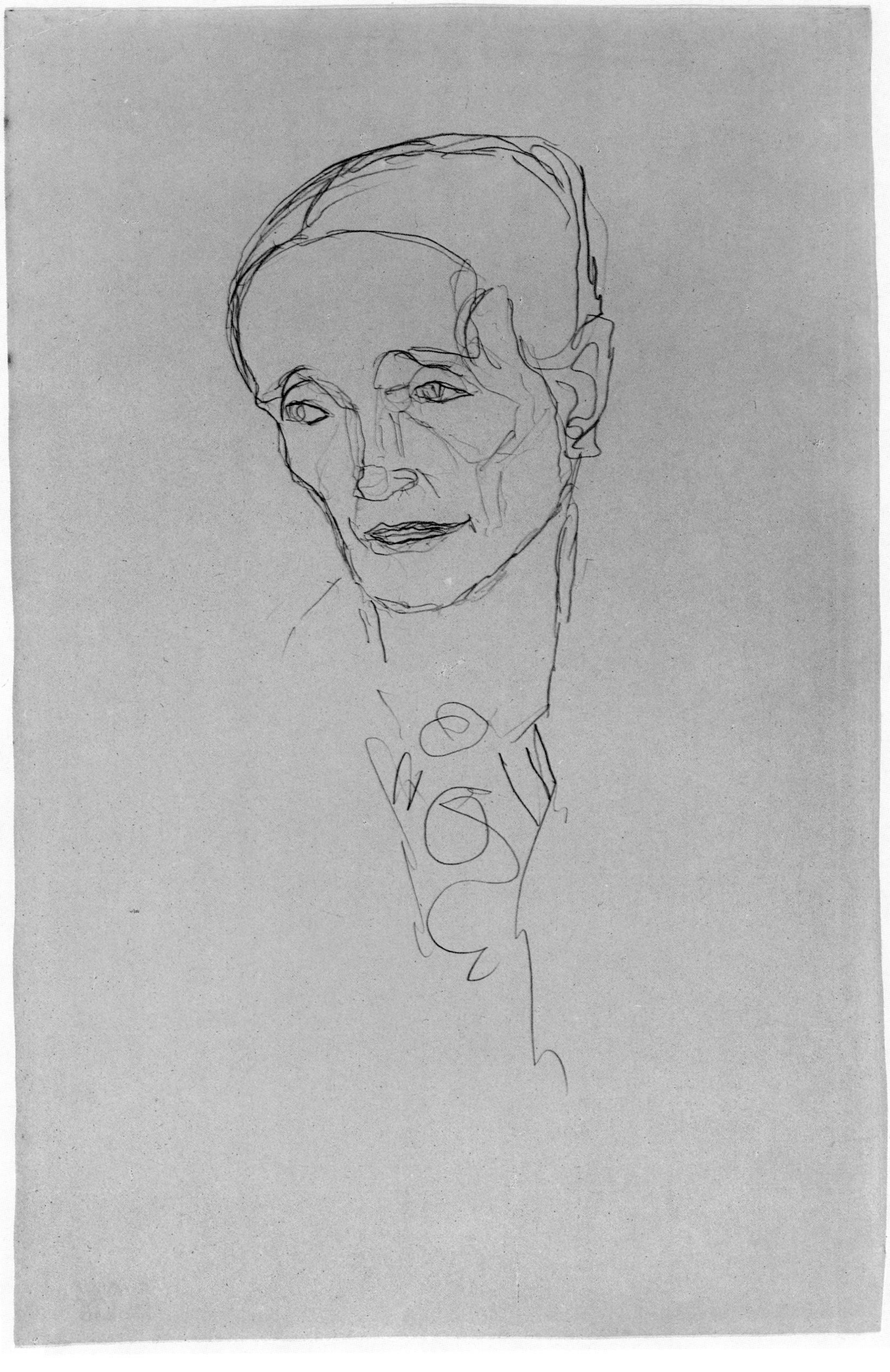

75. *Portrait study of an old woman*, 1915.

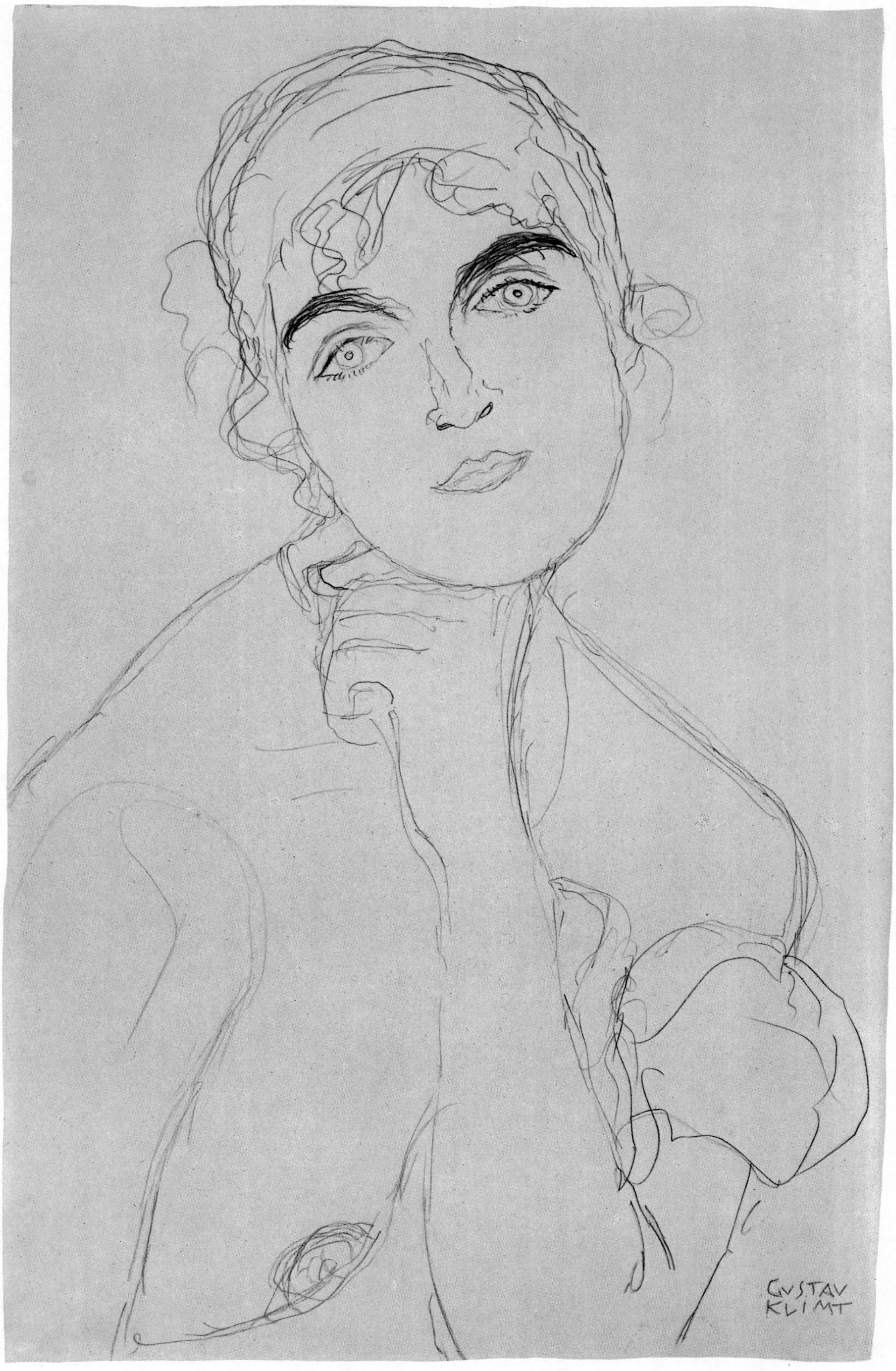

76. *Portrait of a lady*, 1915.

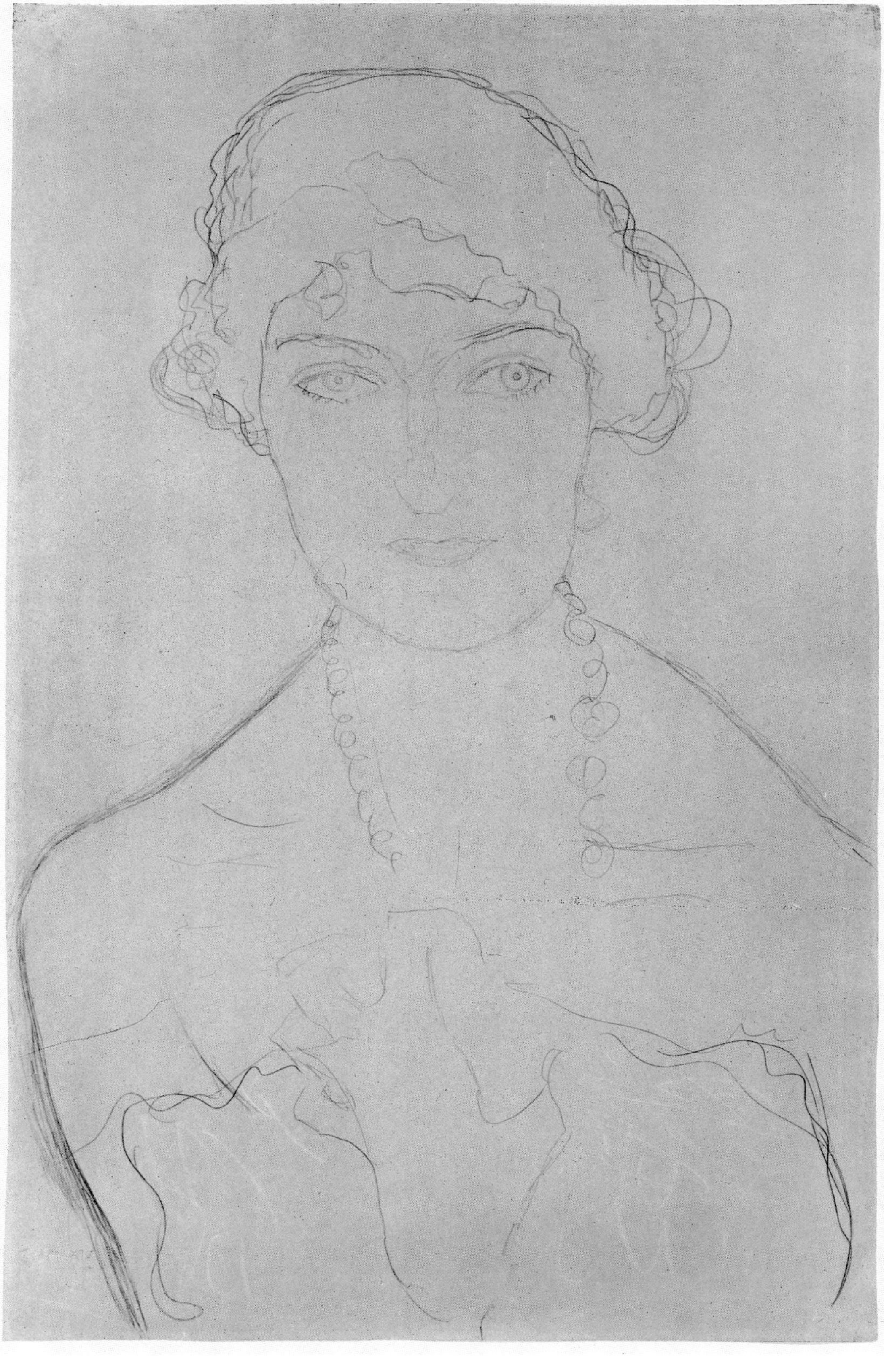

77. *Portrait of a lady*, 1915.

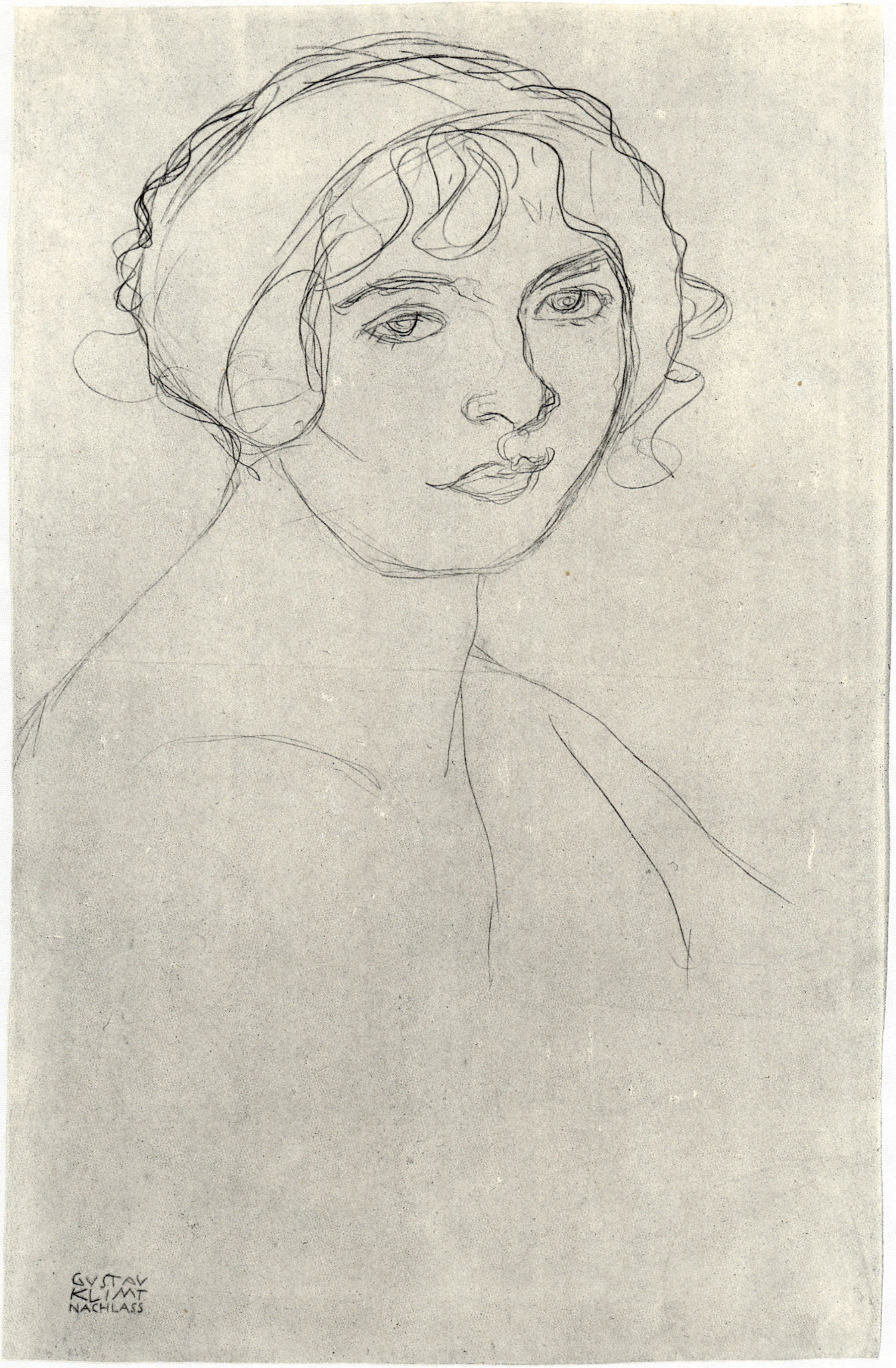

78. *Portrait study of a lady*, 1915.

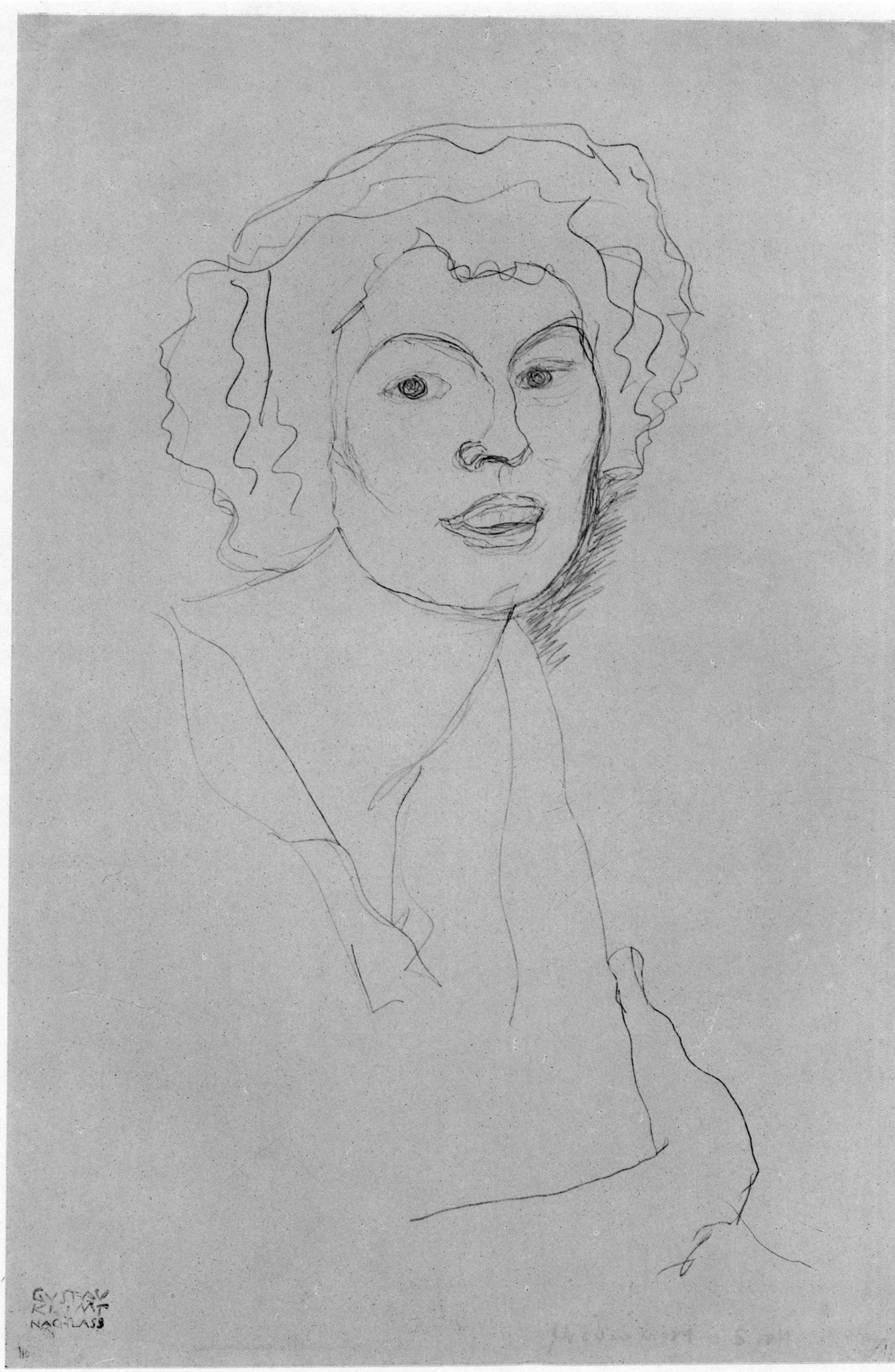

79. *Portrait study of a lady*, 1915.

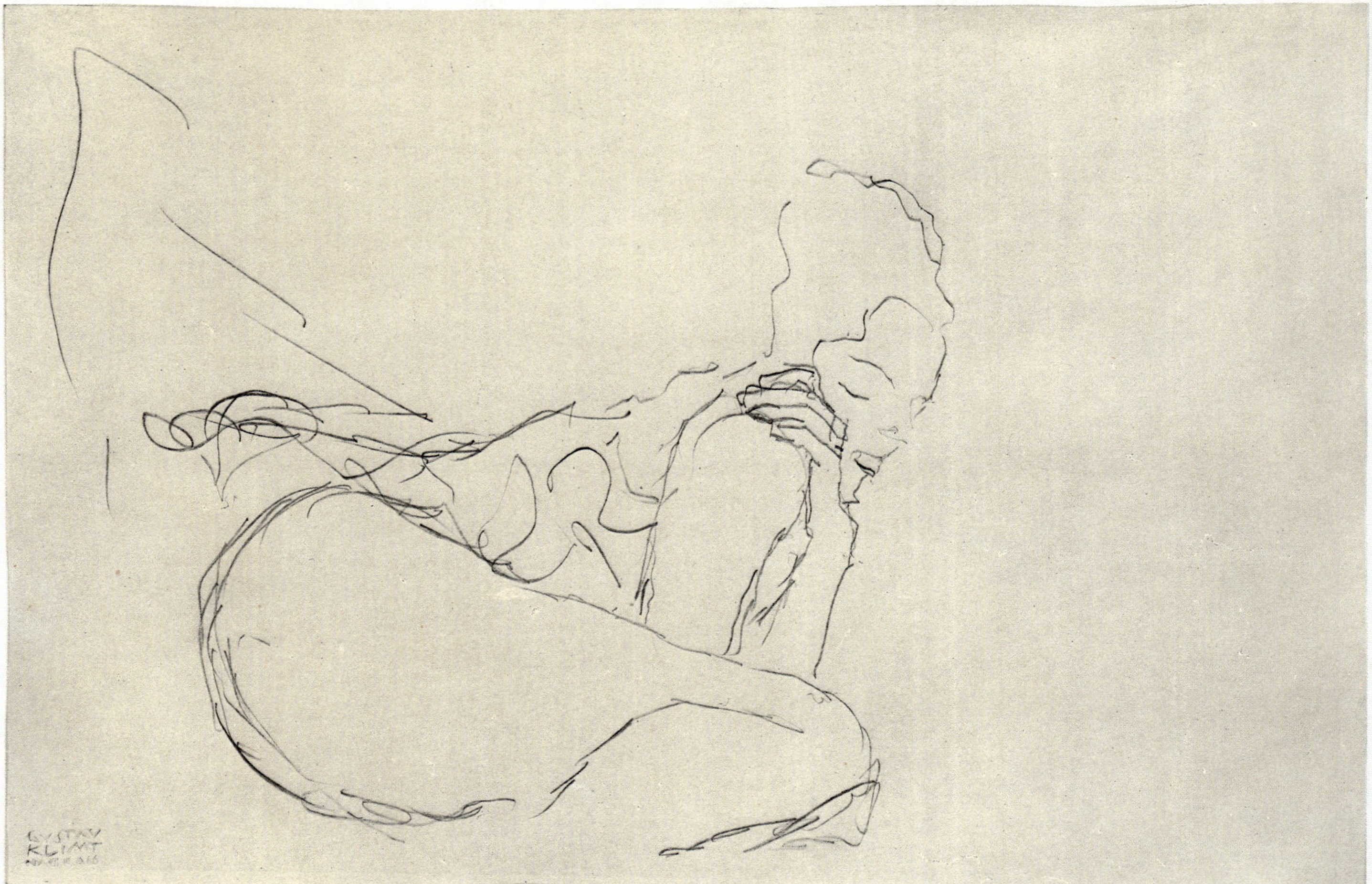

80. *Semi-nude figure sleeping, curled up*, *c.* 1915.

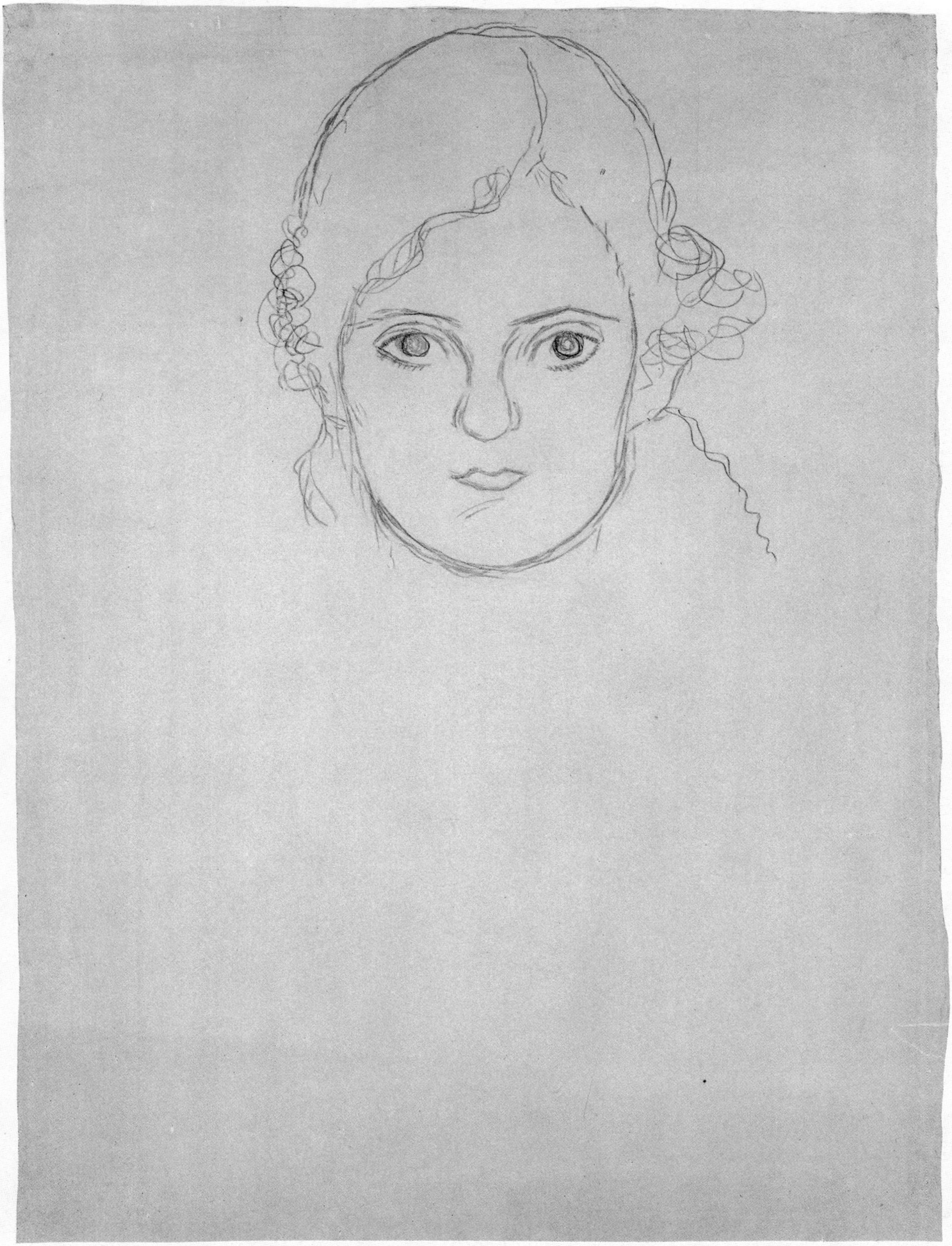

81. *Portrait study of a young woman.* 1915–16.

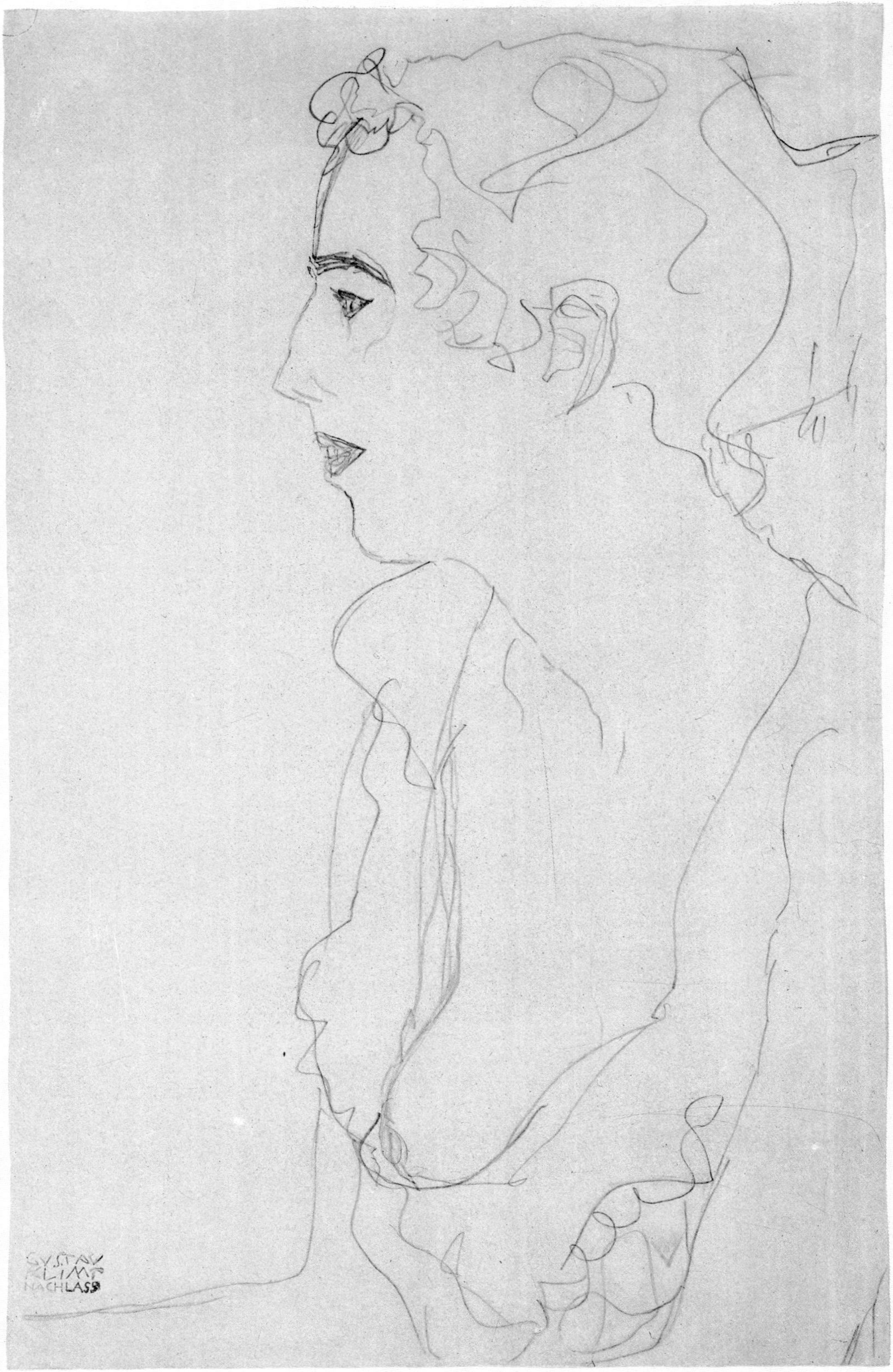

82. *Portrait study of a woman in profile*, 1915–16.

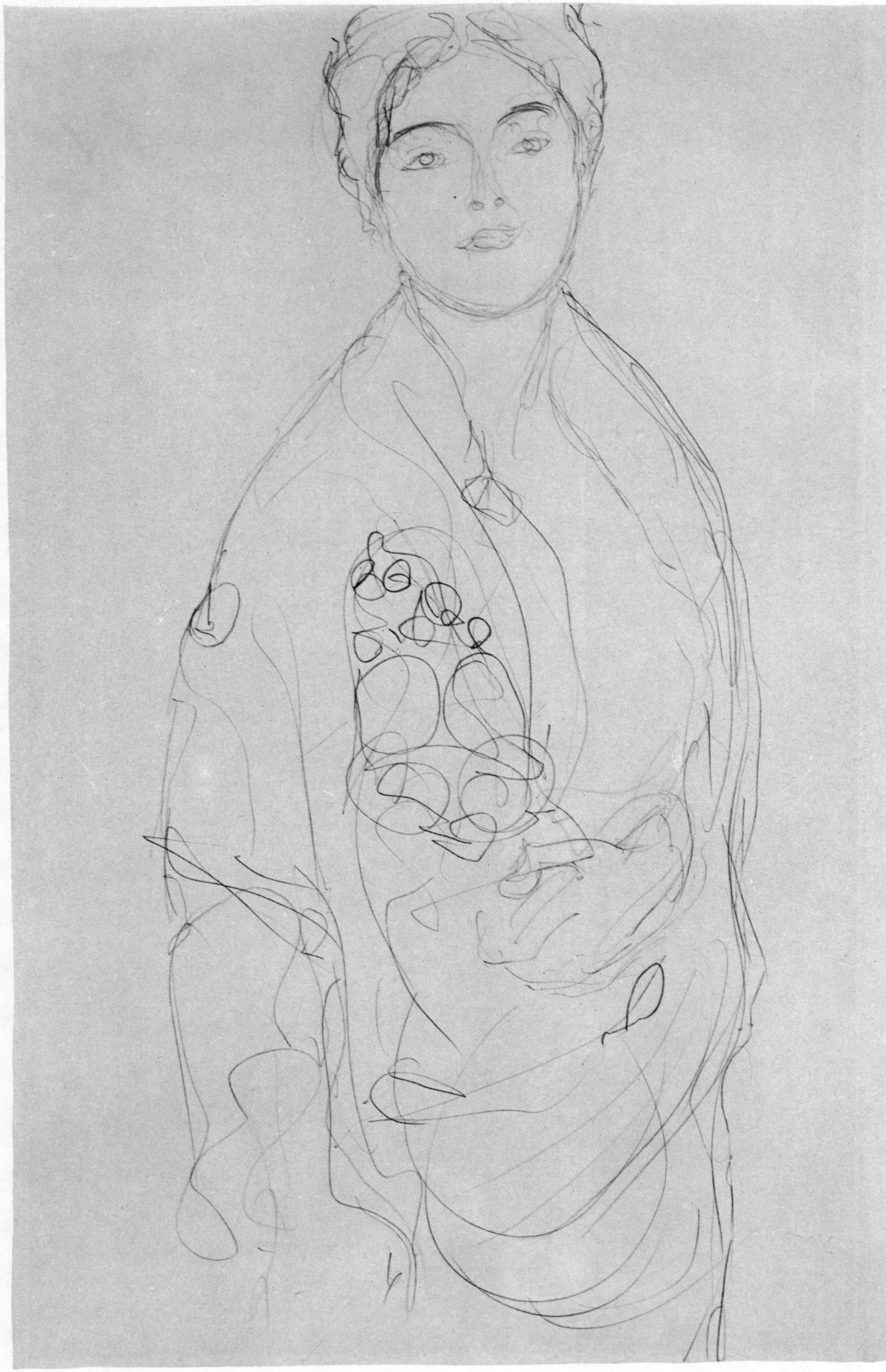

83. *Portrait study of a lady*, 1915–16.

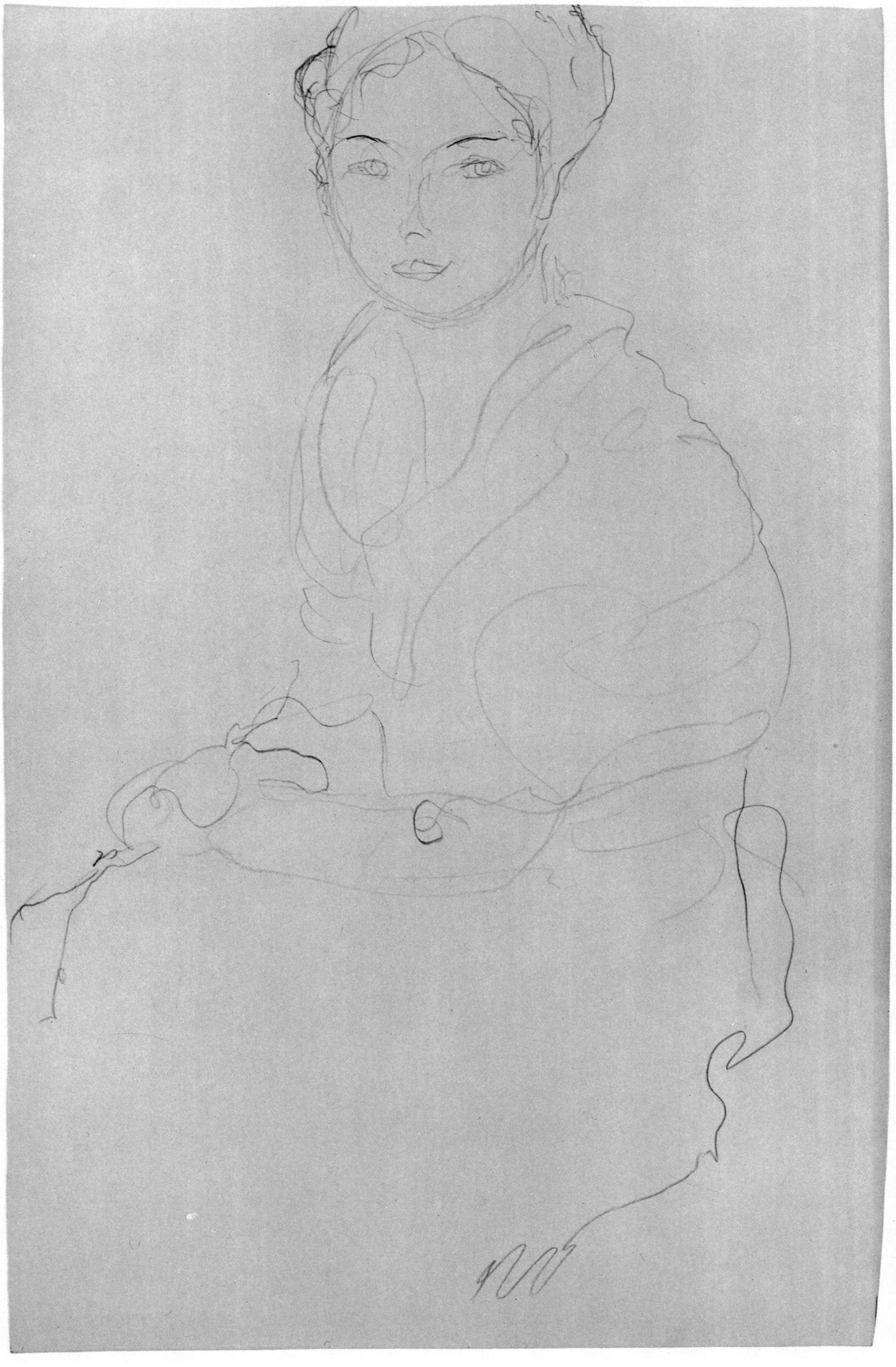

84. *Portrait study of a lady, seated,* 1915–16.

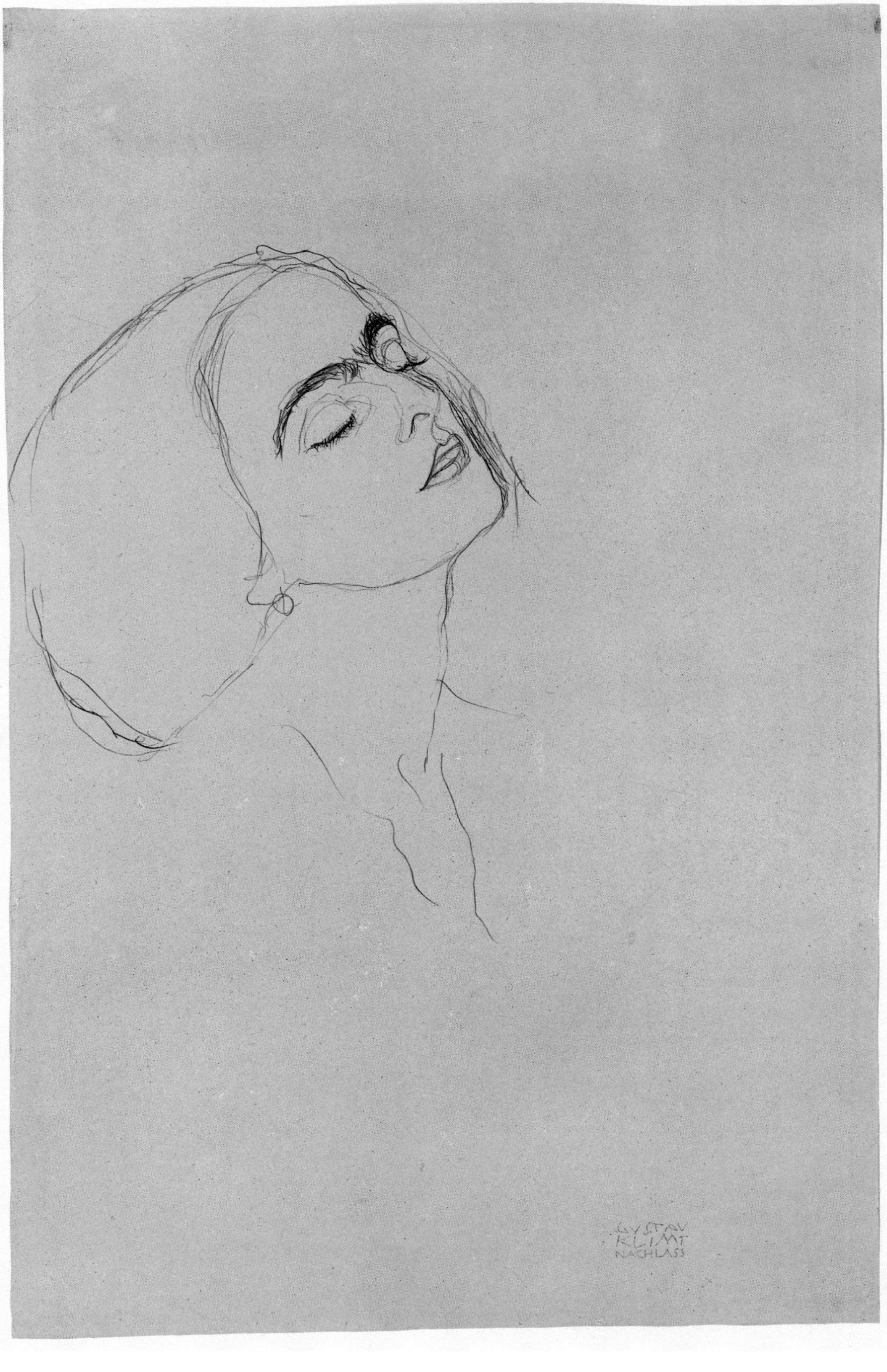

85. *Female head with closed eyes*, 1915–16.

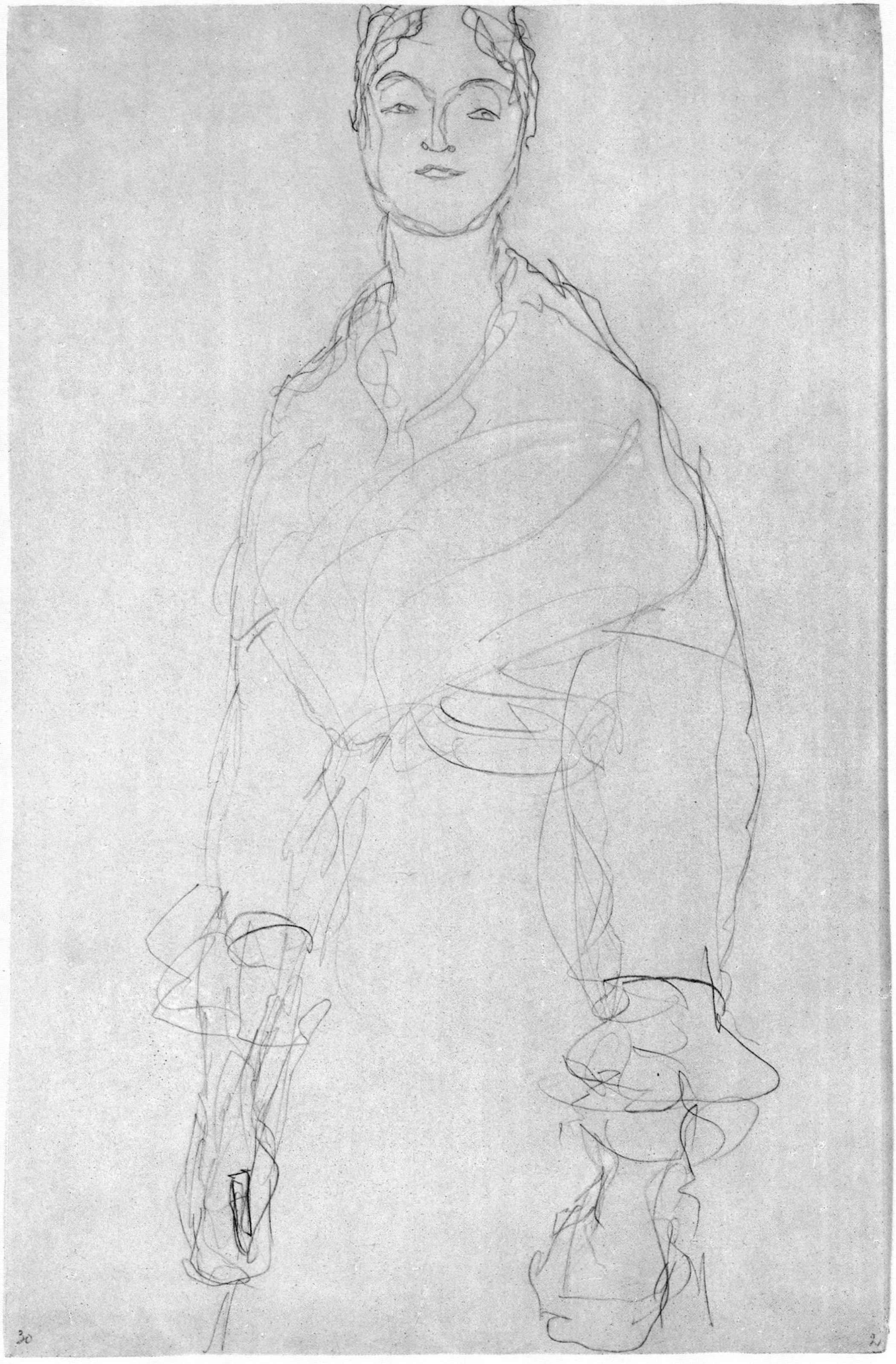

86. *Portrait study of a woman standing*, 1915–16.

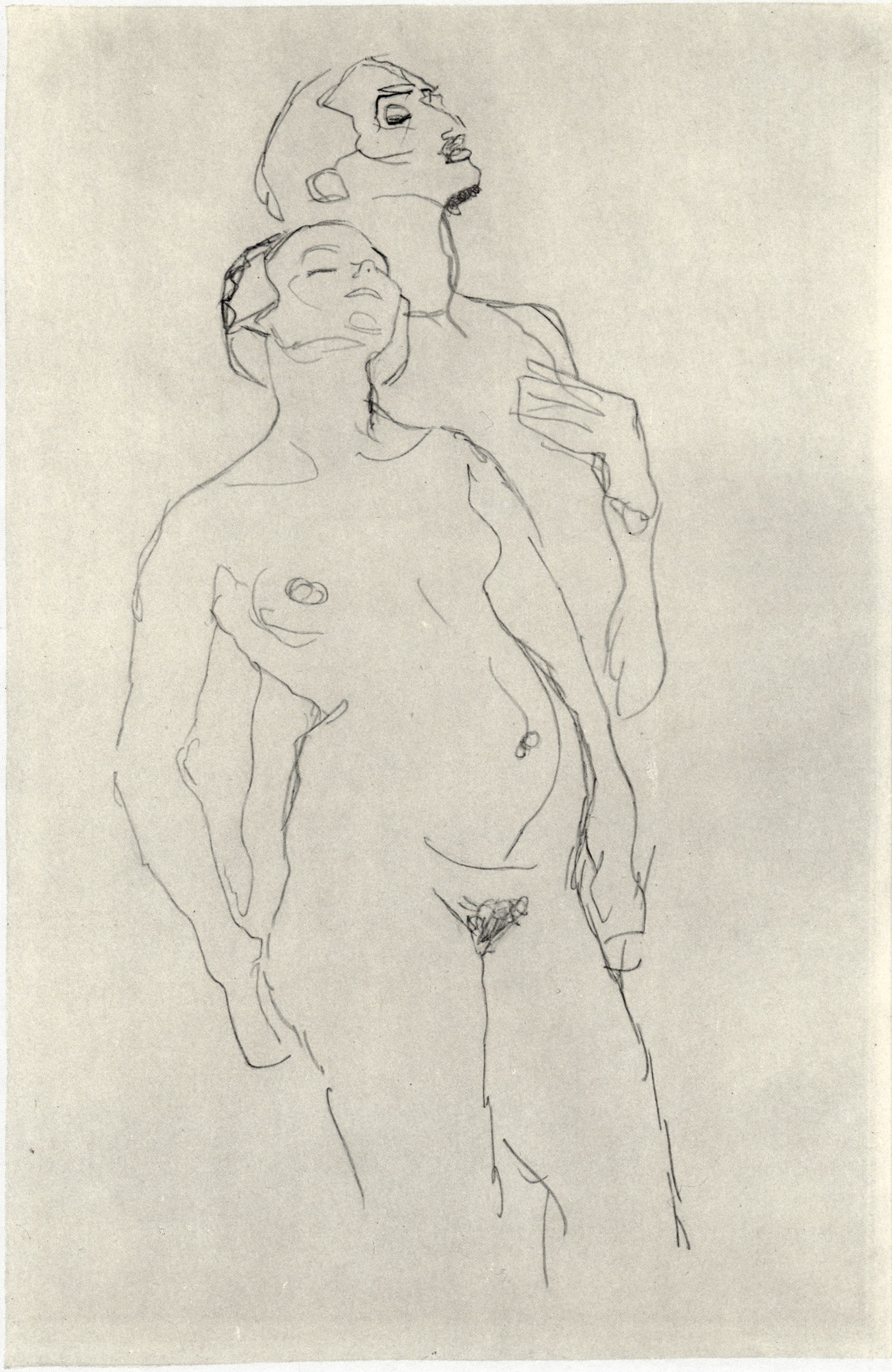

87. *Standing couple, nude*, 1915–16.

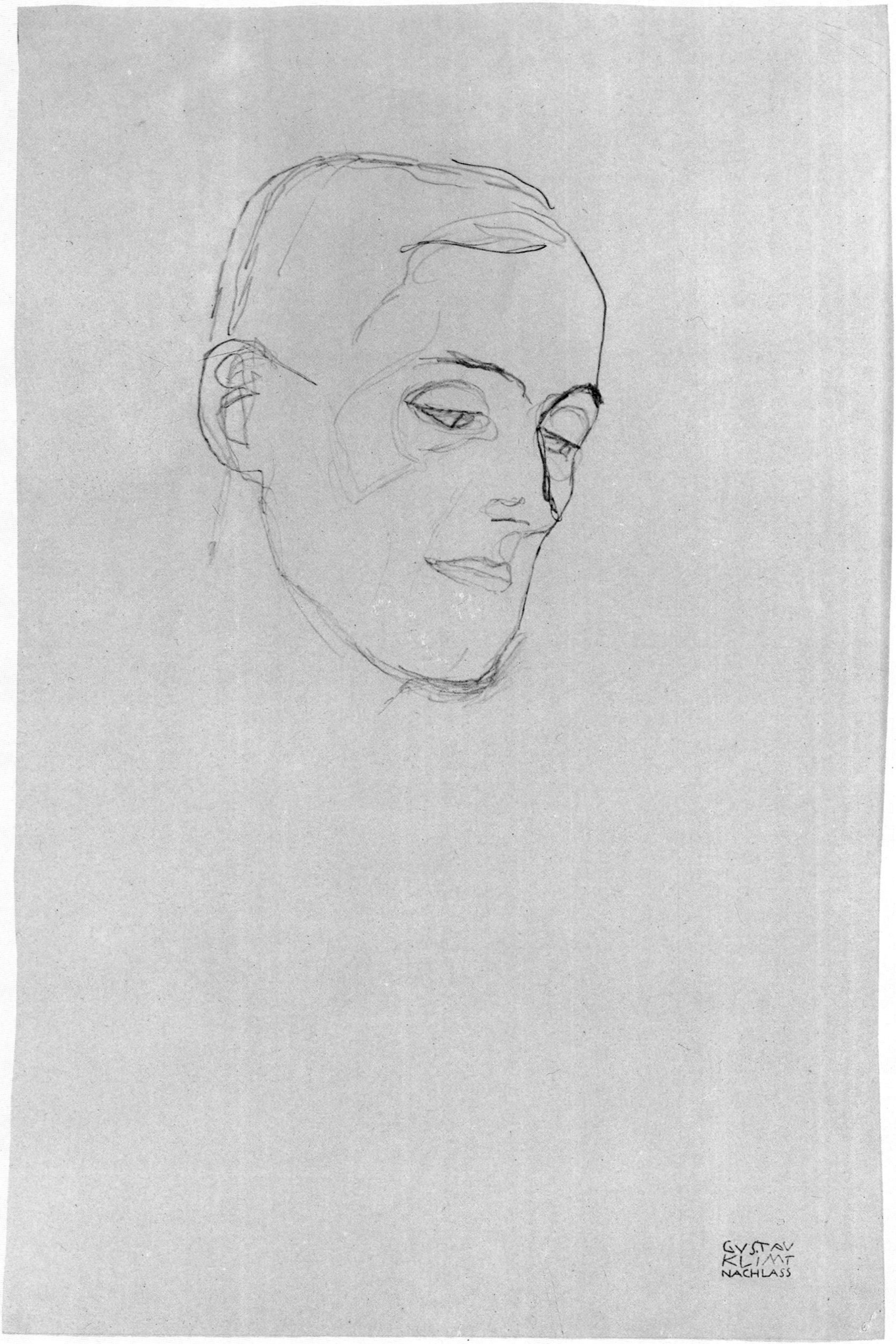

88. *Study of a male head,*
c. 1916.

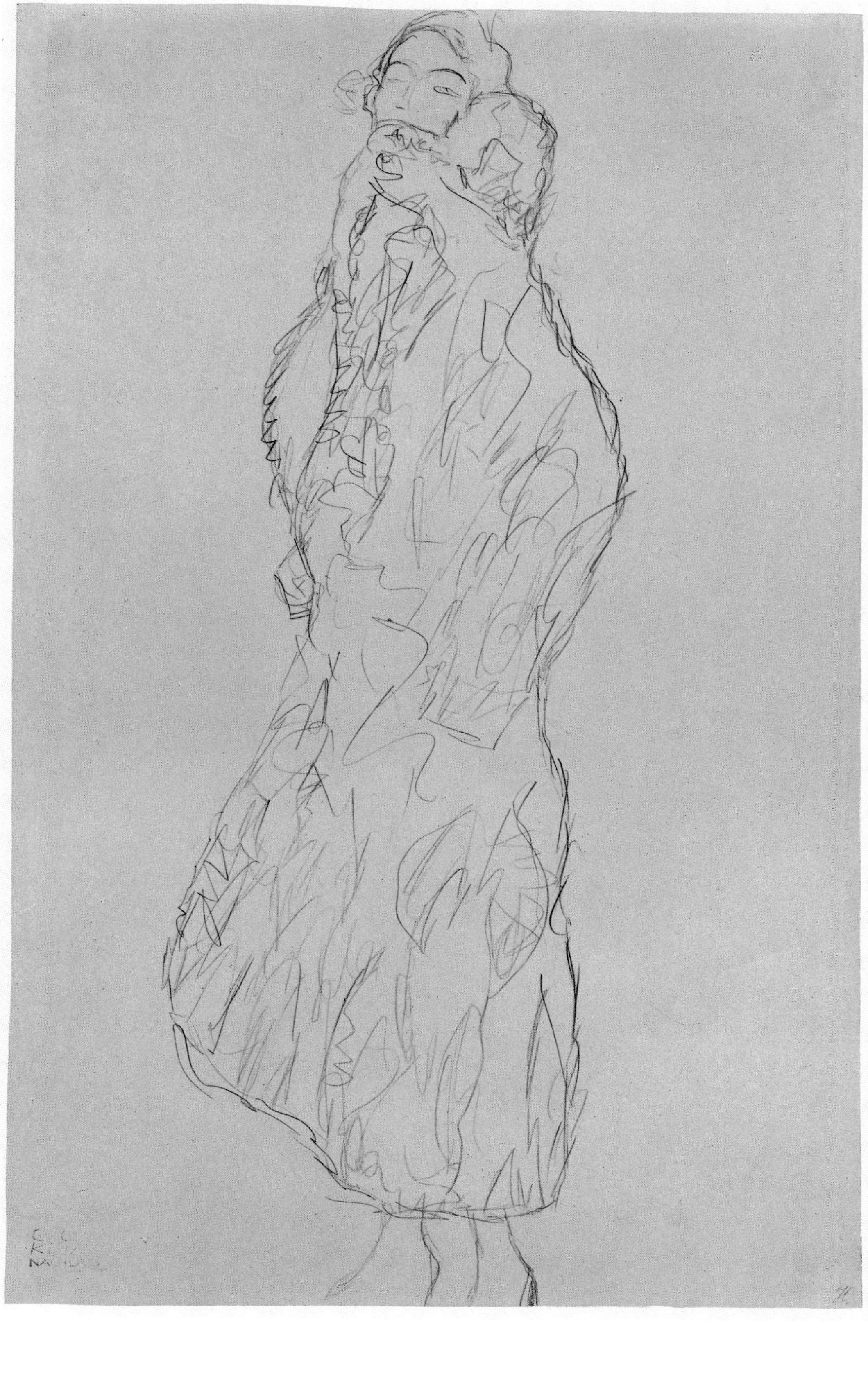

89. *Portrait study of a lady in a fur coat*, 1916.

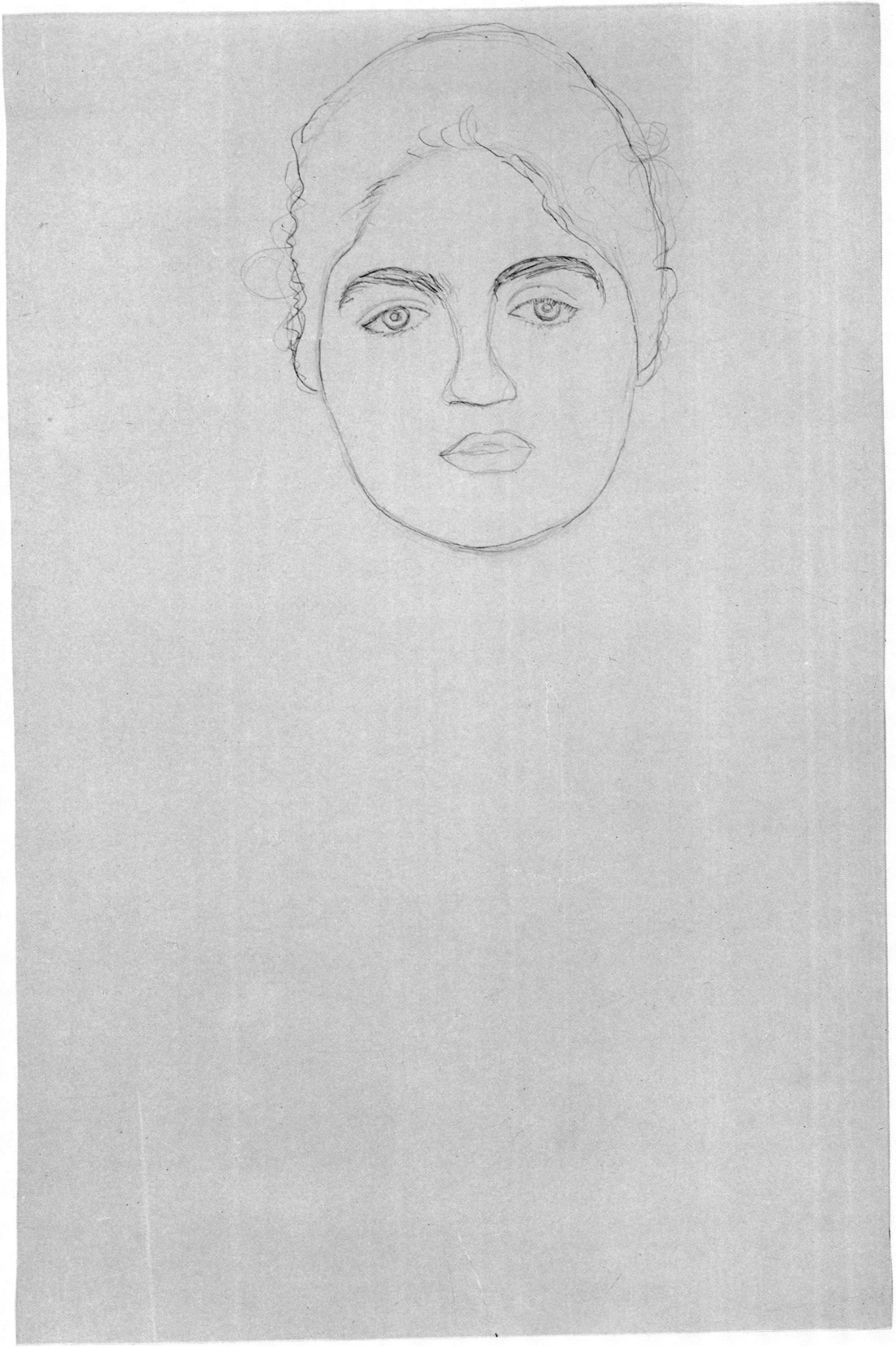

90. *Portrait study of Friederike Beer-Monti*, 1916.

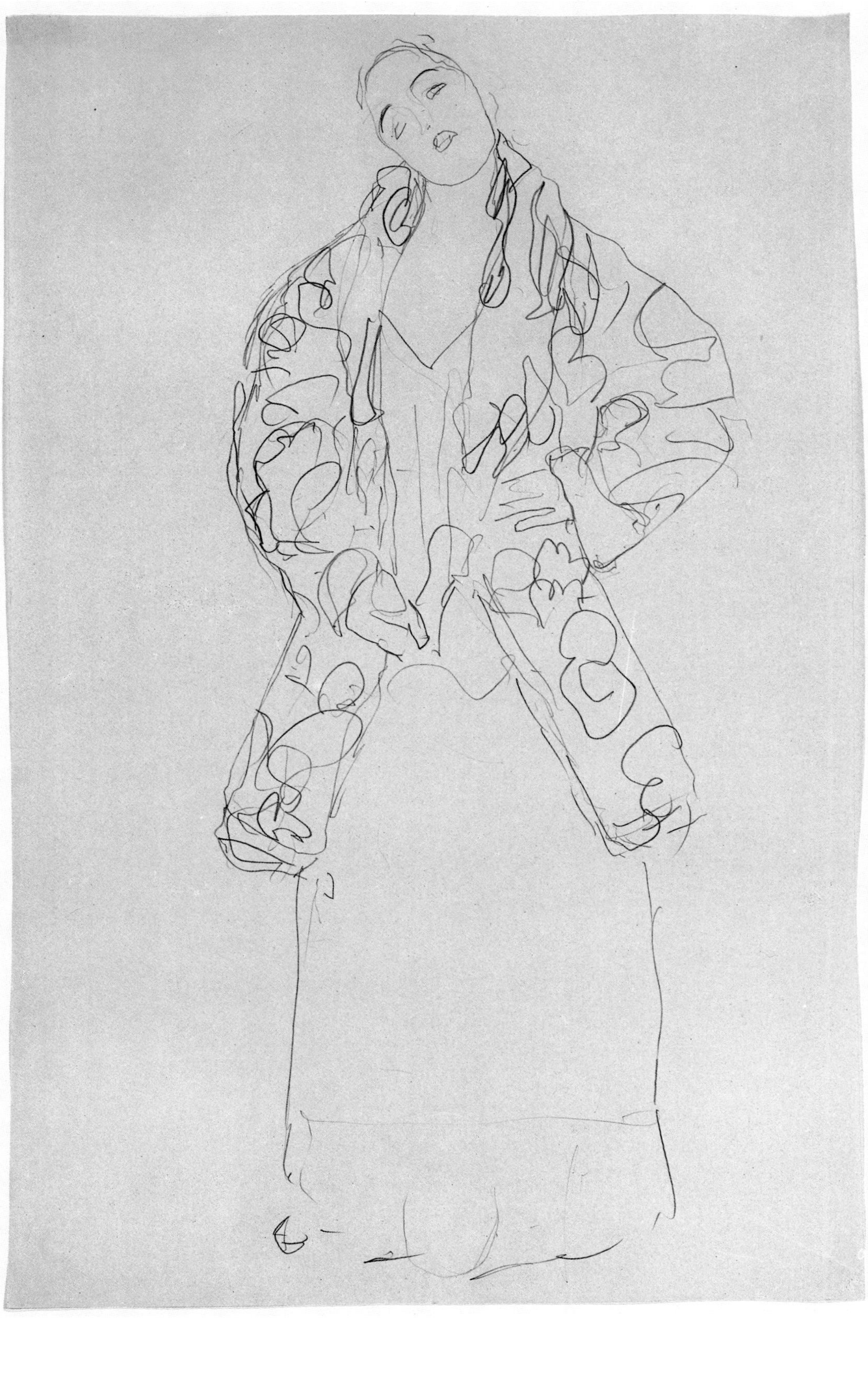

91. *Portrait study of Friederike Beer-Monti*, c. 1916.

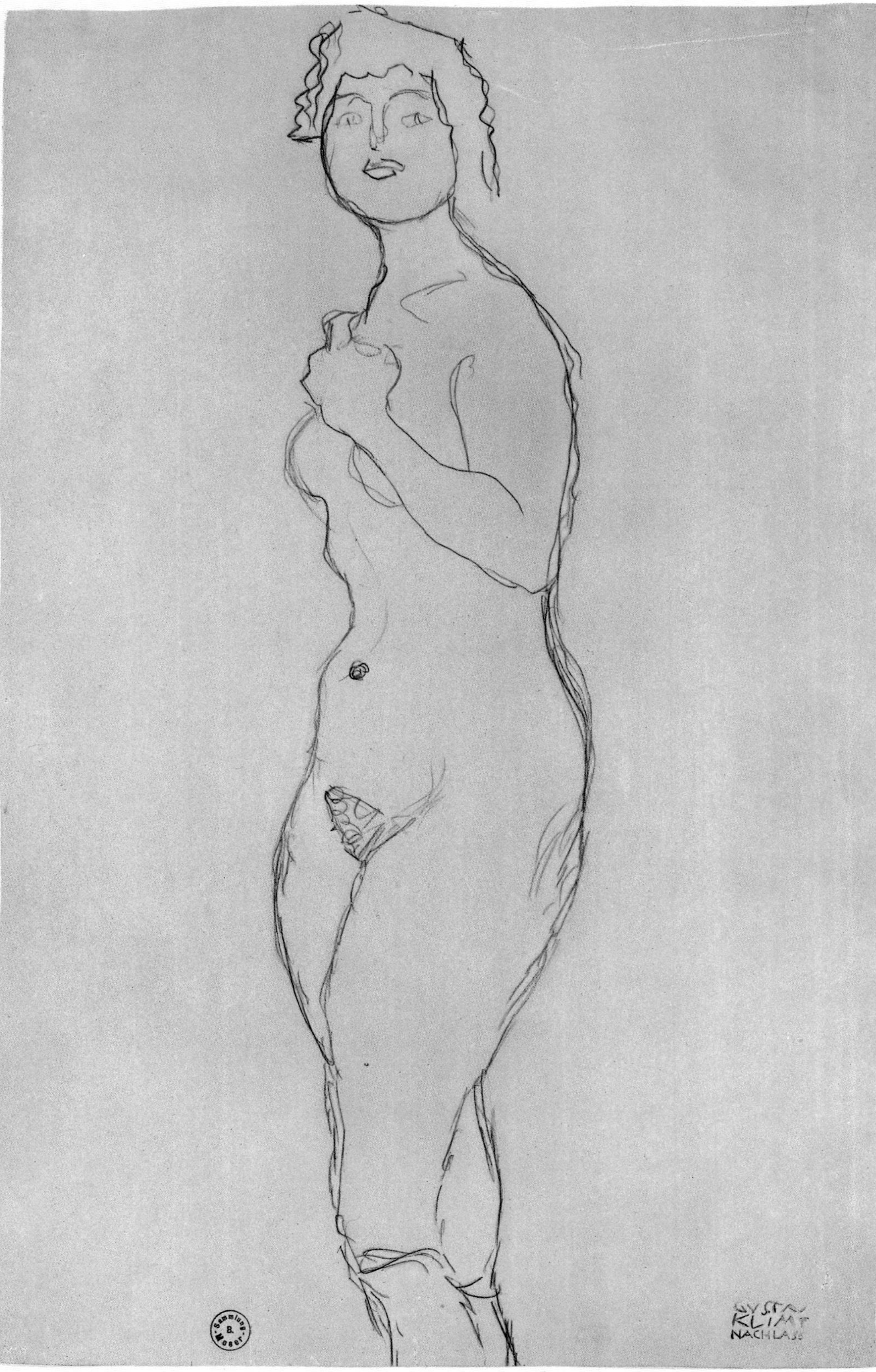

92. *Standing nude*, 1916.

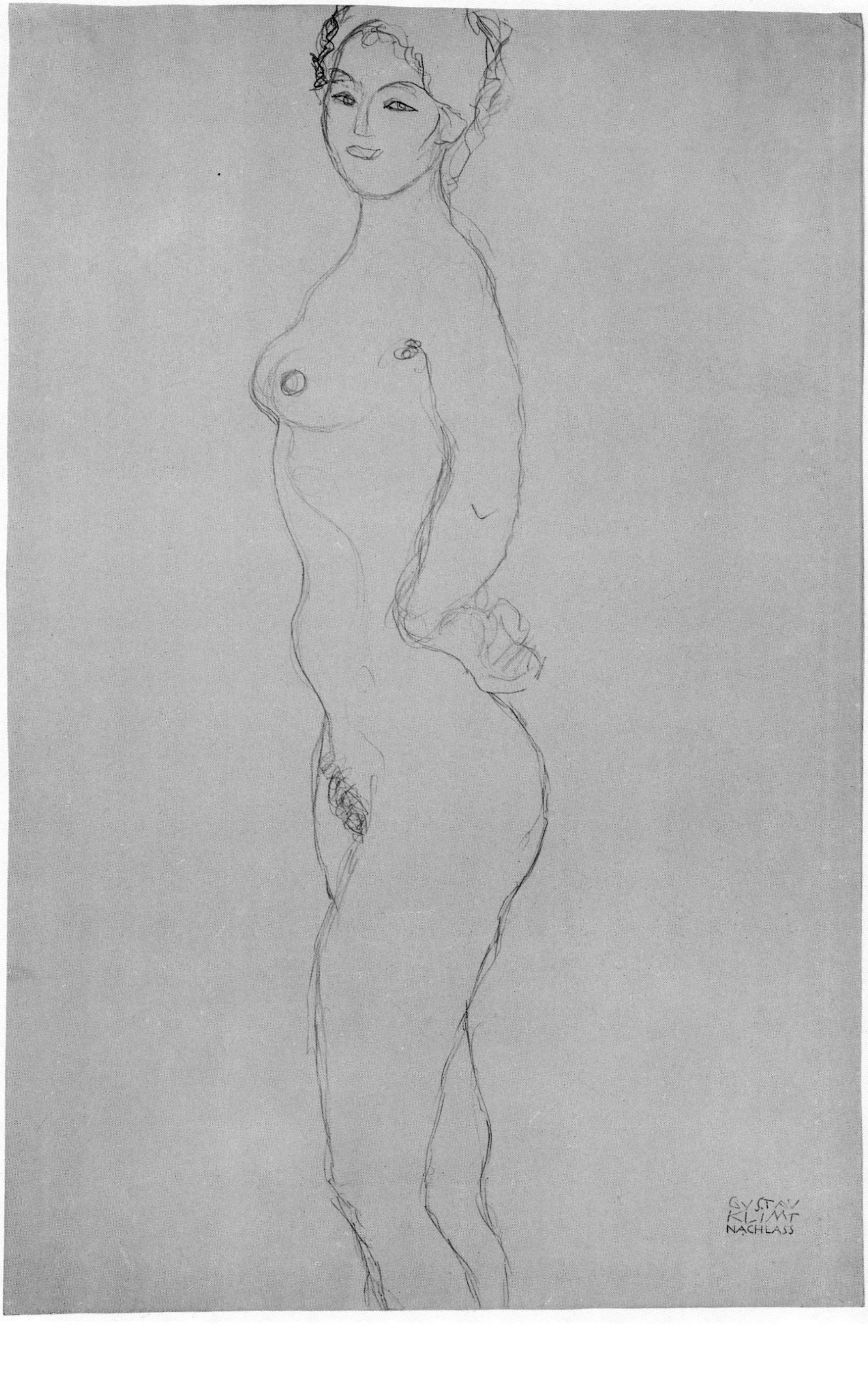

93. *Standing nude*, 1916.

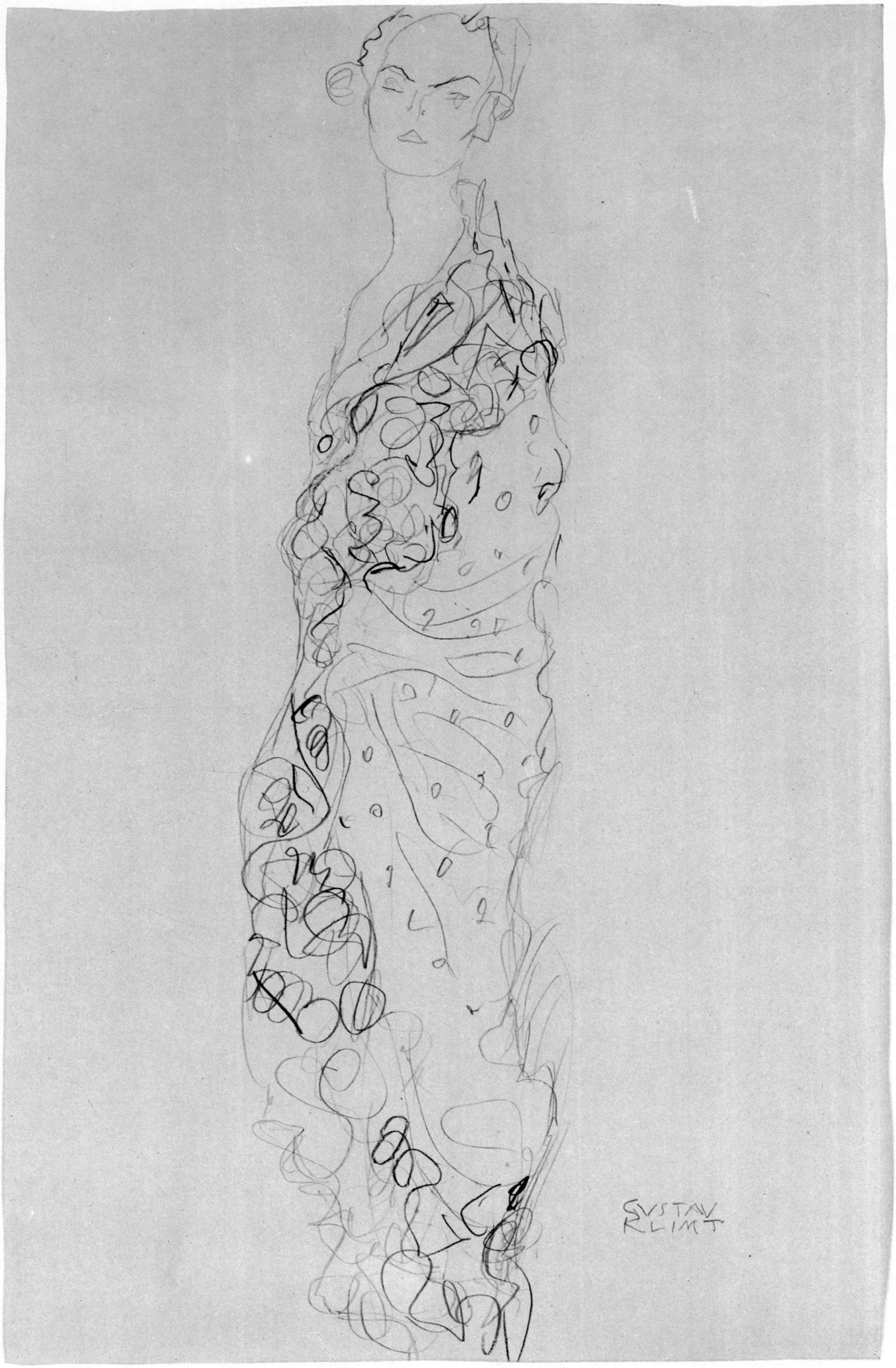

94. *Standing lady in elegant costume*, 1916.

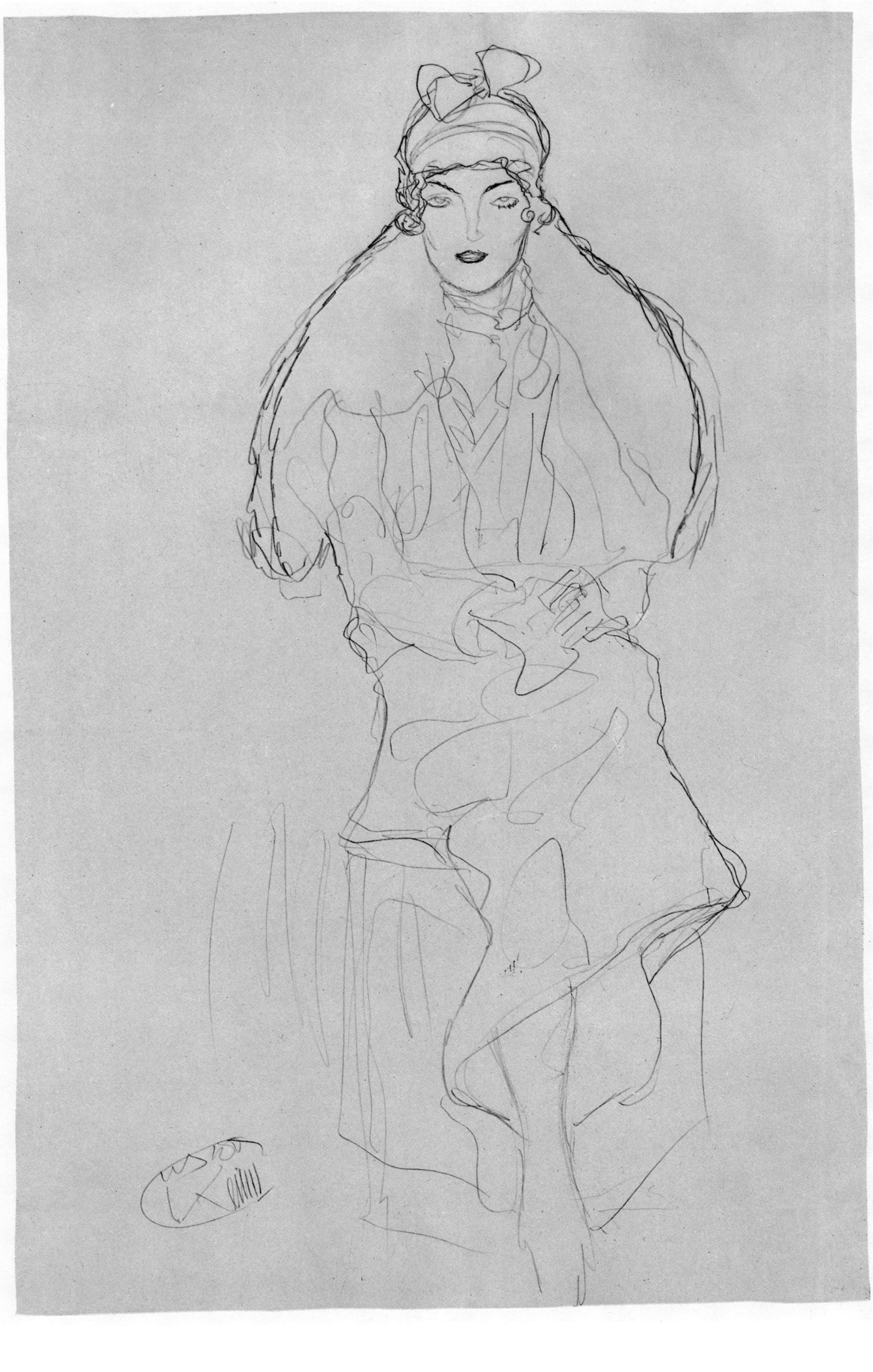

95. *Portrait study of a young lady with hat and boa*, 1916.

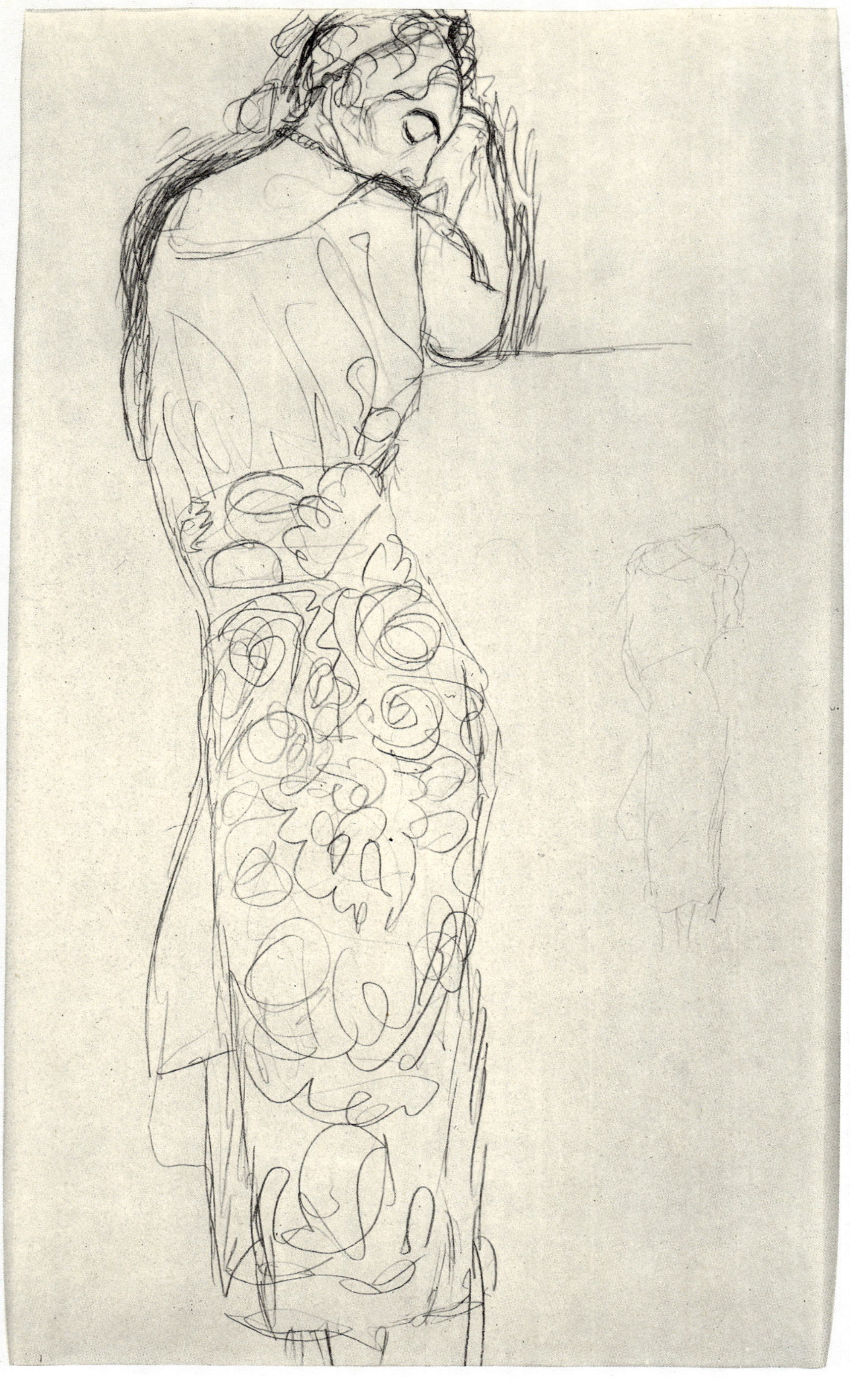

96. *Back view of a standing woman, leaning on her right elbow*, 1916.

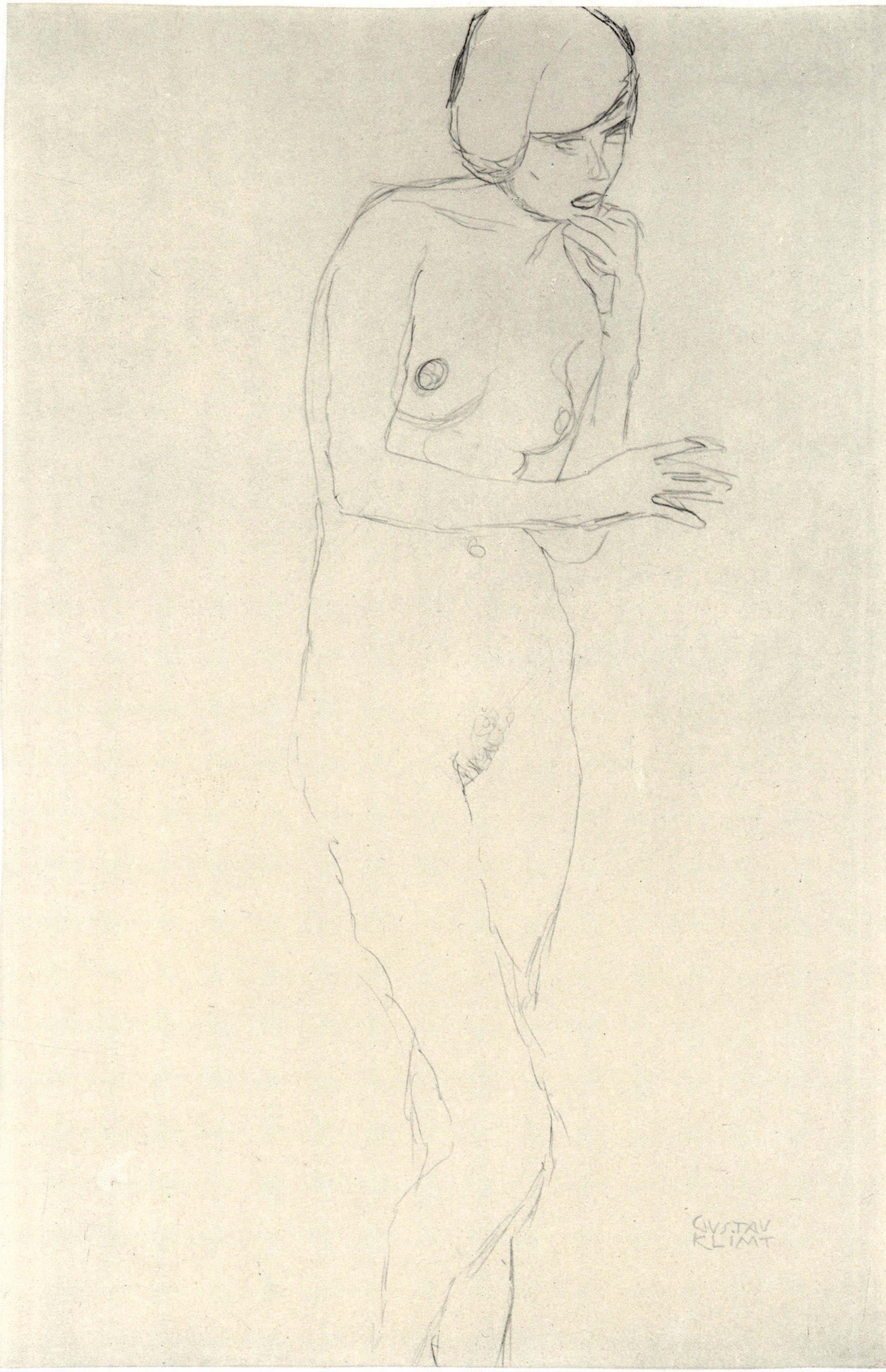

97. *Standing woman with left hand to her chin, c.* 1916–17.

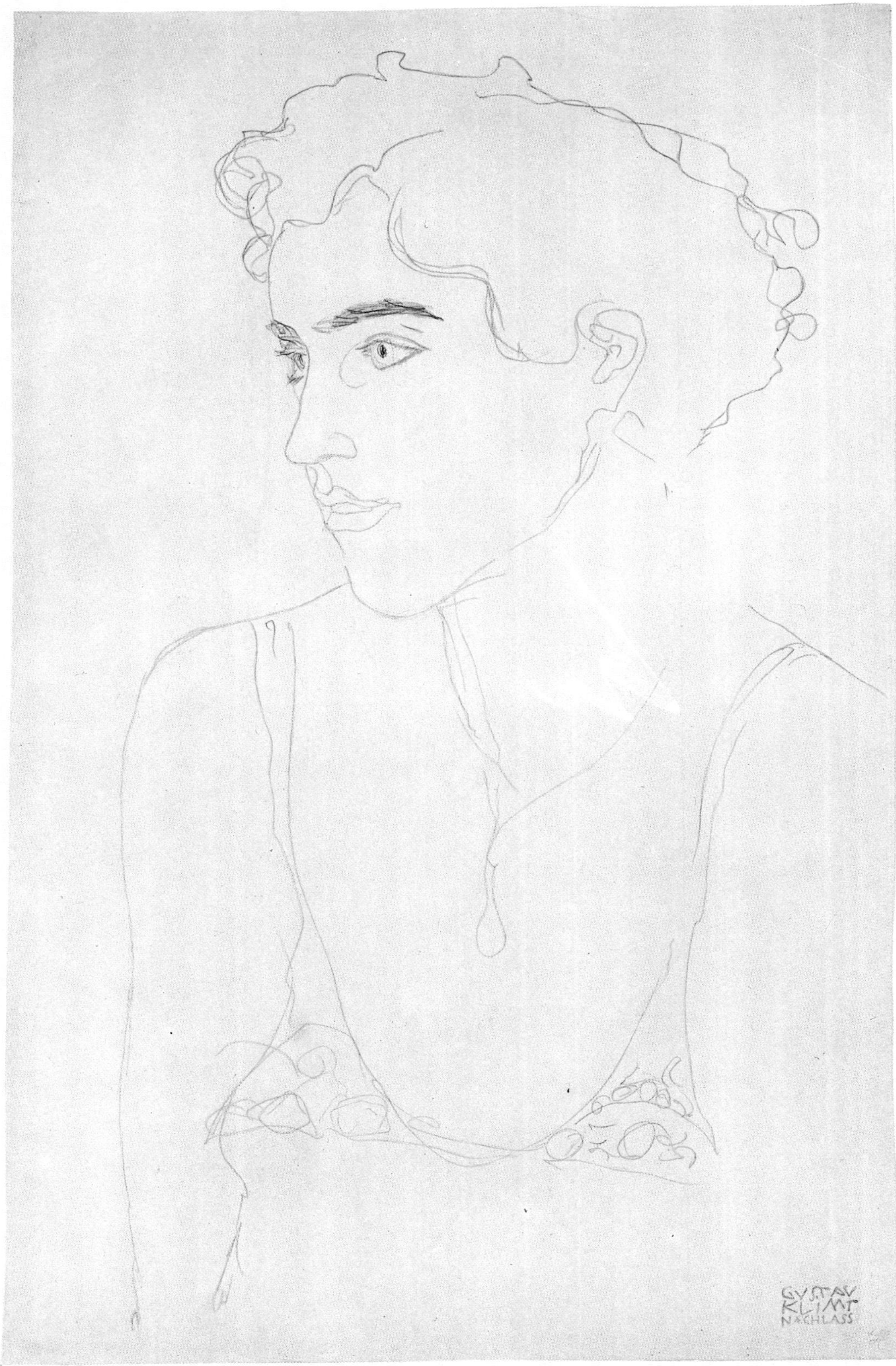

98. *Portrait study of a lady*, 1916–17.

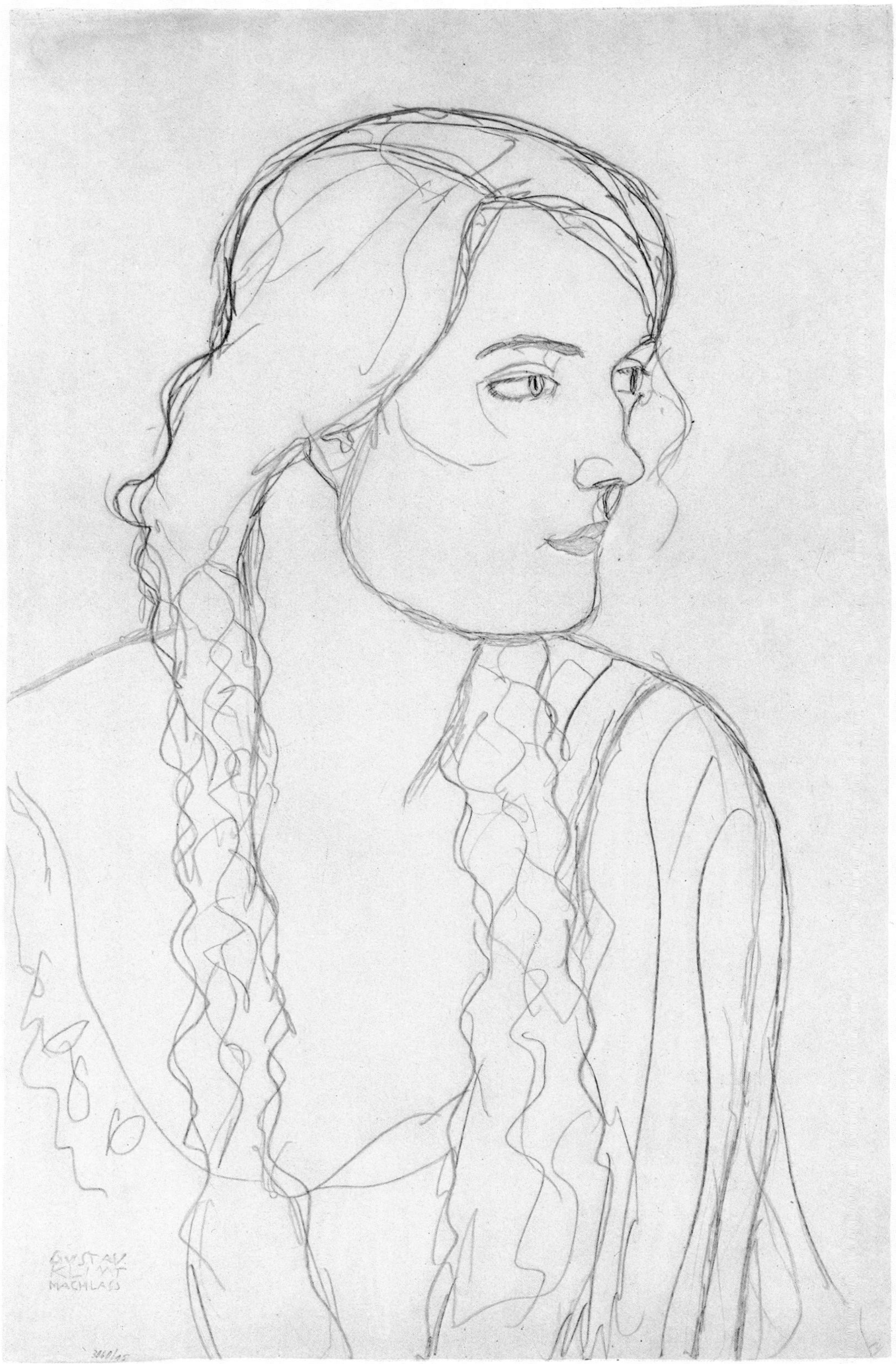

99. *Portrait study of a young woman*, 1916–17.

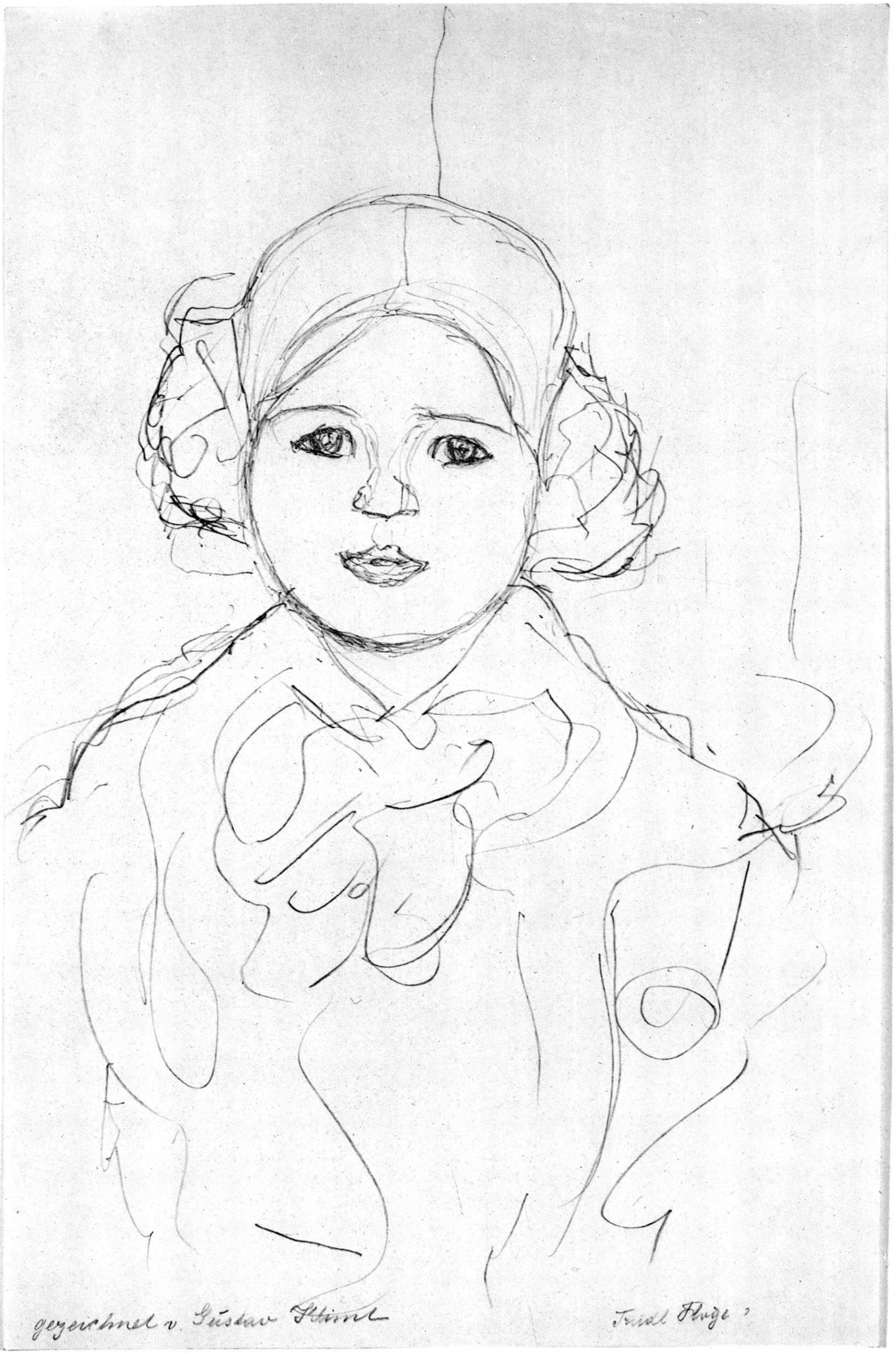

100. *Portrait study of a girl (Trudl Flöge)*, 1916–17.

Catalogue of the drawings

1. *Study of a man with a beard*, 1879.
Black charcoal with highlights in white chalk, 40.3 × 26.7 cm.
Signed and dated, bottom right.
2. *Recumbent male nude*, 1880.
Pencil, 28.9 × 43.2 cm.
Signed and dated, bottom right.
3. *Male nude seated on a pedestal*, 1880.
Pencil, 38.9 × 27 cm.
Signed and dated, bottom right.
4. *Study of a pair of boots*, 1883–4.
Pencil with highlights in white chalk, 45 × 31.5 cm.
5. *Bearded man standing, back view, with two studies of a right hand*, 1886.
Charcoal with highlights in white chalk, 44.8 × 31.1 cm.
(For the ceiling fresco of the Burgtheater of Vienna, 1886–88, Dobai 39).
6. *Young man with beard and skull-cap*, 1886–88.
Charcoal with highlights in white chalk, 45.1 × 31.8 cm.
Stamp of the Klimt estate, bottom right.
7. *Portrait study of a young woman*, 1890–91.
Charcoal with highlights in white chalk, 43.5 × 30.8 cm.
8. *Portrait study of an old man in profile*, *c.* 1890–94.
Charcoal with highlights in white chalk, 45.7 × 31.1 cm.
Stamp of the Klimt estate, bottom right.
9. *Portrait study of a young woman smiling*, 1895–96.
Charcoal, 44.8 × 31.7 cm.
Stamp of the Klimt estate, bottom right.
10. *Study for 'Tragedy'*, *c.* 1897.
Charcoal, 46.2 × 31.6 cm.
Stamp of the Klimt estate, bottom right.
11. *Nude with dark background*, *c.* 1896.
Pencil with white highlights, 45.1 × 32.1 cm.
Stamp of the Klimt estate, bottom right.
(For *Medicine* [ceiling panel in the great hall of the University of Vienna], 1897–98, Dobai 88, 1900–07, Dobai 112).
12. *Portrait study of a man in profile*, 1896–97.
Charcoal with highlights in white chalk, 45.4 × 31.1 cm
13. *Seated woman with chin resting on right hand*, 1897.
Charcoal, 44.5 × 31.7 cm.
Stamp of the Klimt estate, bottom right.
14. *Portrait study of a young woman in profile with tilted head*, 1897–98.
Charcoal, 44.4 × 32.4 cm.
Stamp of the Klimt estate, bottom right,
15. *Nude; bending forwards*, 1898.
Black pastel, 30.8 × 42.9 cm.
(Authentication of Hermine Klimt, bottom left).
16. *Seated nude, fat woman*, 1899–1900.
Charcoal 44.8 × 30.8 cm.
(Study for *Medicine*, 1900–07, Dobai 112).
17. *Nude with right arm extended*, 1900.
Pencil, 46.3 × 31.4 cm.
Stamp of the Klimt estate, bottom right.
(For *Medicine*, 1900–07, Dobai 112).
18. *Nude: young girl standing, looking downwards*, *c.* 1901.
Charcoal, 44.8 × 30.5 cm.
(For the *Beethoven* frieze, 1902, Dobai 127).
19. *Nude: fat woman, standing*, *c.* 1901.
Charcoal, 44.8 × 30.5 cm.
(For the *Beethoven* frieze, 1902, Dobai 127).
20. *Seated nude with right leg raised*, *c.* 1901.
Charcoal, 44.5 × 29.8 cm.
Stamp of the Klimt estate, bottom right.
(For the *Beethoven* frieze, 1902, Dobai 127).
21. *Nude, prone*, *c.* 1901.
Charcoal, 30.5 × 44.8 cm.
(For the *Beethoven* frieze, 1902, Dobai 127).
22. *Seated nude, back view*, *c.* 1901.
Charcoal, 45.1 × 31.8 cm.
(For the *Beethoven* frieze, 1902, Dobai 127).
23. *Standing nude in profile*, 1901.
Charcoal, 45.1 × 32.4 cm.
Stamp of the Klimt estate, bottom left.
(For the Beethoven frieze, 1902, Dobai 127)
24. *Standing nude with right leg raised*, 1901.
Charcoal, 45.1 × 32.4 cm.
(For the *Beethoven* frieze, 1902, Dobai 127).
25. *Nudes: male and pregnant female*, 1902.
Blue and orange pastel, 44.8 × 30.5 cm.
(For *Hope I*, 1903, Dobai 129).
26. *Nudes: male and pregnant female*, 1902.
Blue pastel, 43.8 × 30.5 cm.
(For *Hope I*, 1903, Dobai 129).
27. *Nudes: male and pregnant female*, 1902.
Blue pastel, 44.8 × 30.8 cm.
(For *Hope I*, 1903, Dobai 129).
28. *Standing nude with raised arms*, *c.* 1902.
Charcoal, 44.5 × 31.1 cm.
(For *Jurisprudence*, 1903–07, Dobai 128).

29. *Nude, supine*, 1903.
Blue pastel, 30.6 × 44.6 cm.
(For *Danae*, 1907–08, Dobai 151).
30. *Portrait study of an old woman with hands to her face*, 1903.
Charcoal, 45.1 × 31.8 cm.
Stamp of the Klimt estate, bottom right.
31 *Seated lady*, 1903.
Charcoal, 45.1 × 31.8 cm.
(For the *Portrait of Adele Bloch-Bauer*, 1907, Dobai 150).
32. *Standing nude looking downwards*, 1903.
Black pastel, 45 × 31.4 cm.
Initial 'K', bottom right.
33. *Nude: old woman standing in profile, and study of legs*, 1903.
Charcoal, 45.1 × 31.4 cm.
Stamp of the Klimt estate, bottom left.
(For *The three ages of life*, 1905, Dobai 141).
34. *Lady seated in an armchair*, 1903–04.
Charcoal, 44.8 × 31.8 cm.
Stamp of the Klimt estate, on verso.
(For the *Portrait of Adele Bloch-Bauer*. 1907, Dobai 150).
35. *Sleeping infant*, 1904.
Pencil, 54.9 × 35 cm.
(For *The three ages of life*, 1905, Dobai 141).
36. *Study of an old woman in profile*, 1904.
Blue pastel, 44.1 × 30.5 cm.
(For *The three ages of life*, 1905, Dobai 141).
37. *Old woman, seated, with left hand to her face*, 1904.
Pencil, 44.8 × 31.7 cm.
Stamp of the Klimt estate, bottom right.
38. *Standing lady*, 1904–05.
Pencil, 55.2 × 35 cm.
(For the *Portrait of Adele Bloch-Bauer*, 1907, Dobai 150).
39. *Nude with raised arms*, 1905–06.
Pencil, 44.5 × 30.5 cm.
40. *Prone figure, semi-nude*, 1905–06.
Pencil, 36.8 × 55.9 cm.
41. *Seated figure, semi-nude, with arms resting on her legs*, 1906–07.
Pencil with highlights in red and blue pastel, 55.9 × 37.1 cm.
Stamp of the Klimt estate, bottom right.
42. *Portrait study of a lady in profile with a high-collared blouse*, *c*. 1906–07.
Pencil, 55.2 × 34 cm.
43. *Standing nude with red lips*, 1906–07.
Pencil and orange pastel, 55.9 × 37.1 cm.
Stamp of the Klimt estate, bottom right.
44. *Standing nude in profile*, 1906–07.
Pencil, 55.9 × 39.5 cm.
Stamp of the Klimt estate, bottom left.
45. *Standing nude*, *c*. 1907.
Pencil, 55.9 × 37.1 cm.
46. *Seated nude looking downwards to the left, and study of a hand*, 1907–08.
Pencil, 56.5 × 37.1 cm.
47. *Seated woman*, 1907–08.
Pencil, 55.9 × 36.8 cm.
Stamp of the Klimt estate, bottom right.
48. *Portrait of a lady with a tall hat, and lying female figure*, 1907–08.
Pencil with highlights in orange pastel, 55.9 × 37.1 cm.
Stamp of the Klimt estate, bottom right.
(The lower figure was evidently added later, in *c*. 1912–13).
49. *Standing nude with left arm raised*, 1907–08.
Pencil and orange pastel, 56.2 × 37.1 cm.
50. *Seated figure, semi-nude*, *c*. 1908.
Blue pastel, 52.7 × 38.7 cm.
Stamp of the Klimt estate, bottom right.
51. *Seated nude with hands in her lap*, 1908.
Orange pastel, 55.9 × 36.8 cm.
Stamp of the Klimt estate, bottom left.
52. *Standing woman, with a nude woman crouching behind her*, 1908.
Blue pencil, 56.2 × 37.1 cm.
Stamp of the Klimt estate, bottom right.
53. *Two female nudes embracing*, 1909–10.
Pencil, 55.9 × 36.8 cm.
Stamp of the Klimt estate, bottom right.
54. *Standing nude with head bent to the left and leaning on her hands*, *c*. 1910.
Pencil, 55.9 × 36.2 cm.
(For *Life and death*, 1908–11, Dobai 183).
55. *Prone nude*, 1910.
Blue pastel, 36.5 × 53.3 cm.
Stamp of the Klimt estate, on verso.
56. *Portrait study of a young woman looking downwards*, *c*. 1910–12.
Pencil, 55.9 × 37.1 cm.
Stamp of the Klimt estate, bottom right.

57. *Young girl with apron*, 1912.
Pencil, 56.1 × 36.8 cm.
(For the *Portrait of Mäda Primavesi*).
58. *Standing nude, back view*, 1912–13.
Pencil, 56.8 × 37.1 cm.
(Authentication of Hermine Klimt, top left).
59. *Woman reclining*, 1912–13.
Pencil, 31.7 × 51.7 cm.
60. *Woman reclining, semi-nude*, 1912–13.
Pencil, 36.8 × 55.9 cm.
Stamp of the Klimt estate, bottom right.
61. *Reclining nude with left hand on her face*, 1912–13.
Pencil, 36.8 × 56.2 cm.
62. *Reclining nude with left leg raised*, 1913.
Blue pastel with highlights in orange pastel,
37.1 × 56.2 cm.
63. *Portrait study of a lady with head tilted and eyes closed*, 1913.
Pencil, 57.1 × 37.5 cm.
64. *Two seated nudes, back view*, 1913.
Pencil, 57.1 × 37.5 cm.
65. *Studies of hands and shoes*, *c.* 1914.
Pencil, 51.1 × 37.5 cm.
Stamp of the Klimt estate, bottom right.
(Study for the *Portrait of Baroness Bachofen-Echt*, 1914, Dobai 188).
66. *Nude with arms raised above the head*, 1914.
Pencil, 55.6 × 36.8 cm.
67. *Portrait study of a woman in profile*, 1914.
Pencil, 55.2 × 36.8 cm.
Stamp of the Klimt estate, bottom right.
68. *Portrait study of an old lady*, 1914.
Pencil, 57.1 × 37.5 cm.
69. *Semi-nude figure reclining*, 1914.
Pencil, 36.2 × 55.9 cm.
Stamp of the Klimt estate, bottom left.
70. *Semi-nude figure reclining*, 1914–15.
Pencil, 57.1 × 37.5 cm.
71. *Semi-nude figure reclining with legs drawn up*, 1914–15.
Blue pastel, 55.2 × 36.5 cm.
72. *Two male heads in profile*, 1914–15.
Pencil, 56.2 × 36.8 cm.
Stamp of the Klimt estate, bottom left.
(Study for the figure of Adam in the unfinished painting *Adam and Eve*, 1917–18, Dobai 220).
73. *Reclining nude*, *c.* 1914–18.
Pencil, 36.2 × 55.9 cm.
Stamp of the Klimt estate, bottom right.
74. *Portrait study of a young woman in profile*, *c.* 1915.
Pencil, 54 × 35.6 cm.
75. *Portrait study of an old woman*, 1915.
Pencil, 57.1 × 36.8 cm.
76. *Portrait of a lady*, 1915.
Pencil, 55.6 × 35.8 cm.
Signed, bottom right.
77. *Portrait of a lady*, 1915.
Pencil and orange pastel, 56.8 × 37.8 cm.
Stamp of the Klimt estate, bottom left.
78. *Portrait study of a lady*, 1915.
Pencil, 55.2 × 35.6 cm.
Stamp of the Klimt estate, bottom left.
79. *Portrait study of a lady*, 1915.
Pencil, 57.1 × 37.5 cm.
Stamp of the Klimt estate, bottom left.
80. *Semi-nude figure sleeping, curled up*, *c.* 1915.
Pencil, 36.7 × 55.9 cm.
Stamp of the Klimt estate, bottom left.
81. *Portrait study of a young woman*, 1915–16.
Pencil, 53.6 × 41.3 cm.
82. *Portrait study of a woman in profile*, 1915–16.
Pencil, 56 × 36.5 cm.
Stamp of the Klimt estate, bottom left.
83. *Portrait study of a lady*, 1915–16.
Pencil, 50.1 × 32.4 cm.
Stamp of the Klimt estate, bottom right.
84. *Portrait study of a lady, seated*, 1915–16.
Pencil, 50.1–32.4 cm.
85. *Female head with closed eyes*, 1915–16.
Pencil, 55.9 × 36.5 cm.
Stamp of the Klimt estate, bottom right.
86. *Portrait study of a woman standing*, 1915–16.
Pencil, 50.1 × 32 cm.
87. *Standing couple, nude*, 1915–16.
Pencil, 55.9 × 36.7 cm.
(Study for the unfinished painting *Adam and Eve*, 1917–18, Dobai 220).
88. *Study of a male head*, *c.* 1916.
Pencil, 57.8 × 37.5 cm.
Stamp of the Klimt estate, bottom right.
(Study for the unfinished painting *Adam and Eve*, 1917–18, Dobai 220).

89. *Portrait study of a lady in a fur coat*, 1916.
Pencil, 50.2 × 32.5 cm.
Stamp of the Klimt estate, bottom left.
(Study for the unfinished painting
The polecat fur coat, 1916–18, Dobai 206).

90. *Portrait study of Friederike Beer-Monti*, 1916.
Pencil, 56.8 × 37.5 cm.
(Study for the *Portrait of Friederike Beer-Monti*, 1916,
Dobai 196).

91. *Portrait study of Friederike Beer-Monti*, *c.* 1916.
Pencil, 57 × 37.5 cm.

92. *Standing nude*, 1916.
Pencil, 55.9 × 36.2 cm.
Stamp of the Klimt estate, bottom right.

93. *Standing nude*, 1916.
Pencil, 57 × 37.3 cm.
Stamp of the Klimt estate, bottom right.

94. *Standing lady in elegant costume*, 1916.
Pencil, blue and orange pastel, 50.1 × 32.4 cm.
Signed, bottom right.

95. *Portrait study of a young lady with hat and boa*, 1916.
Pencil, 56.8 × 37.5 cm.
Signed, bottom left.

96. *Back view of a standing woman, leaning on her right elbow*, 1916.
Pencil, 49.5 × 29.8 cm.

97. *Standing woman with left hand to her chin*, *c.* 1916–17.
Pencil, 56.5 × 36.8 cm.
Signed, bottom right.

98. *Portrait study of a lady*, 1916–17.
Pencil, 56.8 × 37.1 cm.
Stamp of the Klimt estate, bottom right.

99. *Portrait study of a young woman*, 1916–17.
Pencil with red, blue and white highlights, 56.8 × 37.5 cm.
Stamp of the Klimt estate, bottom left.
(For the unfinished painting *The Bride*, 1917–18,
Dobai 222).

100. *Portrait study of a girl (Trudl Flöge)*, 1916–17.
Pencil, 55.9 × 36.8 cm.

Select Bibliography

H. Bahr, *Rede über Klimt*, Vienna, 1901.
H. Bahr, *Gegen Klimt*, Vienna, 1903.
L. Hevesi, *Acht Jahre Sezession, 1897–1905*, Vienna, 1906.
L. Hevesi, *Altkunst-Neukunst, Wien 1894–1908*, Vienna, 1918.
H. Bahr, P. Altenberg, *Das Werk Gustav Klimts*, Vienna, 1918.
M. Eisler, *Gustav Klimt*, Vienna, 1920.
E. Pirchan, *Gustav Klimt, Ein Künstler aus Wien*, Vienna, 1942.
C. Moll, *Ricordo Gustav Klimt*, Vienna, 1943.
M. J. Liechtenstein, *Kunst in Österreich 1815–1951*, Linz, 1951.
E. Pirchan, *Gustav Klimt*, Vienna, 1956.
I. Hatle, *Gustave Klimt, Ein Wiener Maler des Jugendstils*, Vienna, 1958.
A. Strobl, *Gustav Klimt*, Salzburg, 1962 and 1965.
A. Strobl, *Gustav Klint, 1862–1918, Zeichnungen*, exhibition catalogue, Graphische Sammlung, Albertina, Vienna, 1962.
C. M. Nebehay, *Gustav Klimt – 150 bedeutende Zeichnungen*, Vienna, 1962.
C. M. Nebehay, *Gustav Klimt, Eine Nachlese, 70 bedeutende Zeichnungen*, Graz, 1964.
A. Strobl, *Gustav Klimt, 25 Zeichnungen*, Graz, 1964.
W. Hofmann, *Moderne Malerei in Österreich*, Vienna, 1965.
F. Novotny, J. Dobai, *Gustav Klimt*, Salzburg, 1967.
Gustav Klimt, in *I maestri del colore*, Milan, 1967.
C. M. Nebehay, *Gustav Klimt Dokumentation*, Vienna, 1969.
W. Hofmann, *Gustav Klimt*, Salzburg, 1971.
P. Vergo, *Art in Vienna*, London, 1975.
A. Comini, *Gustav Klimt*, London, 1975.
A. Strobl, *Gustav Klimt: Drawings and Paintings*, London, 1975.
C. M. Nebehay, *Gustav Klimt, Sein Leben nach zeitgenösischen Berichten und Quellen*, Monaco, 1976.
J. Dobai, S. Coradeschi, *L'opera completa di Klimt*, Milan, 1978.
H. H. Hofstatter, *Gustav Klimt: Erotic Drawings*, London, 1980.
A. Strobl, *Gustav Klimt – Die Zeichnungen*, Salzburg, 1980.
Klimt – I classici della pittura, Milan, 1980.
Gustav Klimt – Disegni erotici, Milan, 1980.
O. Breicha (ed.), *Gustav Klimt*, Milan, 1981.
S. Sabarsky, (ed.), *Gustav Klimt*, exhibition catalogue, Isetan Museum of Art, Tokyo, 1981.

Finito di stampare nel giugno 1984
presso le Arti Grafiche Leva A & G di Sesto S. Giovanni (MI)
per conto delle Nuove Edizioni Gabriele Mazzotta srl